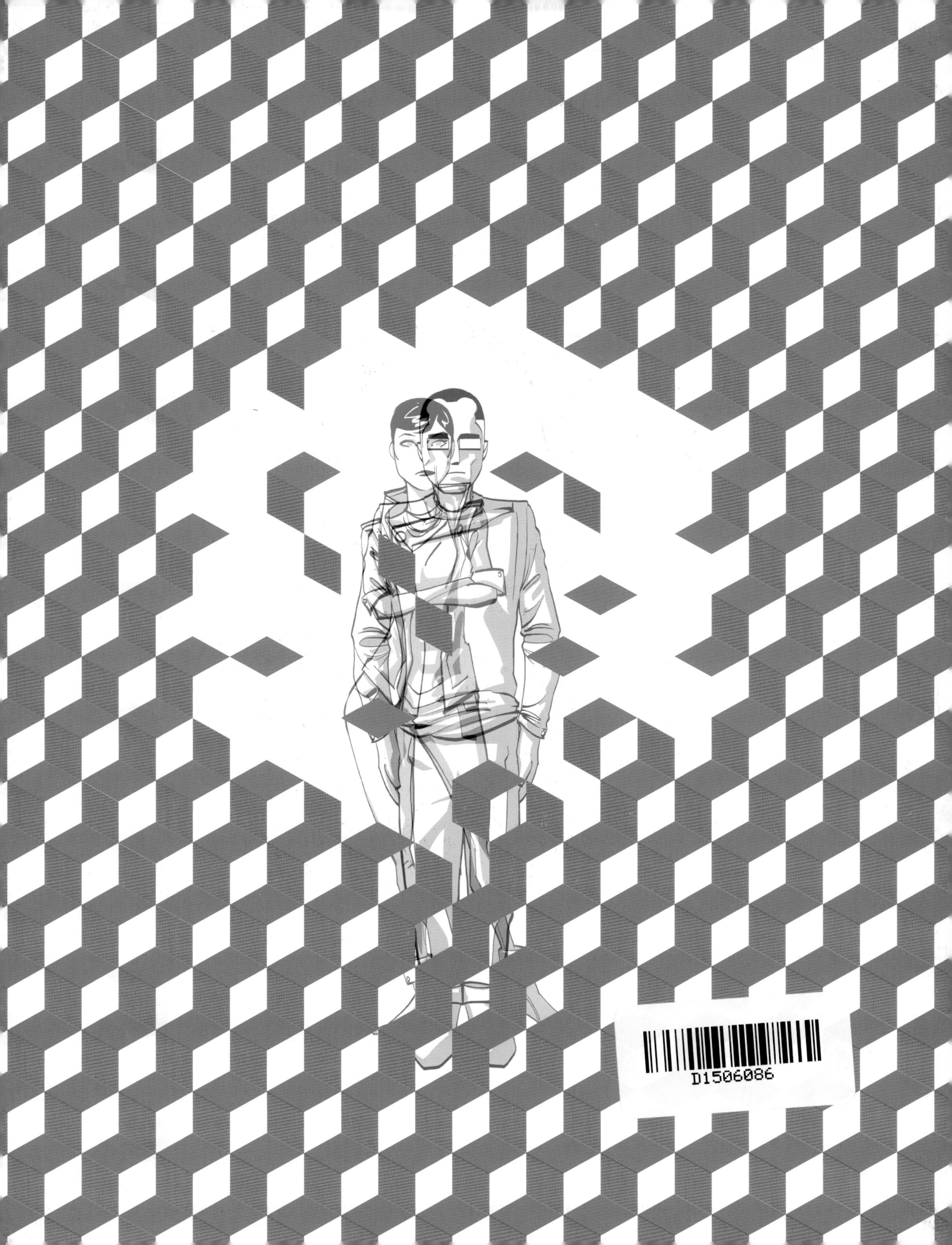

DEAR READER,

The book you have purchased is presented in ANAGLYPH 3D, meaning with the help of the enclosed glasses, a "red" image and a "blue" image composite (technically, confuse) inside your brain to present the simple but irresistible illusion of depth.

For the sharpest result, please make an effort to read this volume in generous natural or artificial light.

We recommend "snack breaks" between the chapters in the event that the persistence of the 3D effect causes lightheadedness, memory loss, or heartache.

Humbly,

THE AUTHORS

Please find your glasses located
in the back of this book.

DEAR READER,

The book you have purchased is presented in ANAGLYPH 3D, meaning with the help of the enclosed glasses, a "red" image and a "blue" image composite (technically, confuse) inside your brain to present the simple but irresistible illusion of depth.

For the sharpest result, please make an effort to read this volume in generous natural or artificial light.

We recommend "snack breaks" between the chapters in the event that the persistence of the 3D effect causes lightheadedness, memory loss, or heartache.

Humbly,
THE AUTHORS

i

Please find your glasses located
in the back of this book.

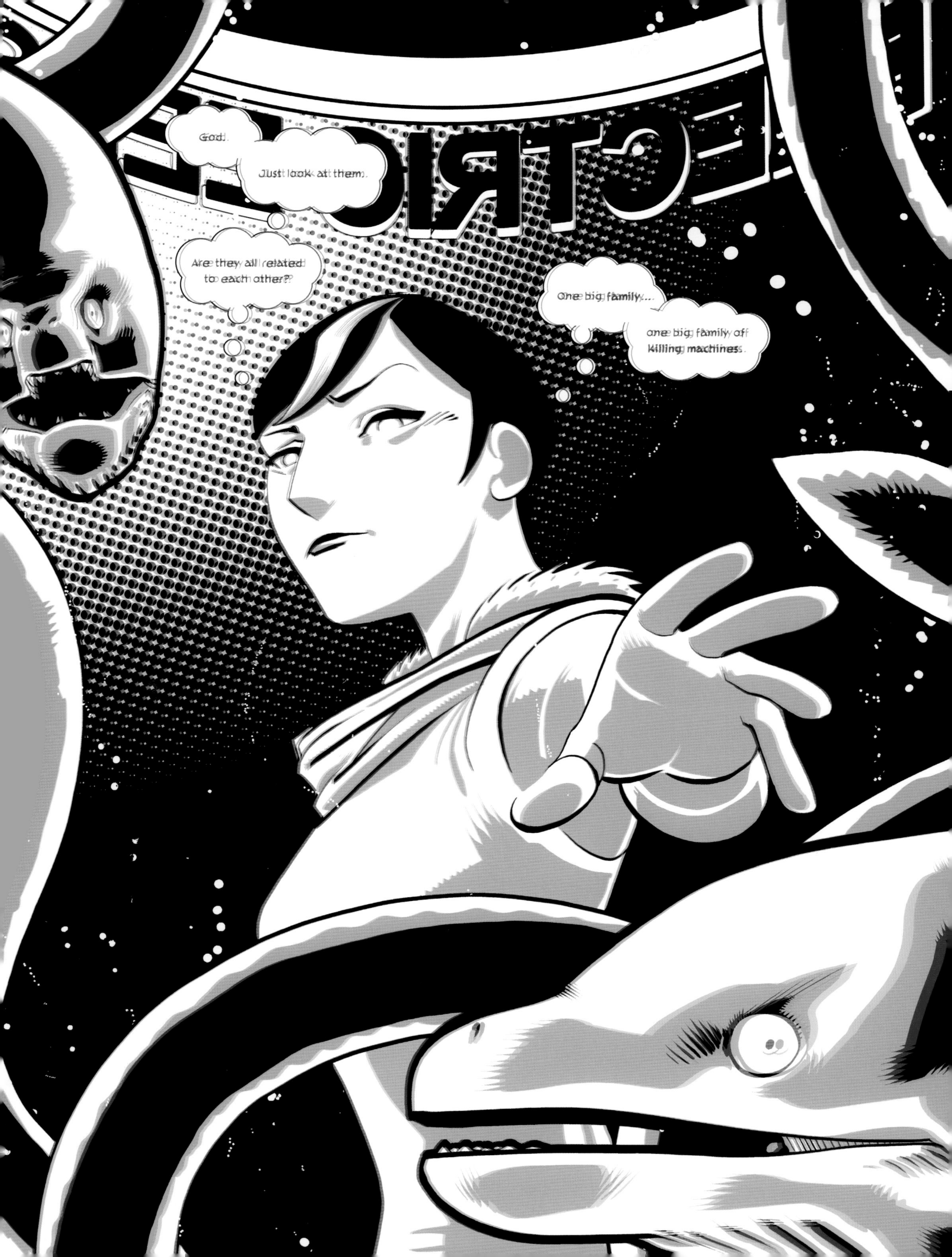
God.
Just look at them.
Are they all related to each other?
One big family...
one big family of killing machines.

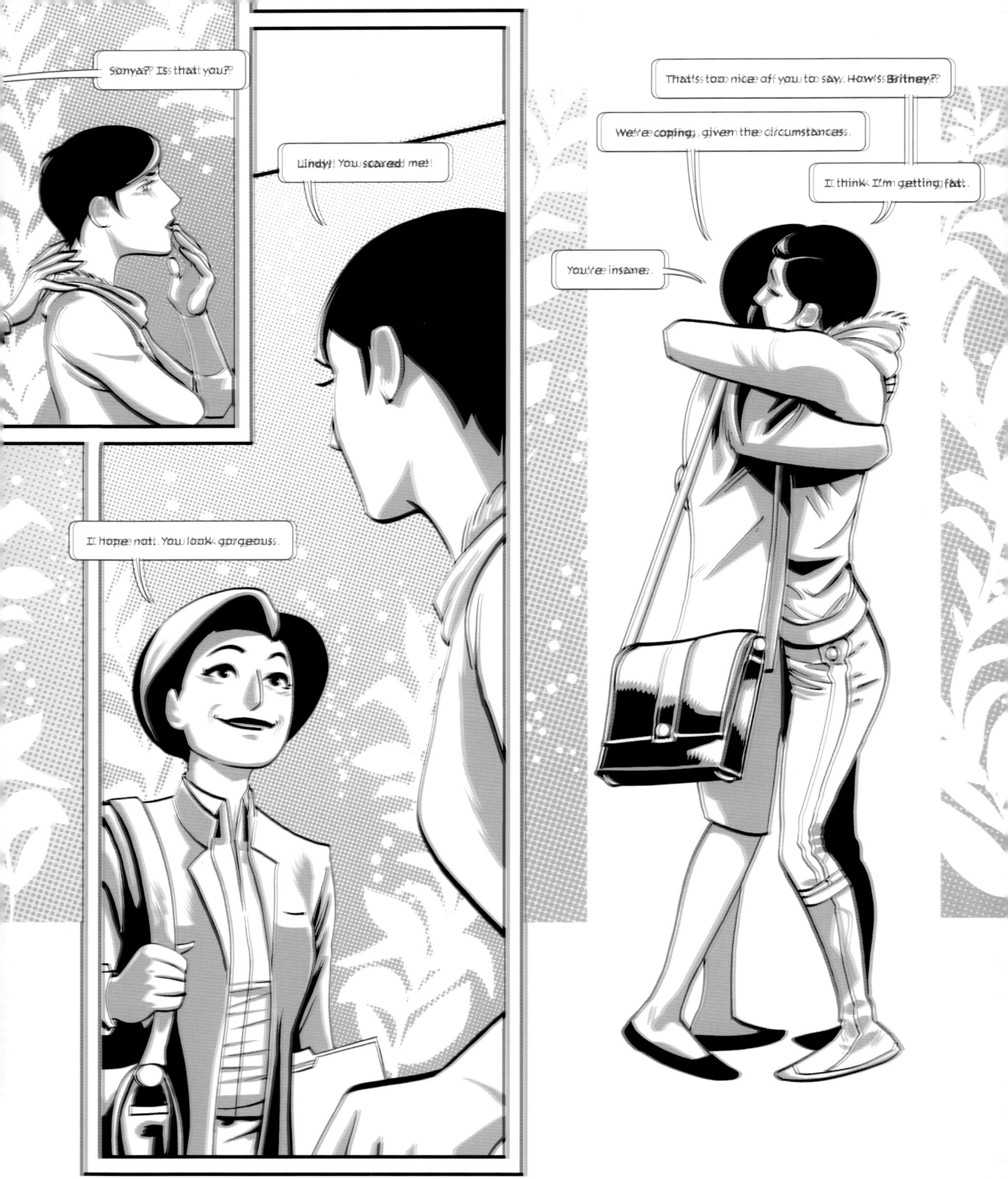
Sonya? Is that you?
Lindy! You scared me!
I hope not. You look gorgeous.
That's too nice of you to say. How's Britney?
We're coping, given the circumstances.
I think I'm getting fat.
You're insane.

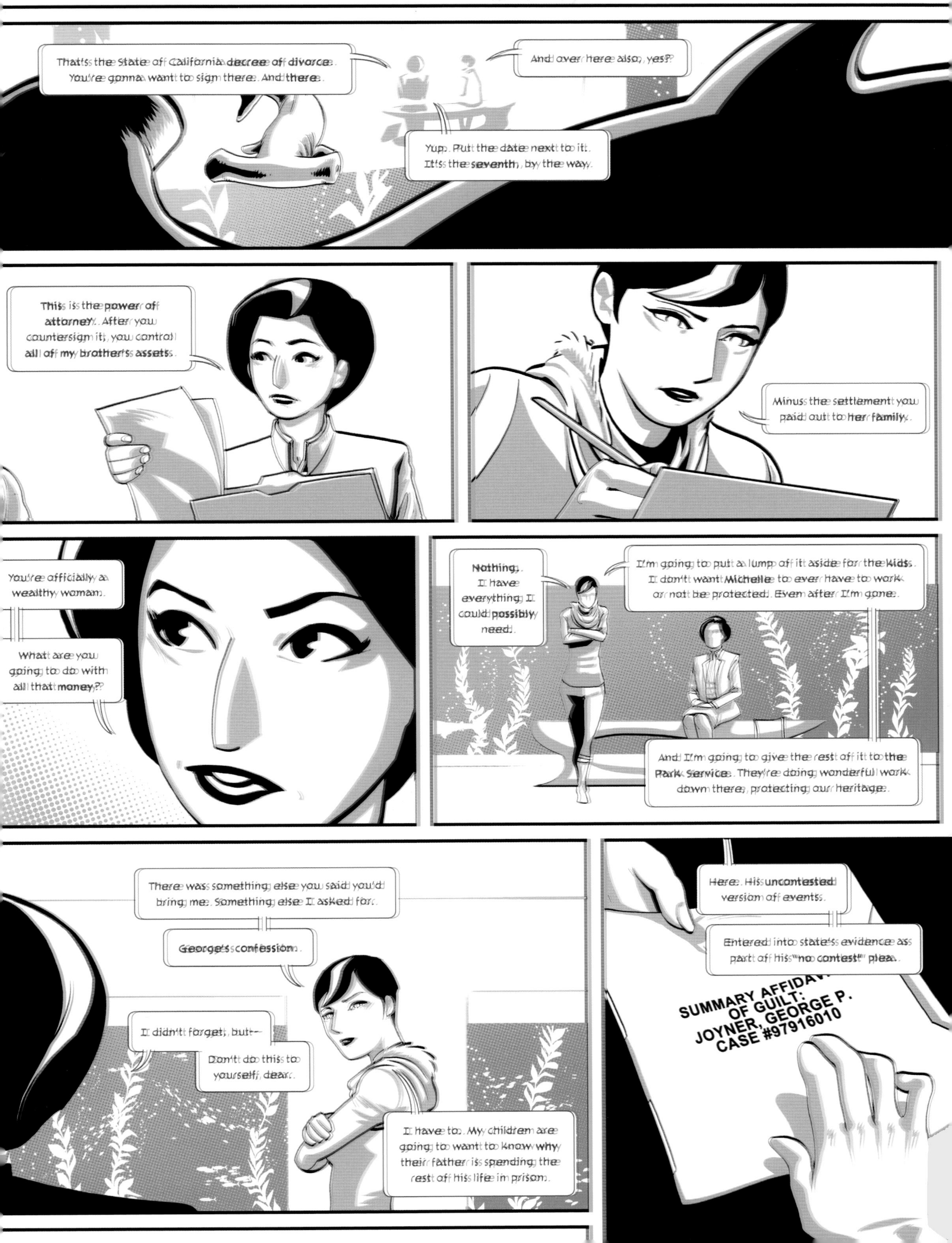
That's the State of California decree of divorce. You're gonna want to sign there. And there.
And over here also, yes?
Yup. Put the date next to it. It's the seventh, by the way.
This is the power of attorney. After you countersign it, you control all of my brother's assets.
Minus the settlement you paid out to her family.
You're officially a wealthy woman.
What are you going to do with all that money?
Nothing. I have everything I could possibly need.
I'm going to put a lump of it aside for the kids. I don't want Michelle to ever have to work or not be protected. Even after I'm gone.
And I'm going to give the rest of it to the Park Service. They're doing wonderful work down there, protecting our heritage.
There was something else you said you'd bring me. Something else I asked for.
George's confession.
I didn't forget, but--
Don't do this to yourself, dear.
I have to. My children are going to want to know why their father is spending the rest of his life in prison.
Here. His uncontested version of events.
Entered into state's evidence as part of his "no contest" plea.
SUMMARY AFFIDAV
OF GUILT:
JOYNER, GEORGE P.
CASE #97916010

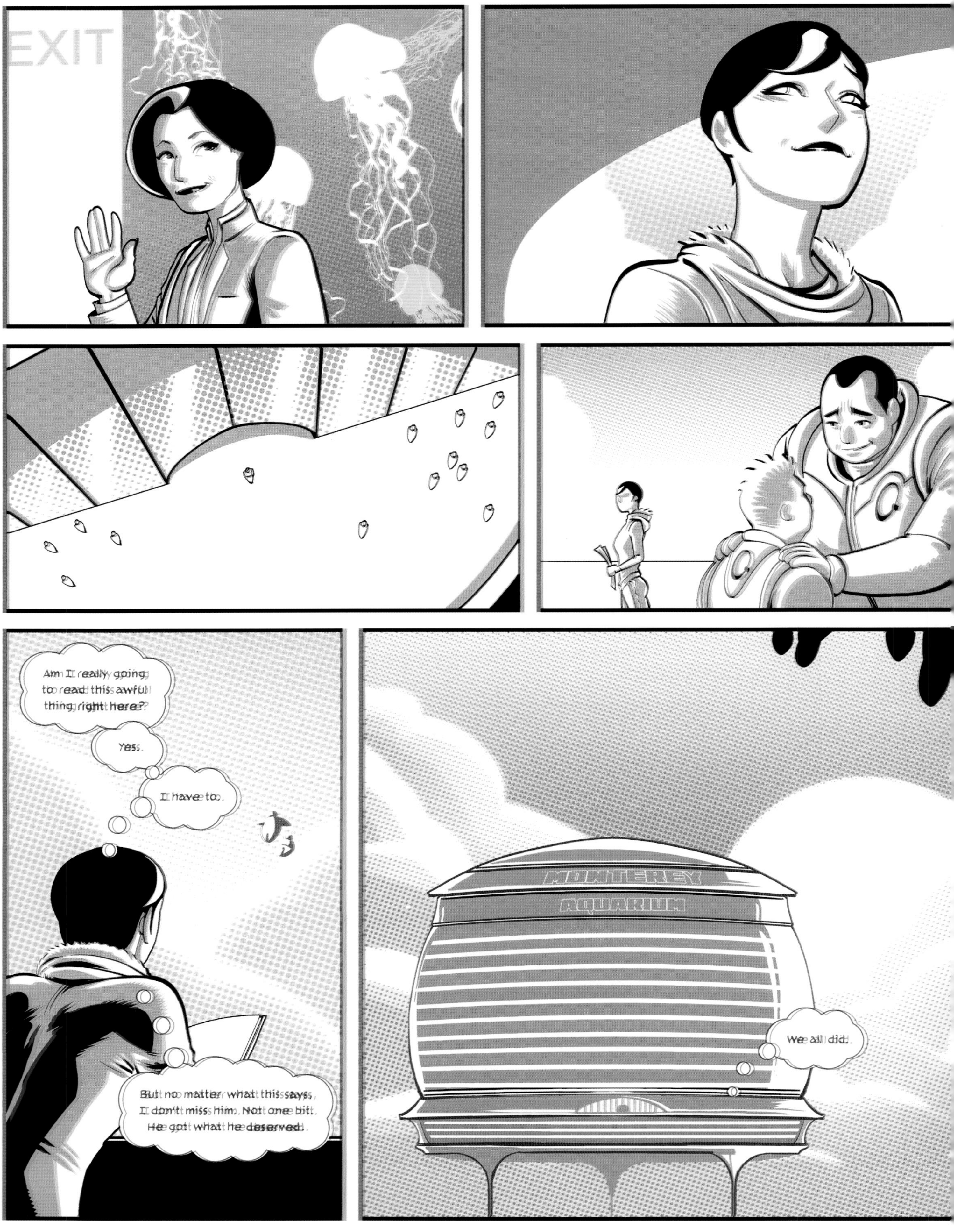
EXIT
Am I really going to read this awful thing right here?
Yes.
I have to.
But no matter what this says, I don't miss him. Not one bit. He got what he deserved.
MONTEREY
AQUARIUM
We all did.

AN
ARCHAIA ORIGINAL
GRAPHIC NOVEL

THE JOYNERS IN 3D

BY
R.J. RYAN & DAVID MARQUEZ

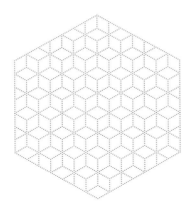

ANAGLYPH 3D BY DAVID MARQUEZ & TARA RHYMES

DESIGN AND LETTERING BY JON ADAMS

EDITED BY STEPHEN CHRISTY

ARCHAIA ENTERTAINMENT
PROUDLY PRESENTS

THE JOYNERS IN 3D

BY

R.J. RYAN AND DAVID MARQUEZ

ANAGLYPH 3D BY DAVID MARQUEZ & TARA RHYMES

DESIGN AND LETTERING BY JON ADAMS

EDITED BY STEPHEN CHRISTY

TABLE OF CONTENTS

CHAPTER ONE

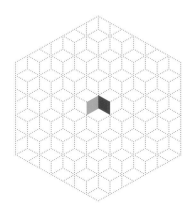

MEET GEORGE JOYNER

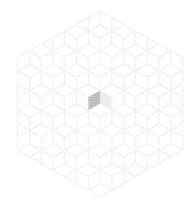

CHAPTER ONE
MEET GEORGE JOYNER

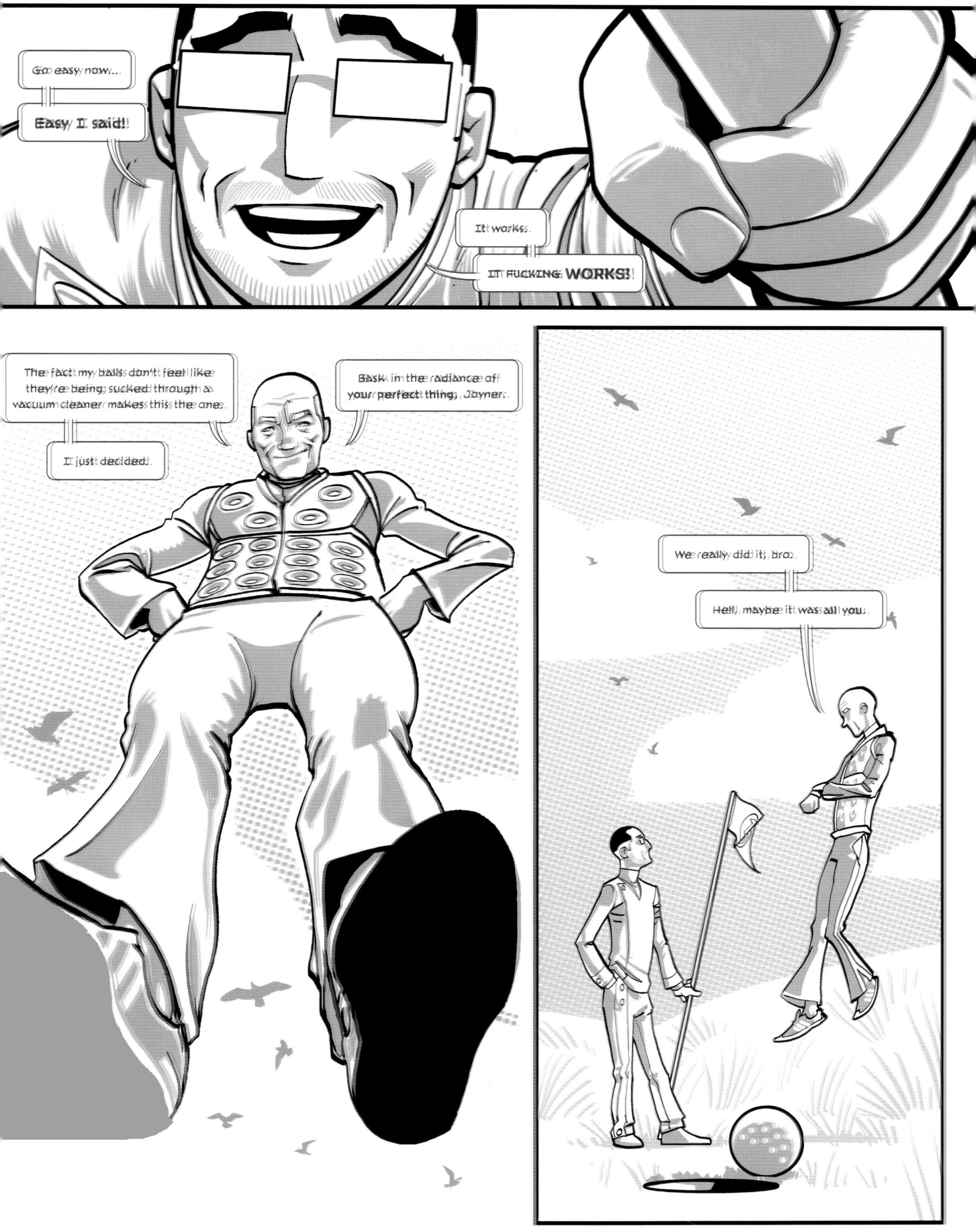
Go easy now...
Easy I said!
It works.
IT FUCKING WORKS!
The fact my balls don't feel like they're being sucked through a vacuum cleaner makes this the one.
I just decided.
Bask in the radiance of your perfect thing, Joyner.
We really did it, bro.
Hell, maybe it was all you.

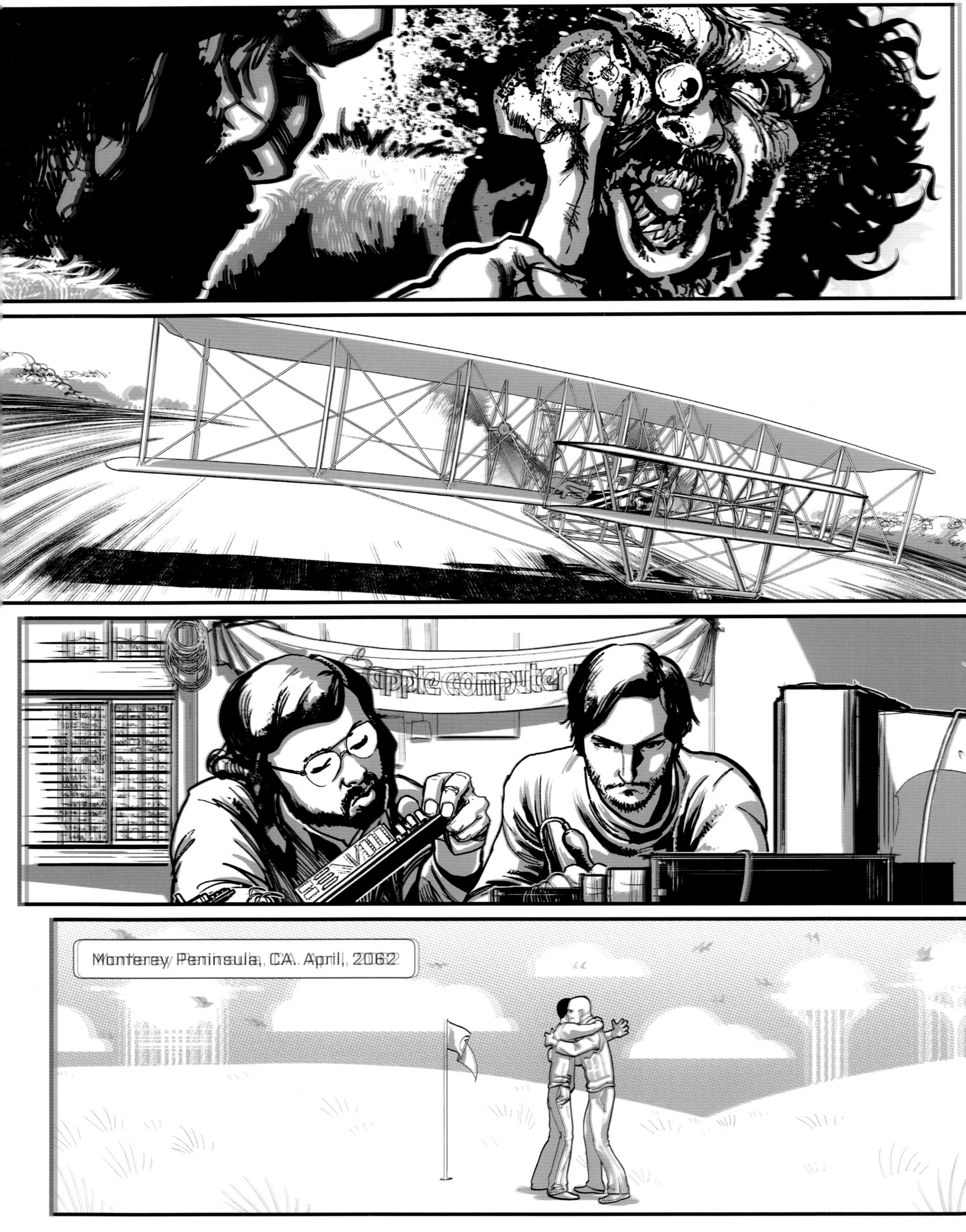
Monterey Peninsula, CA. April, 2062

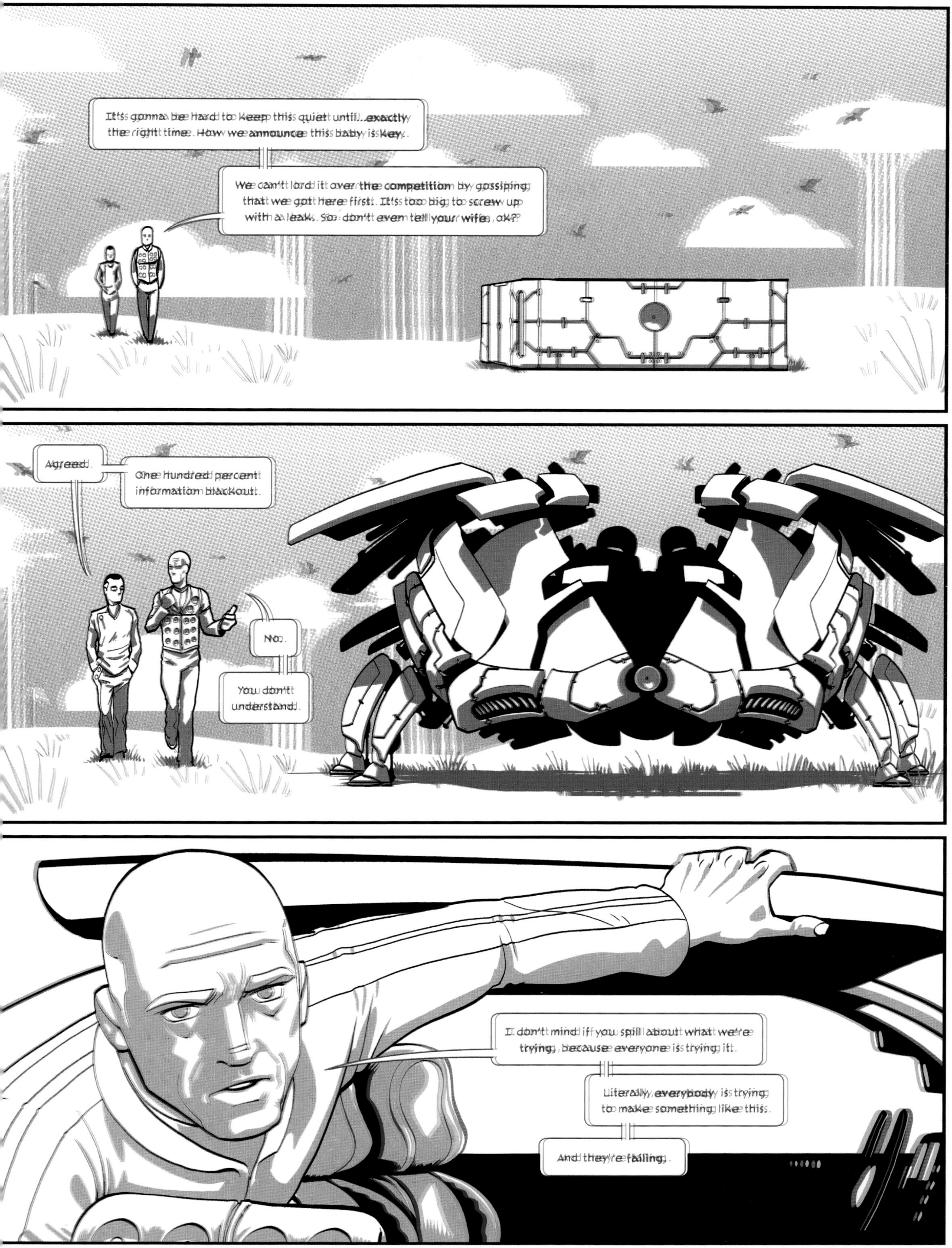
It's gonna be hard to keep this quiet until...exactly the right time. How we announce this baby is key.
We can't lord it over the competition by gossiping that we got here first. It's too big to screw up with a leak. So don't even tell your wife, ok?
Agreed.
One hundred percent information blackout.
No.
You don't understand.
I don't mind if you spill about what we're trying, because everyone is trying it.
Literally, everybody is trying to make something like this.
And they're failing.

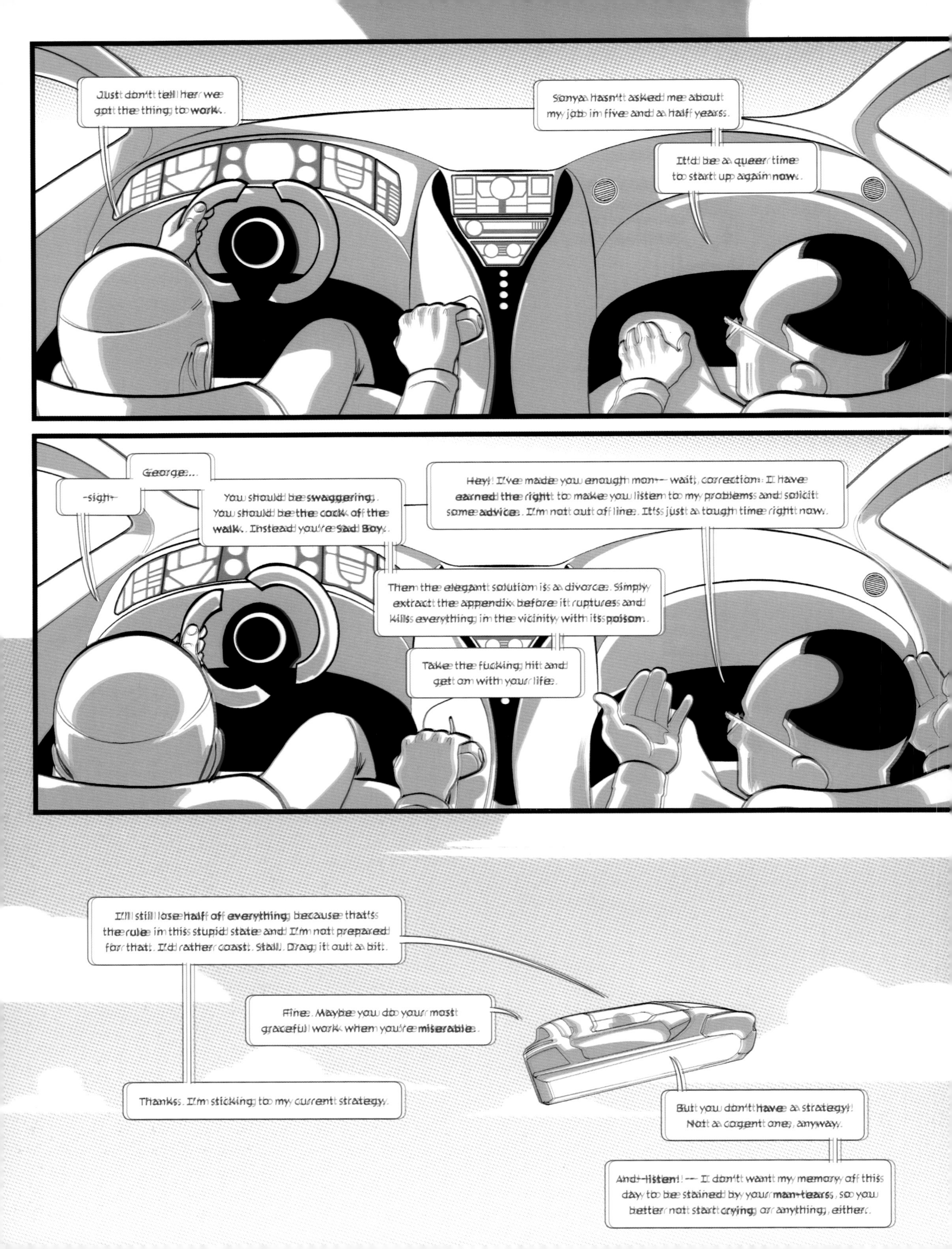
Just don't tell her we got the thing to work.
Sonya hasn't asked me about my job in five and a half years.
It'd be a queer time to start up again now.
-sigh-
George...
You should be swaggering. You should be the cock of the walk. Instead you're Sad Boy.
Hey! I've made you enough mon-- wait, correction: I have earned the right to make you listen to my problems and solicit some advice. I'm not out of line. It's just a tough time right now.
Then the elegant solution is a divorce. Simply extract the appendix before it ruptures and kills everything in the vicinity with its poison.
Take the fucking hit and get on with your life.
I'll still lose half of everything because that's the rule in this stupid state and I'm not prepared for that. I'd rather coast. Stall. Drag it out a bit.
Fine. Maybe you do your most graceful work when you're miserable.
Thanks. I'm sticking to my current strategy.
But you don't have a strategy! Not a cogent one, anyway.
And--listen! -- I don't want my memory of this day to be stained by your man-tears, so you better not start crying or anything, either.

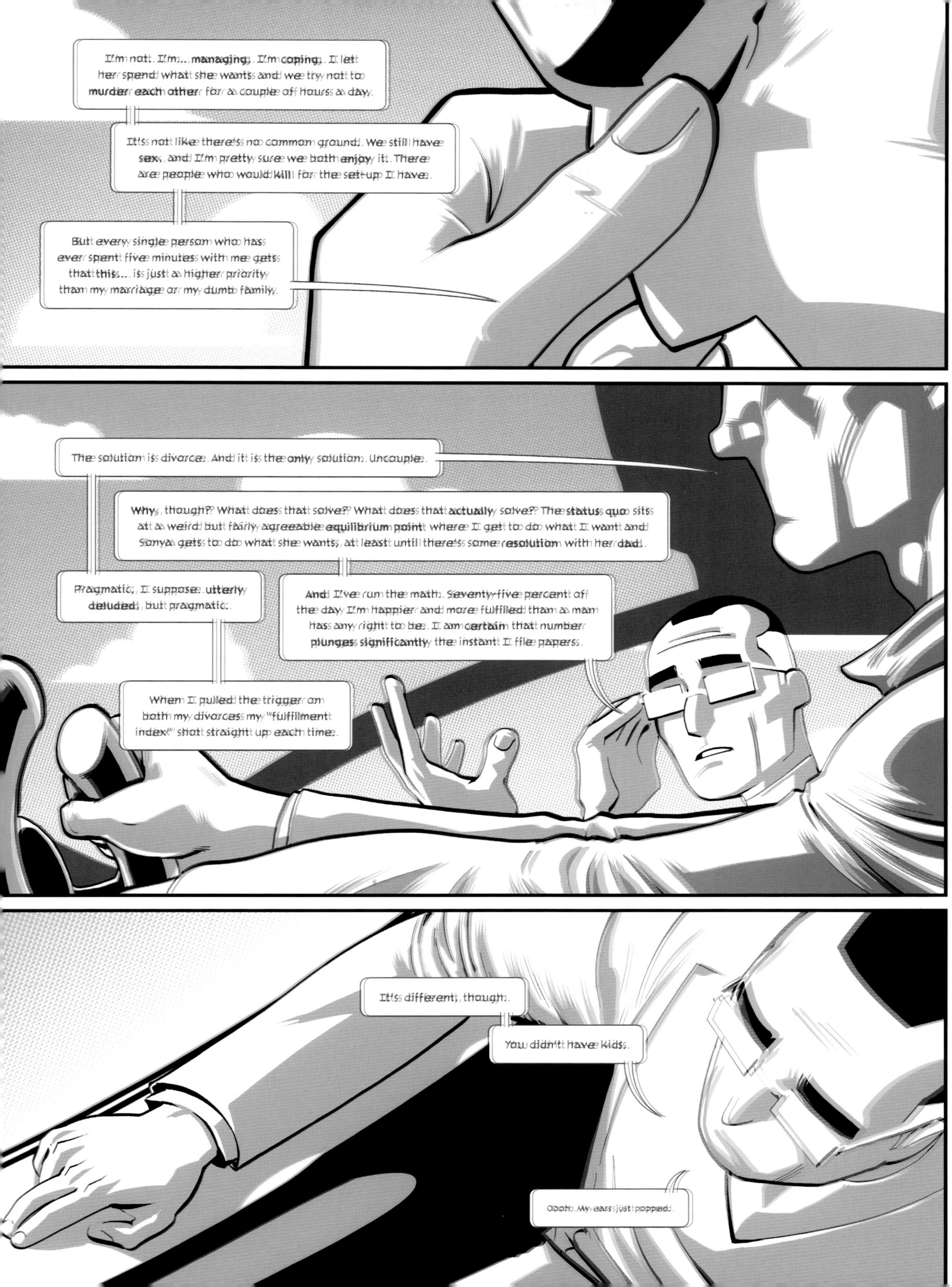
I'm not. I'm... managing. I'm coping. I let her spend what she wants and we try not to murder each other for a couple of hours a day.
It's not like there's no common ground. We still have sex, and I'm pretty sure we both enjoy it. There are people who would kill for the set-up I have.
But every single person who has ever spent five minutes with me gets that this... is just a higher priority than my marriage or my dumb family.
The solution is divorce. And it is the only solution. Uncouple.
Why, though? What does that solve? What does that actually solve? The status quo sits at a weird but fairly agreeable equilibrium point where I get to do what I want and Sonya gets to do what she wants, at least until there's some resolution with her dad.
Pragmatic, I suppose. utterly deluded, but pragmatic.
And I've run the math. Seventy-five percent of the day I'm happier and more fulfilled than a man has any right to be. I am certain that number plunges significantly the instant I file papers.
When I pulled the trigger on both my divorces my "fulfillment index" shot straight up each time.
It's different, though.
You didn't have kids.
Oooh. My ears just popped.

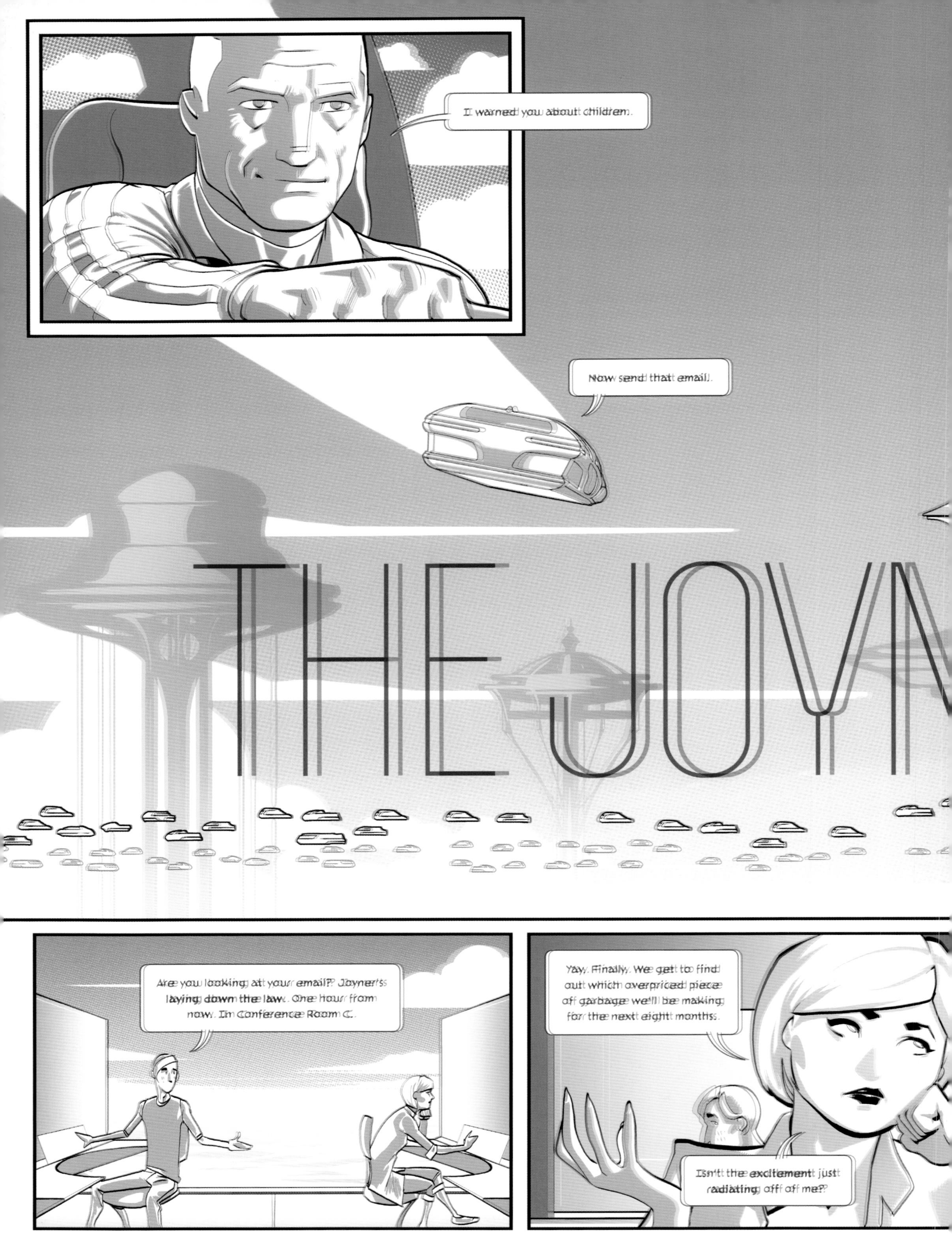
I warned you about children.
Now send that email.
THE JOYN
Are you looking at your email? Joyner's laying down the law. One hour from now. In Conference Room C.
Yay. Finally. We get to find out which overpriced piece of garbage we'll be making for the next eight months.
Isn't the excitement just radiating off of me?

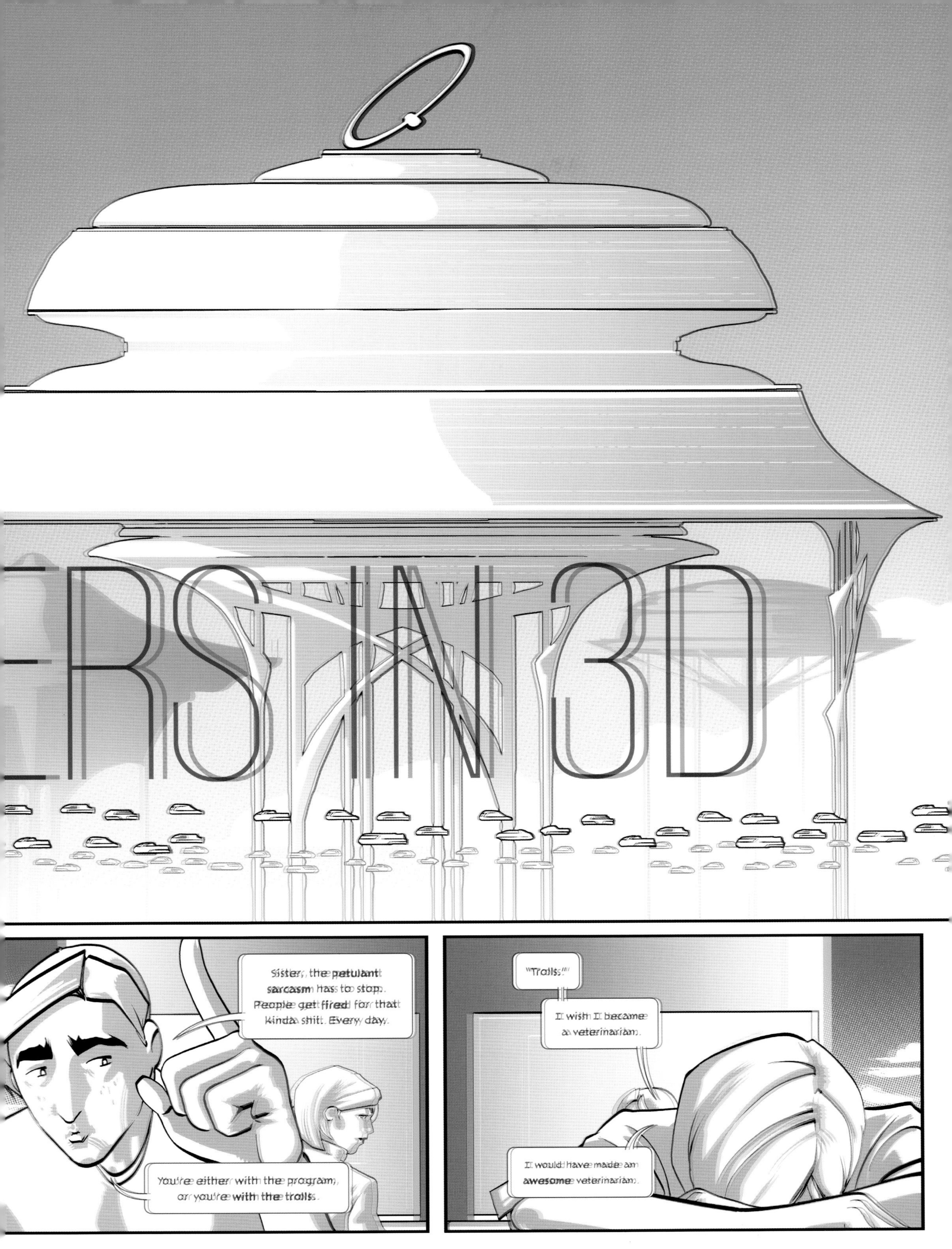
ERS IN 3D
Sister, the petulant sarcasm has to stop. People get fired for that kinda shit. Every day.
You're either with the program, or you're with the trolls.
"Trolls."
I wish I became a veterinarian.
I would have made an awesome veterinarian.

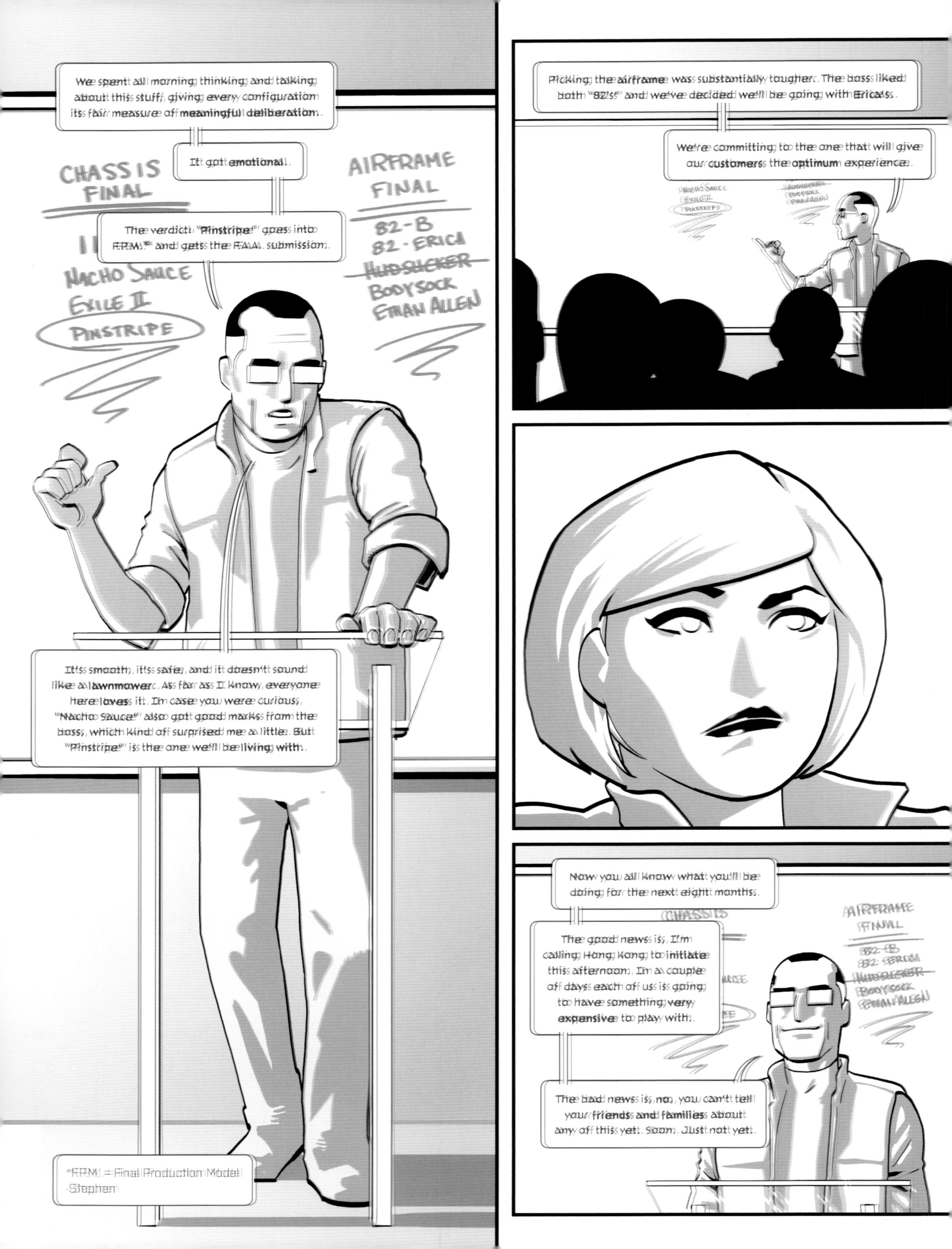

We spent all morning thinking and talking about this stuff, giving every configuration its fair measure of meaningful deliberation.
It got emotional.
CHASSIS FINAL
NACHO SAUCE
EXILE II
PINSTRIPE
AIRFRAME FINAL
82-B
82-ERICA
HUDSUCKER
BODYSOCK
ETHAN ALLEN
The verdict: "Pinstripe" goes into F.P.M.* and gets the F.A.A. submission.
It's smooth, it's safe, and it doesn't sound like a lawnmower. As far as I know, everyone here loves it. In case you were curious, "Nacho Sauce" also got good marks from the boss, which kind of surprised me a little. But "Pinstripe" is the one we'll be living with.
*F.P.M. = Final Production Model -Stephen
Picking the airframe was substantially tougher. The boss liked both "82's" and we've decided we'll be going with Erica's.
We're committing to the one that will give our customers the optimum experience.
Now you all know what you'll be doing for the next eight months.
The good news is, I'm calling Hong Kong to initiate this afternoon. In a couple of days each of us is going to have something very expensive to play with.
The bad news is, no, you can't tell your friends and families about any of this yet. Soon. Just not yet.

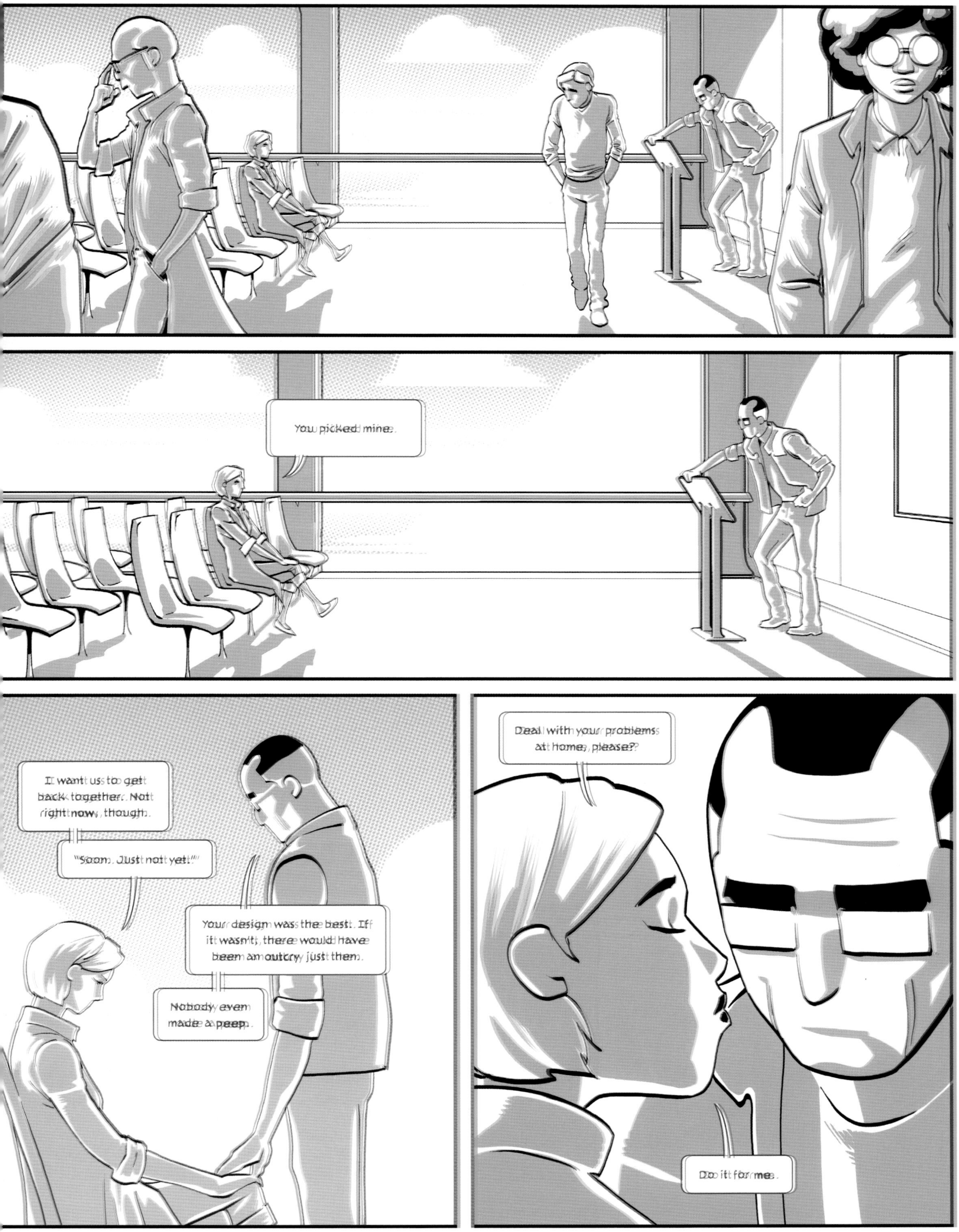
You picked mine.
I want us to get back together. Not right now, though.
"Soon. Just not yet."
Your design was the best. If it wasn't, there would have been an outcry just then.
Nobody even made a peep.
Deal with your problems at home, please?
Do it for me.

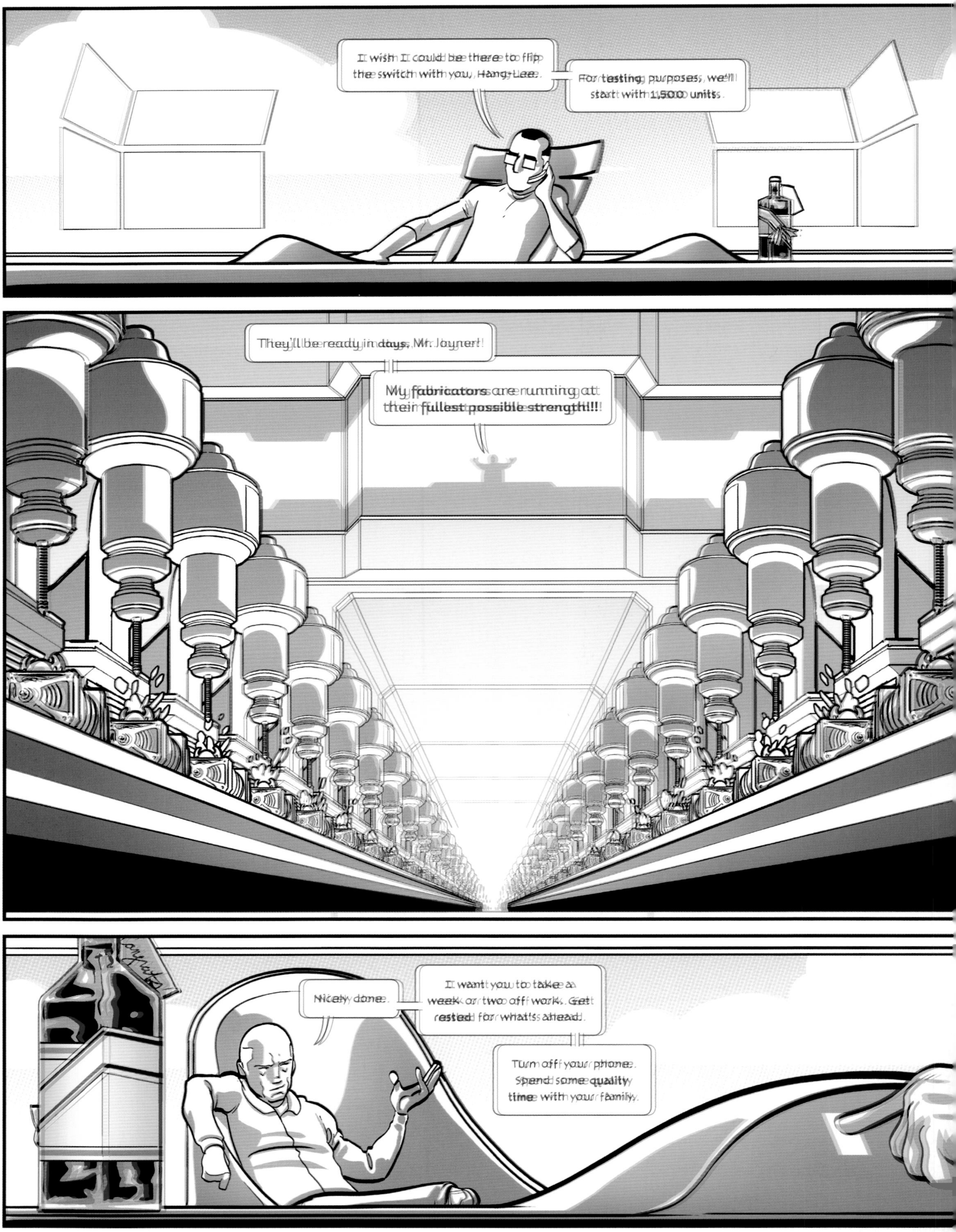
I wish I could be there to flip the switch with you, Hang-Lee.
For testing purposes, we'll start with 1,500 units.
They'll be ready in days, Mr. Joyner!
My fabricators are running at their fullest possible strength!!!
Nicely done.
I want you to take a week or two off work. Get rested for what's ahead.
Turn off your phone. Spend some quality time with your family.

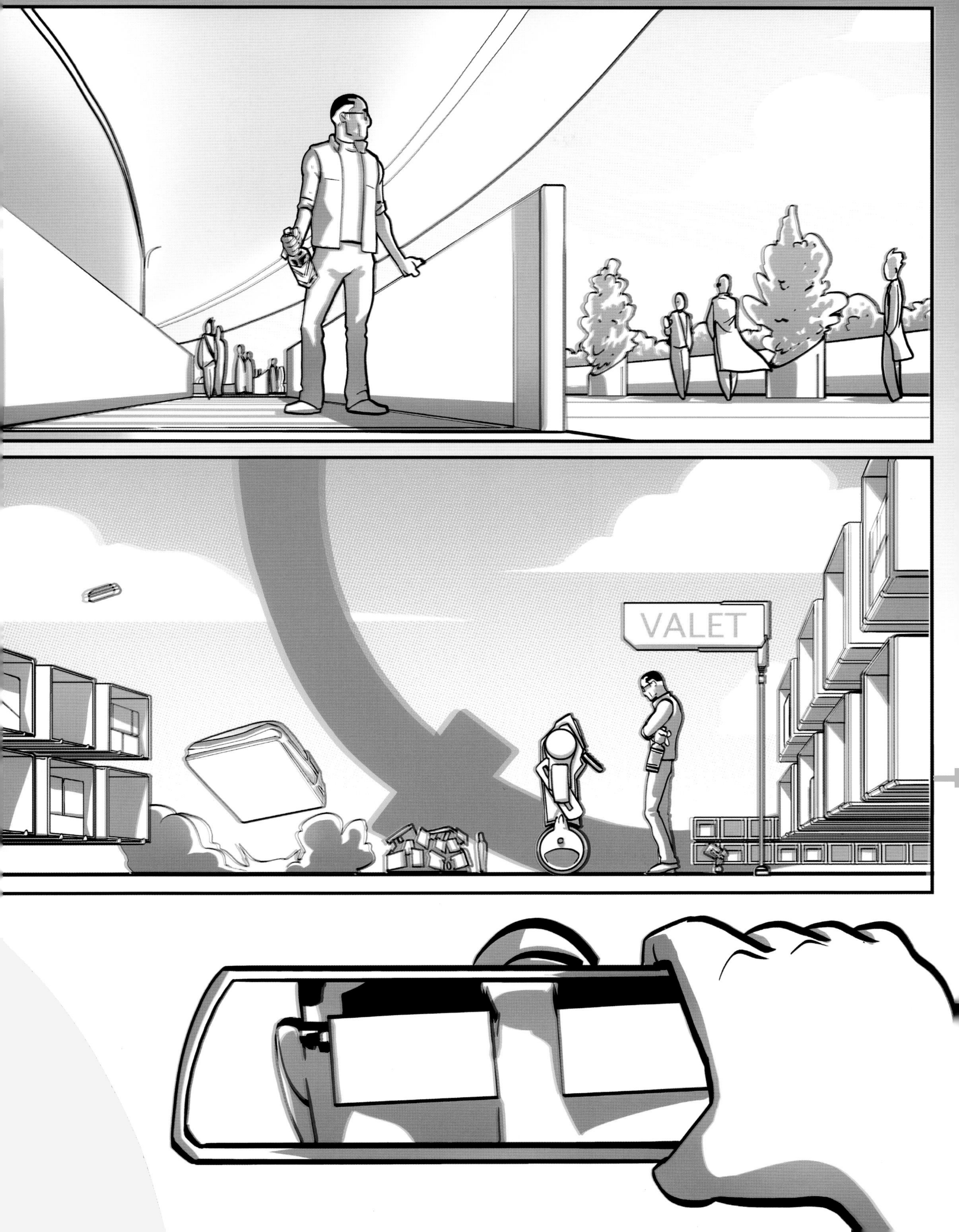
VALET

WHAT'S ON
MY MIND? 7:19PM APRIL 25, 2062

9% GETTING SEX/ FEELING SEXY
I probably could have "done it" with Erica today, right? So why didn't I?

18% FOOD/DINNER
Hungry. Haven't eaten today. L-A-S-A-G-N-A.

50% WHAT THE FUTURE HOLDS
We have finished something impressive that the press and people in general predictably will talk about, desire and use. I'm genuinely excited about this fact even though I can't tell anybody the specifics. This is Huge.

7% MY NET WORTH
I am on track to make $85,900,000.00 this year, increasing my net worth (including the apartment) to nearly $595,000,000.00 -- im that ballpark anyway, I officially have more money than I could ever possibly spend.

10% THE IMPACT A DIVORCE WOULD HAVE ON MY NET WORTH
She would have to take half. She has too much dirt on me to fight her on that.

5.5% NEW AND SPECIFIC SEXUAL CURIOSITY A.K.A. "WICKED THOUGHTS" RE: MICHELLE'S NEW BEHAVIORAL THERAPIST
She just started working for us. Why can't I remember her name? Jessie? Jackie?

6% MY DAUGHTER MICHELLE
There is no cure. There's not going to be one. I'm living with that :((

0.2% AM I SPENDING ENOUGH TIME WITH ROCHESTER?
Pretty confident I am but it's a subject always worth thinking about.

3% WHEN EXACTLY IS DAVID GOING TO EXPIRE??

6.5% DEEPER WORRIES/ANXIETY RE: THE ANY NUMBER OF RANDOM, TERRIBLE THINGS THAT COULD BEFALL
My person. My business. My family. My home. Erica.

1% [PERMANENT MINIMUM] THAT TIME I HAD TO KILL ANOTHER MAN
Got away with it though.

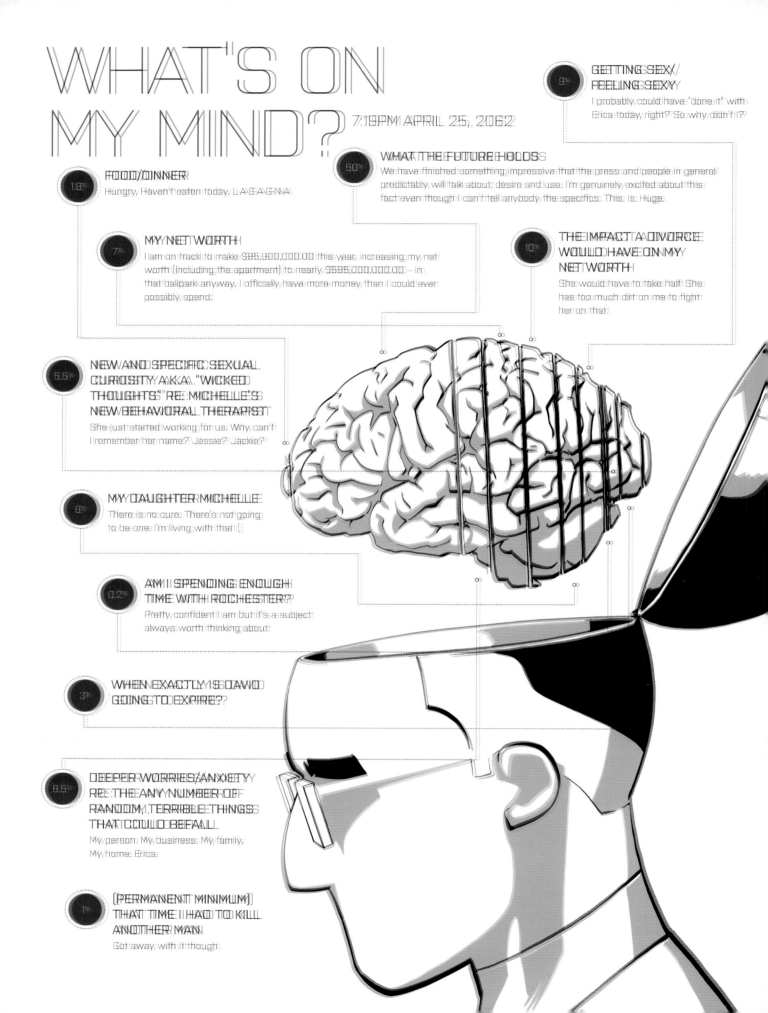

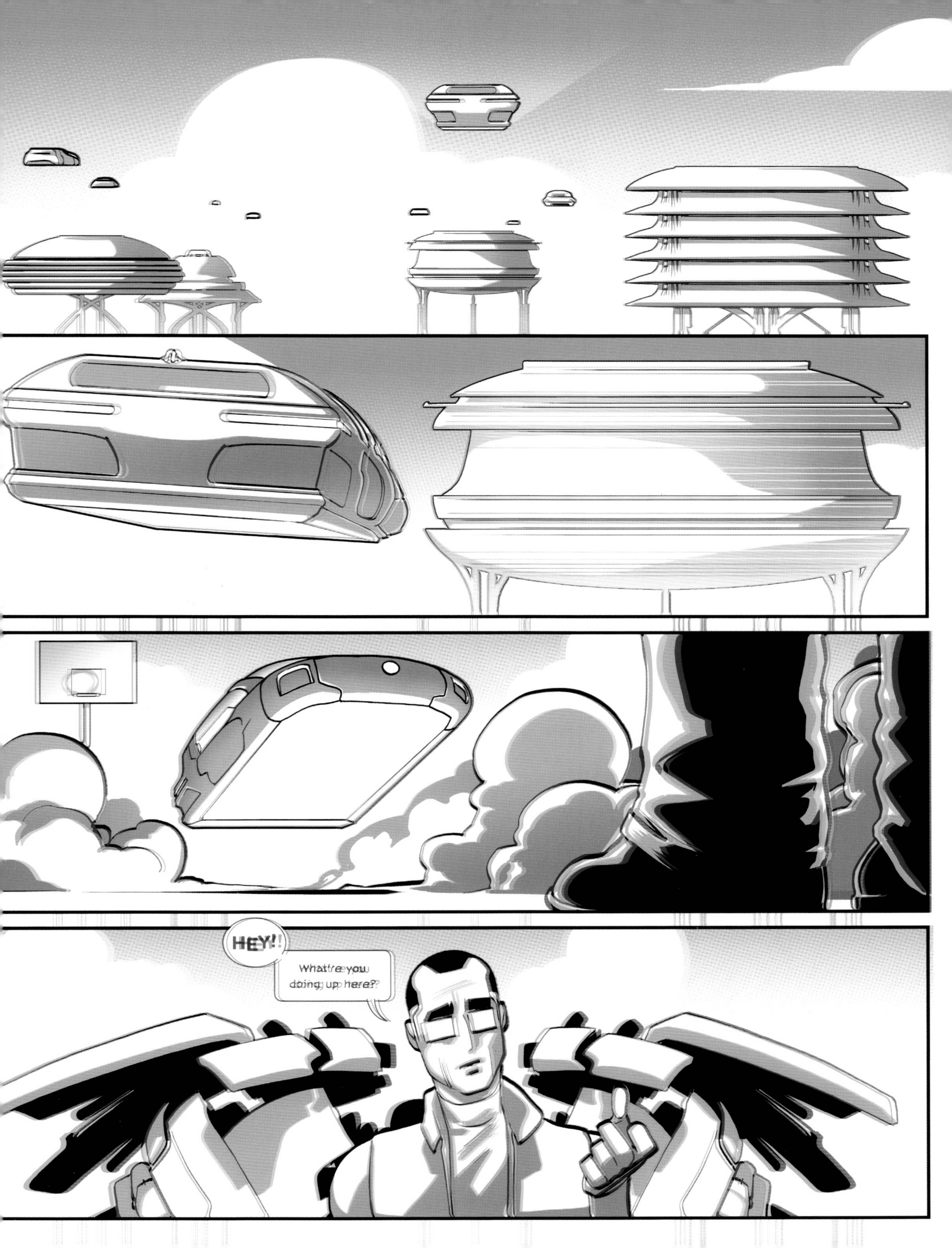
HEY!!
Whatt're you doing up here??

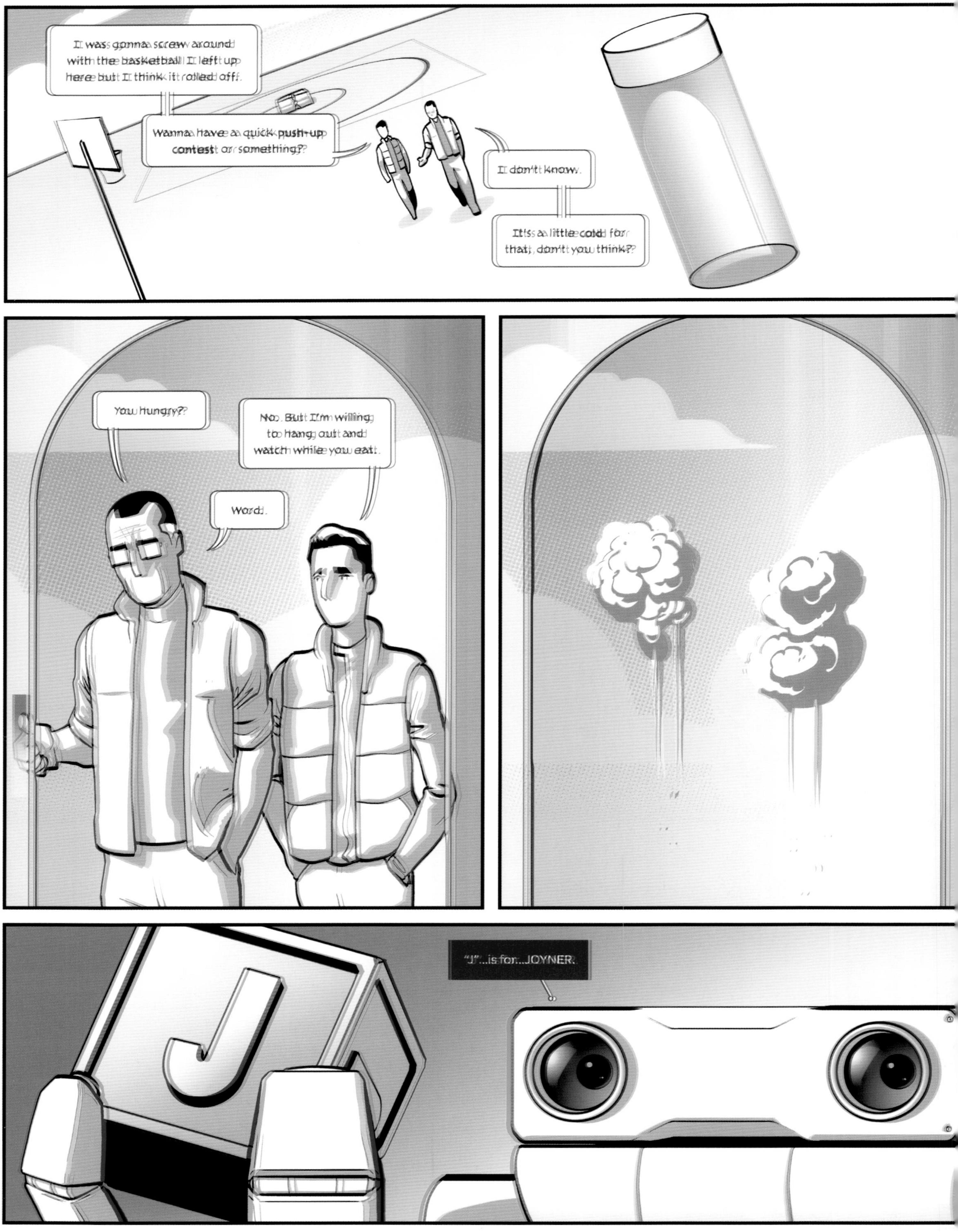
I was gonna screw around with the basketball I left up here but I think it rolled off.
Wanna have a quick push-up contest or something?
I don't know.
It's a little cold for that, don't you think?
You hungry?
No. But I'm willing to hang out and watch while you eat.
Word.
"J"...is for...JOYNER.

I KNOW THAT!
DADDY'S home!
Anyone seen my basketball?
Where's their mother?
...
Master Suite. Dressing Area.
What's the new therapist's name again?
Jamie.
Right. I knew it was 'J'-something. Why doesn't she have a car?
She just moved here. From the Moon.
Hmm.
I guess there's better public transportation up there.

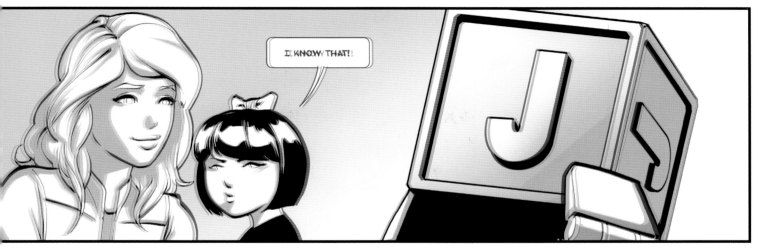

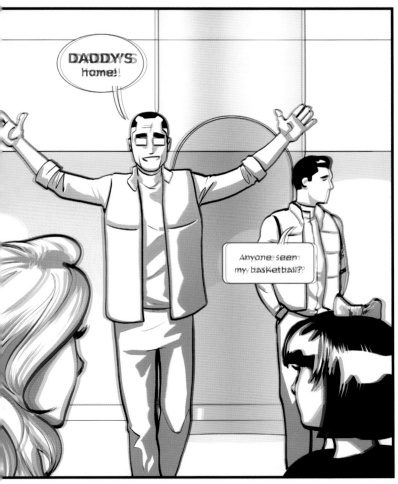

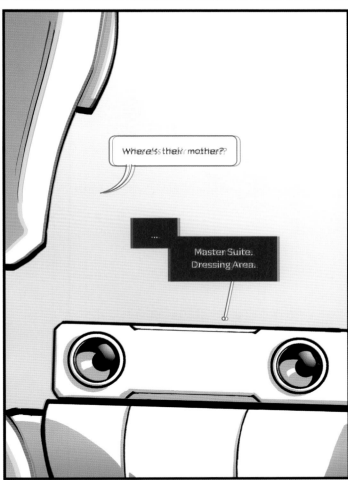

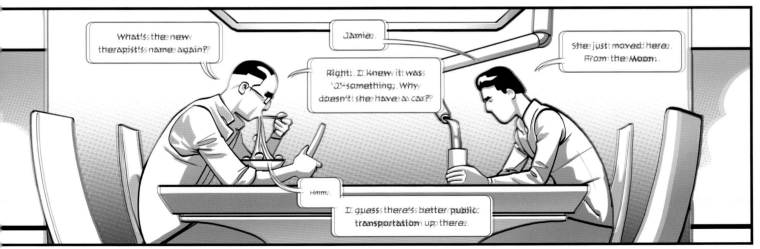

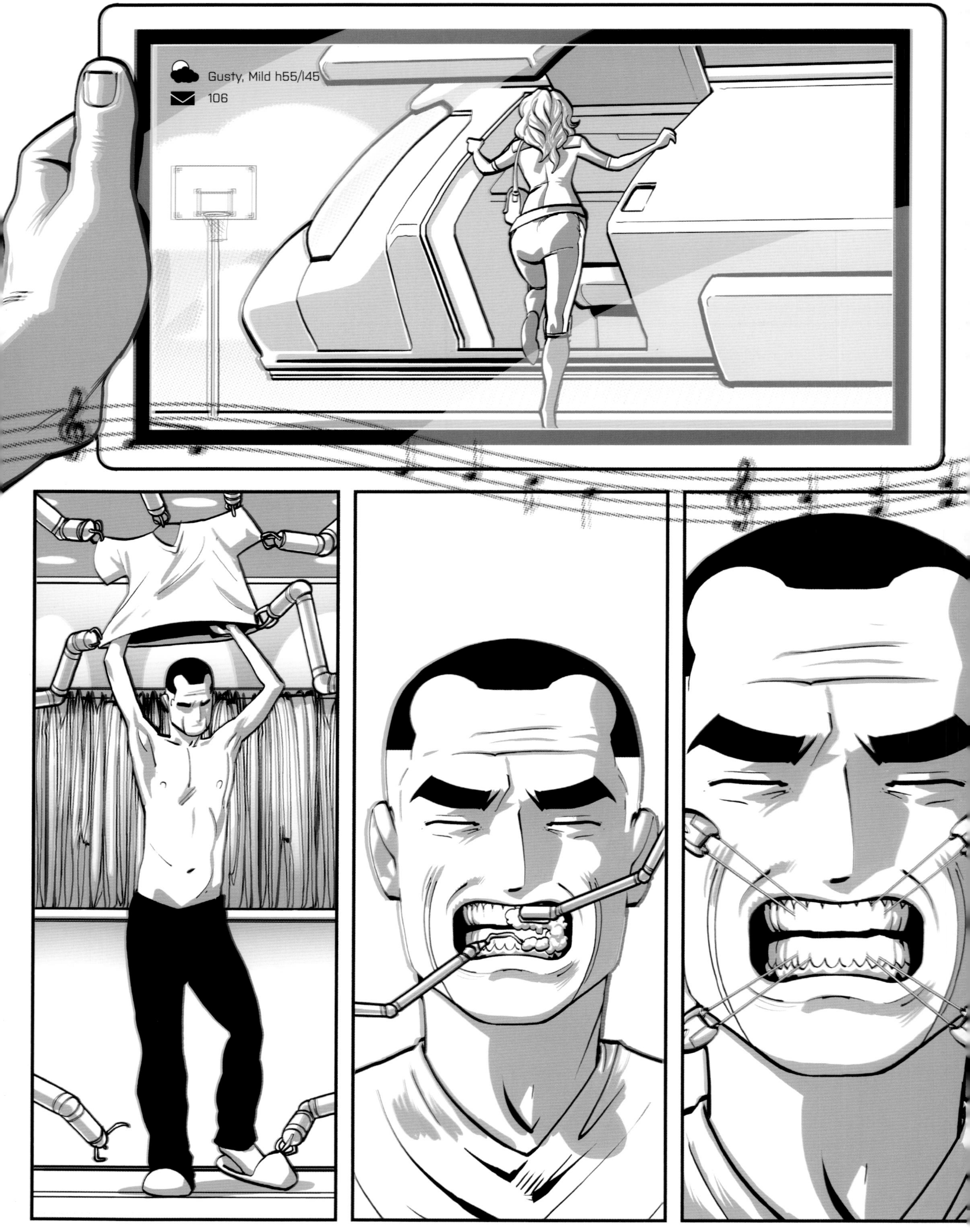
Gusty, Mild h55/l45
106

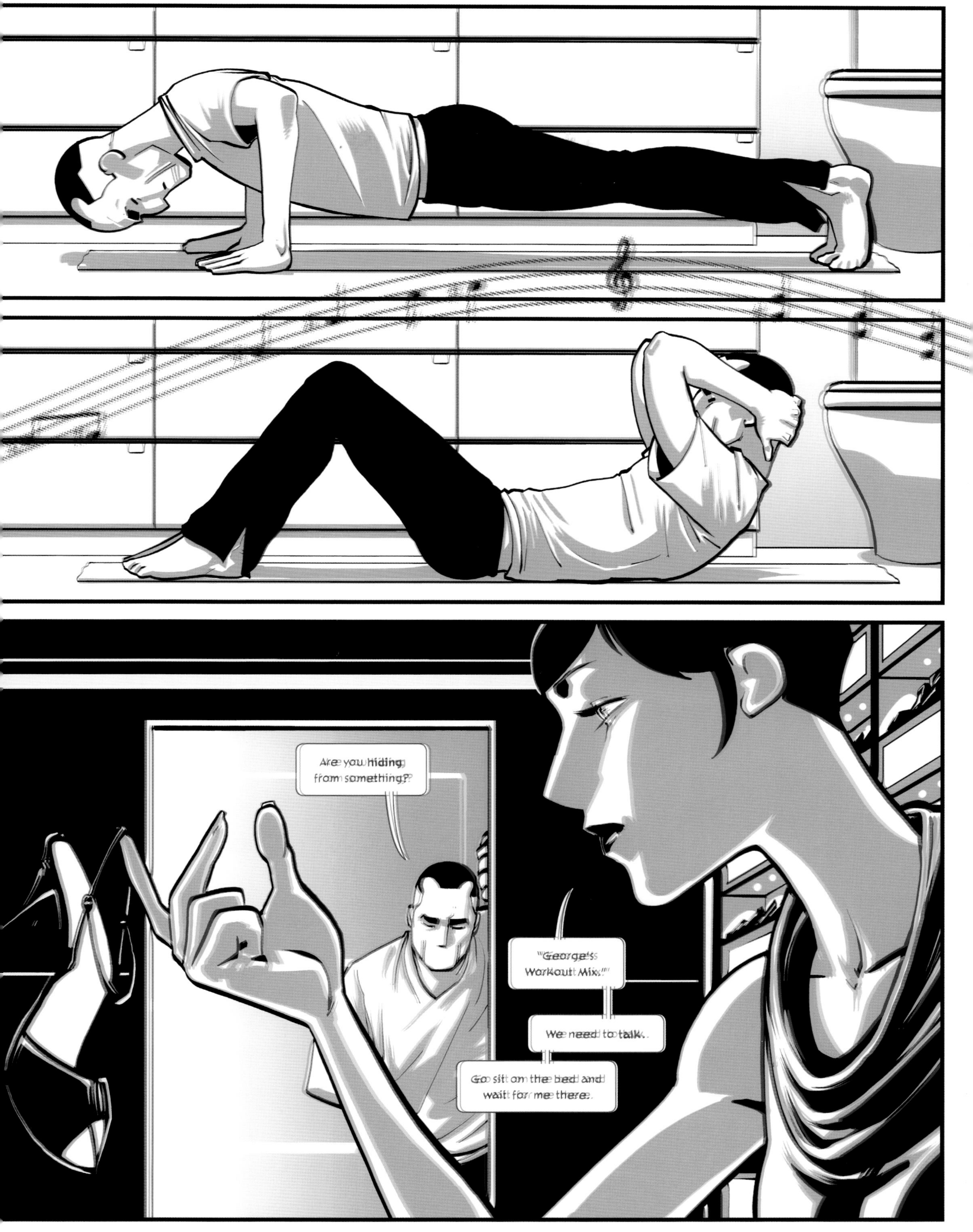

Are you hiding from something?
"George's Workout Mix."
We need to talk.
Go sit on the bed and wait for me there.

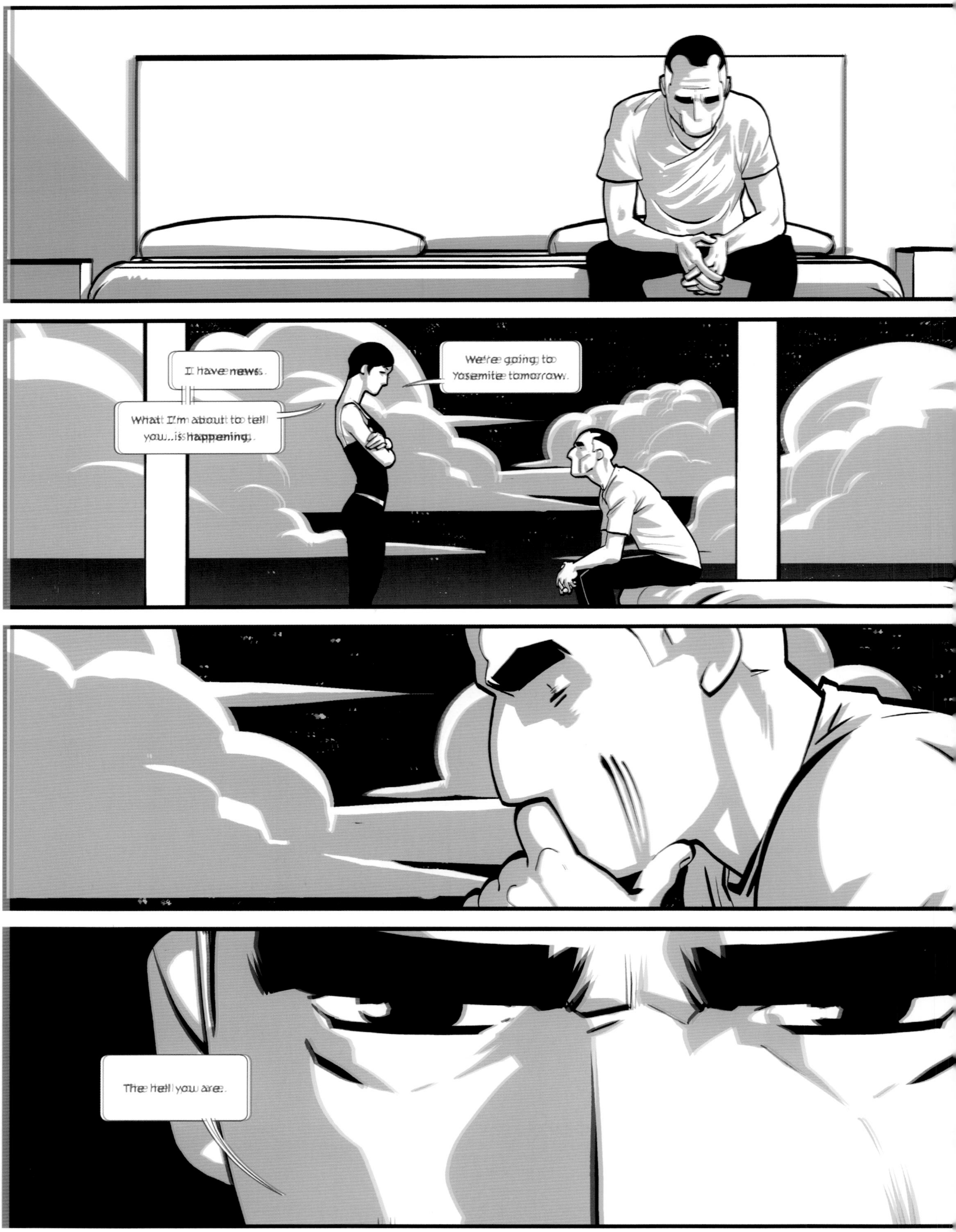

I have news.
What I'm about to tell you...is happening.
We're going to Yosemite tomorrow.
The hell you are.

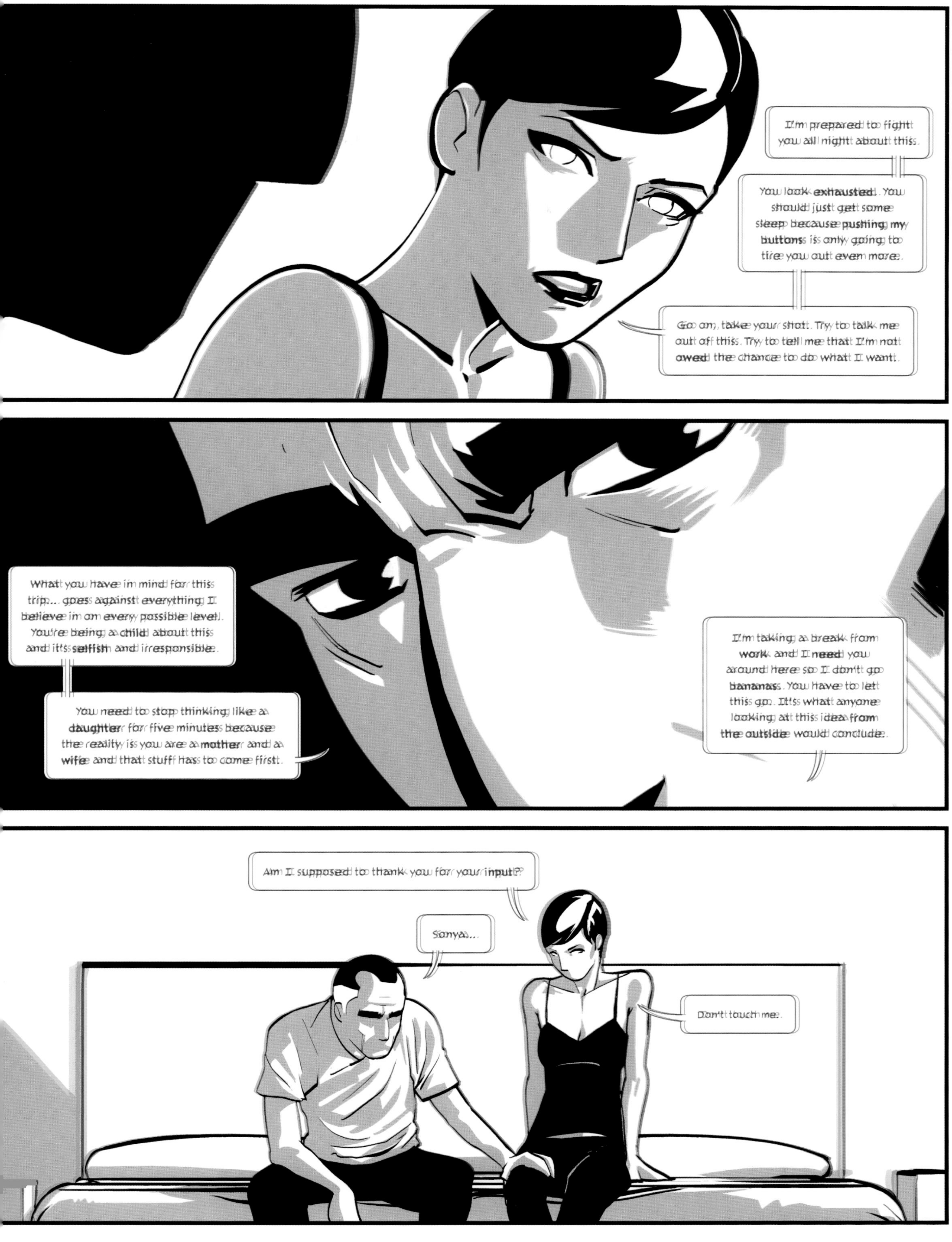
I'm prepared to fight you all night about this.
You look exhausted. You should just get some sleep because pushing my buttons is only going to tire you out even more.
Go on, take your shot. Try to talk me out of this. Try to tell me that I'm not owed the chance to do what I want.
What you have in mind for this trip... goes against everything I believe in on every possible level. You're being a child about this and it's selfish and irresponsible.
You need to stop thinking like a daughter for five minutes because the reality is you are a mother and a wife and that stuff has to come first.
I'm taking a break from work and I need you around here so I don't go bananas. You have to let this go. It's what anyone looking at this idea from the outside would conclude.
Am I supposed to thank you for your input?
Sonya...
Don't touch me.

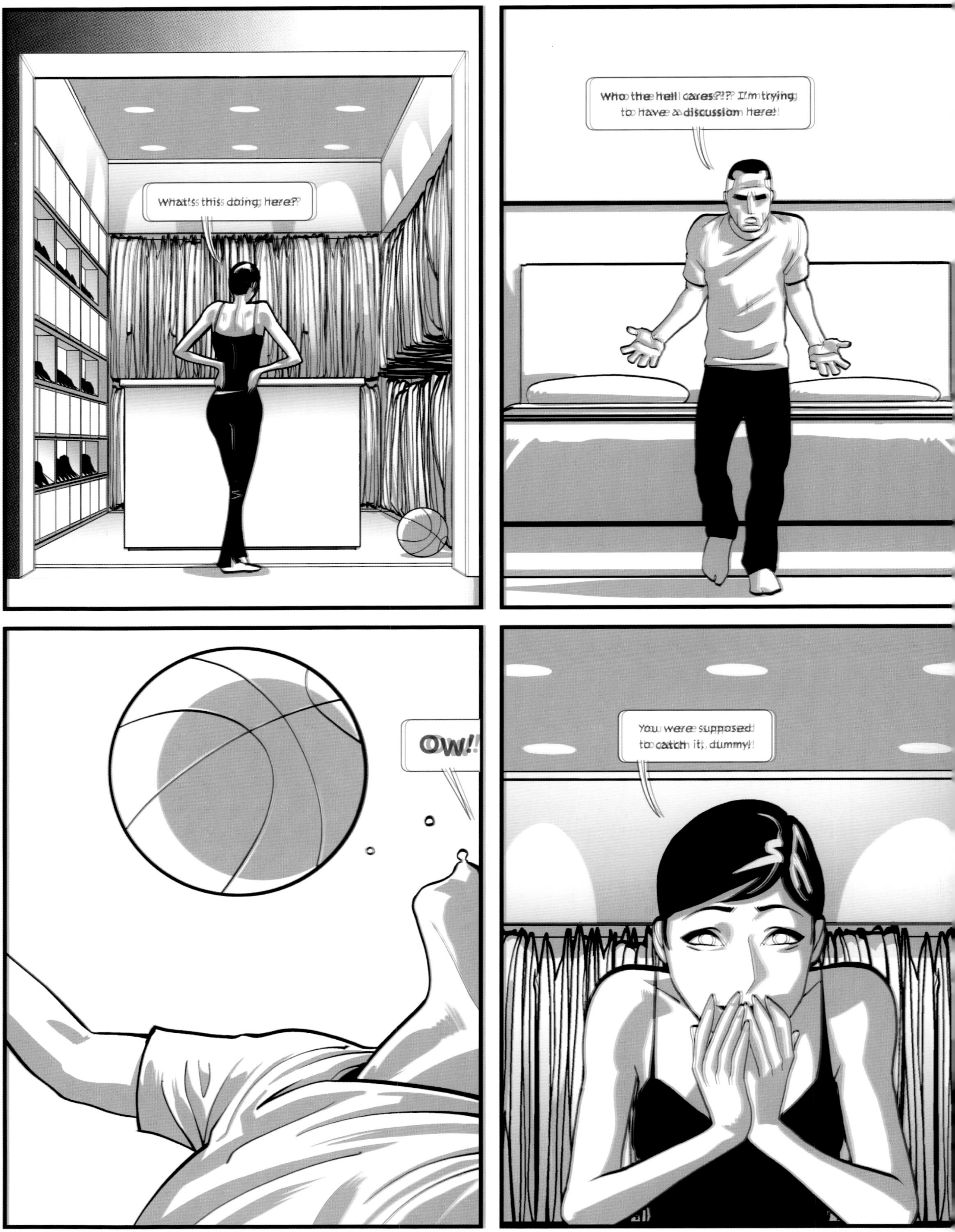
What's this doing here?
Who the hell cares?!? I'm trying to have a discussion here!
OW!!
You were supposed to catch it, dummy!

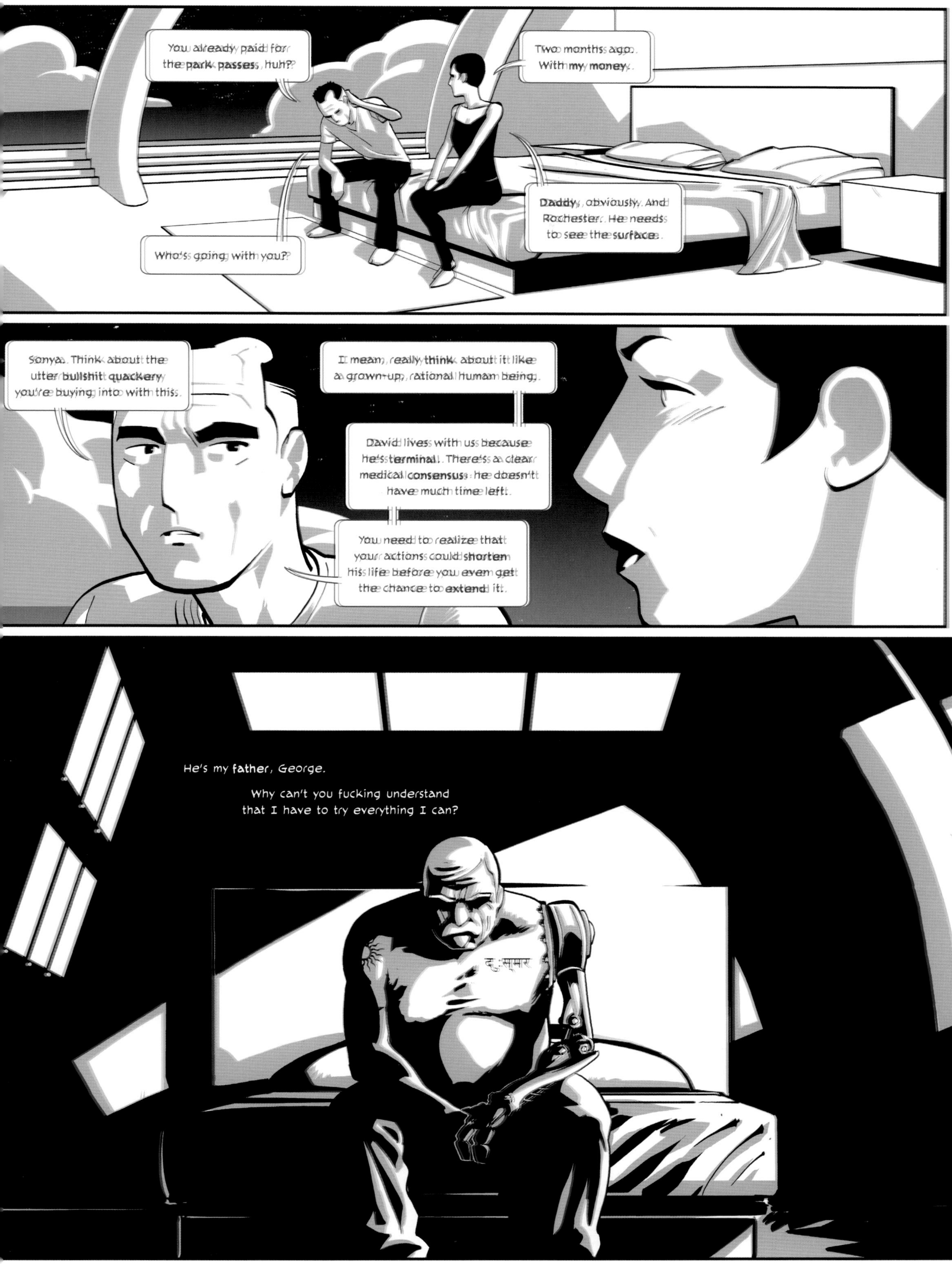
You already paid for the park passes, huh?
Two months ago. With my money.
Who's going with you?
Daddy, obviously. And Rochester. He needs to see the surface.
Sonya. Think about the utter bullshit quackery you're buying into with this.
I mean, really think about it like a grown-up, rational human being.
David lives with us because he's terminal. There's a clear medical consensus: he doesn't have much time left.
You need to realize that your actions could shorten his life before you even get the chance to extend it.
He's my father, George.
Why can't you fucking understand that I have to try everything I can?

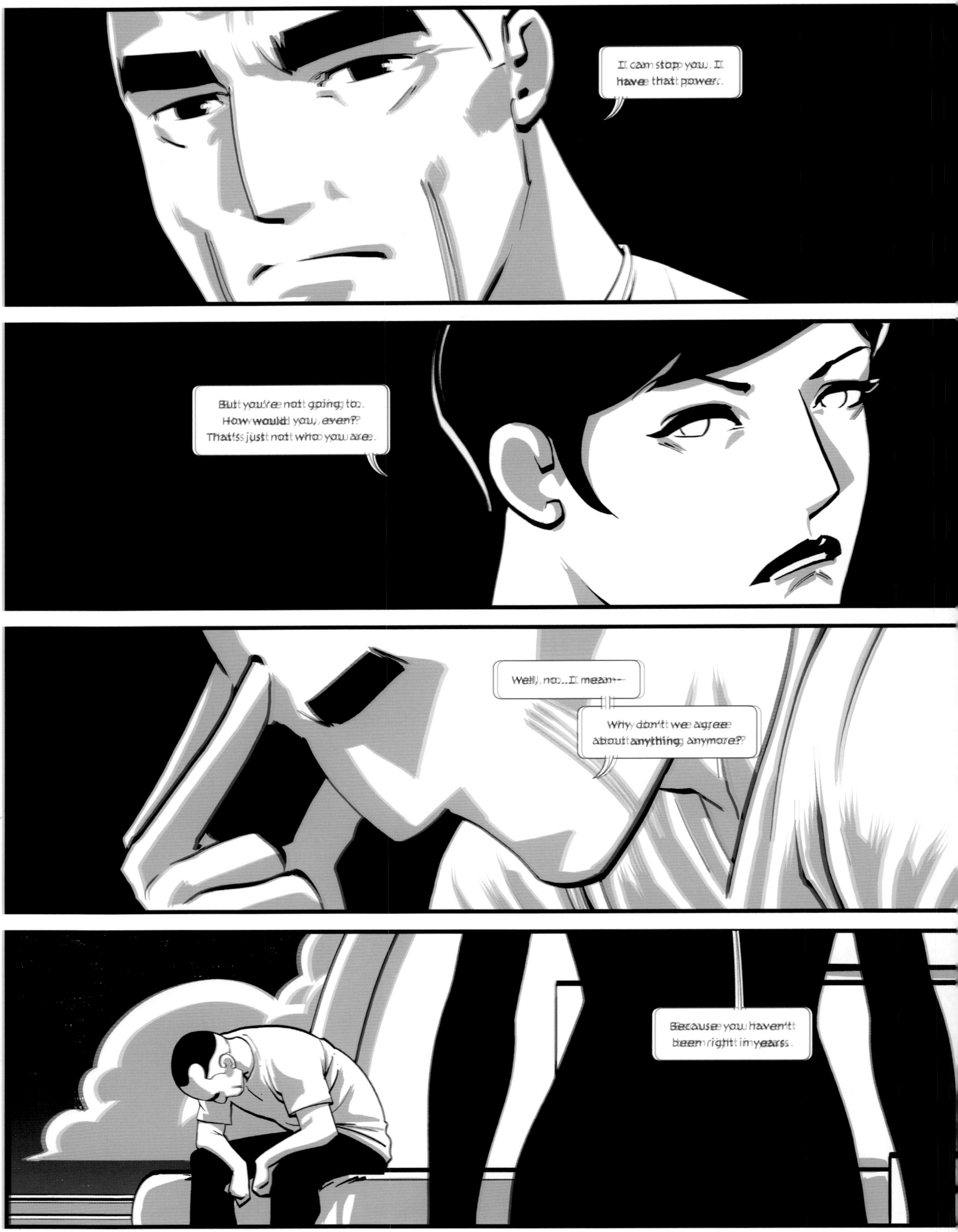
I can stop you. I **have** that power.
But you're not going to. How **would** you, *even*? That's just not who you are.
Well, no...I mean--
Why don't we agree about **anything** anymore?
Because you haven't been right in **years**.

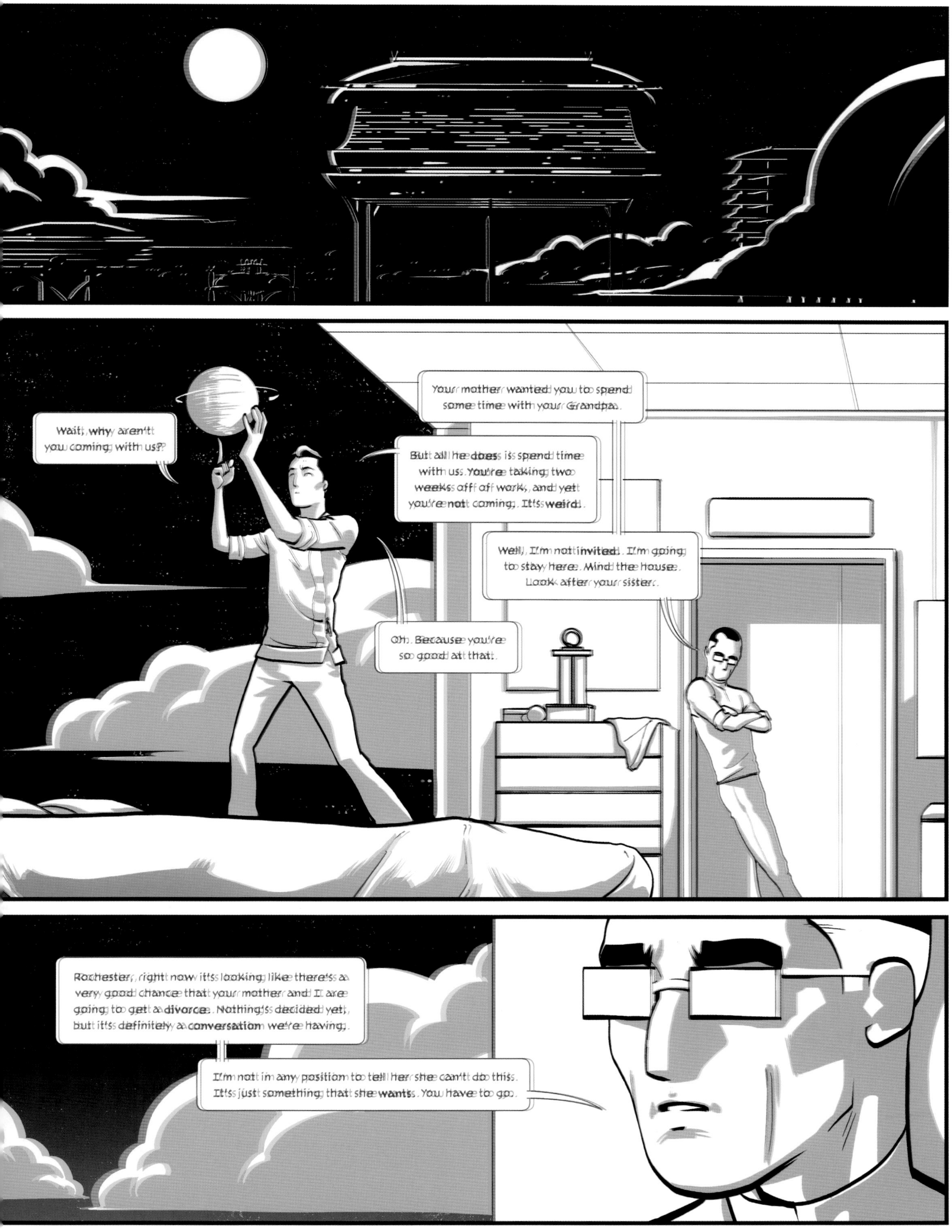
Wait, why aren't you coming with us?
Your mother wanted you to spend some time with your Grandpa.
But all he does is spend time with us. You're taking two weeks off of work, and yet you're not coming. It's weird.
Well, I'm not invited. I'm going to stay here. Mind the house. Look after your sister.
Oh. Because you're so good at that.
Rochester, right now it's looking like there's a very good chance that your mother and I are going to get a divorce. Nothing's decided yet, but it's definitely a conversation we're having.
I'm not in any position to tell her she can't do this. It's just something that she wants. You have to go.

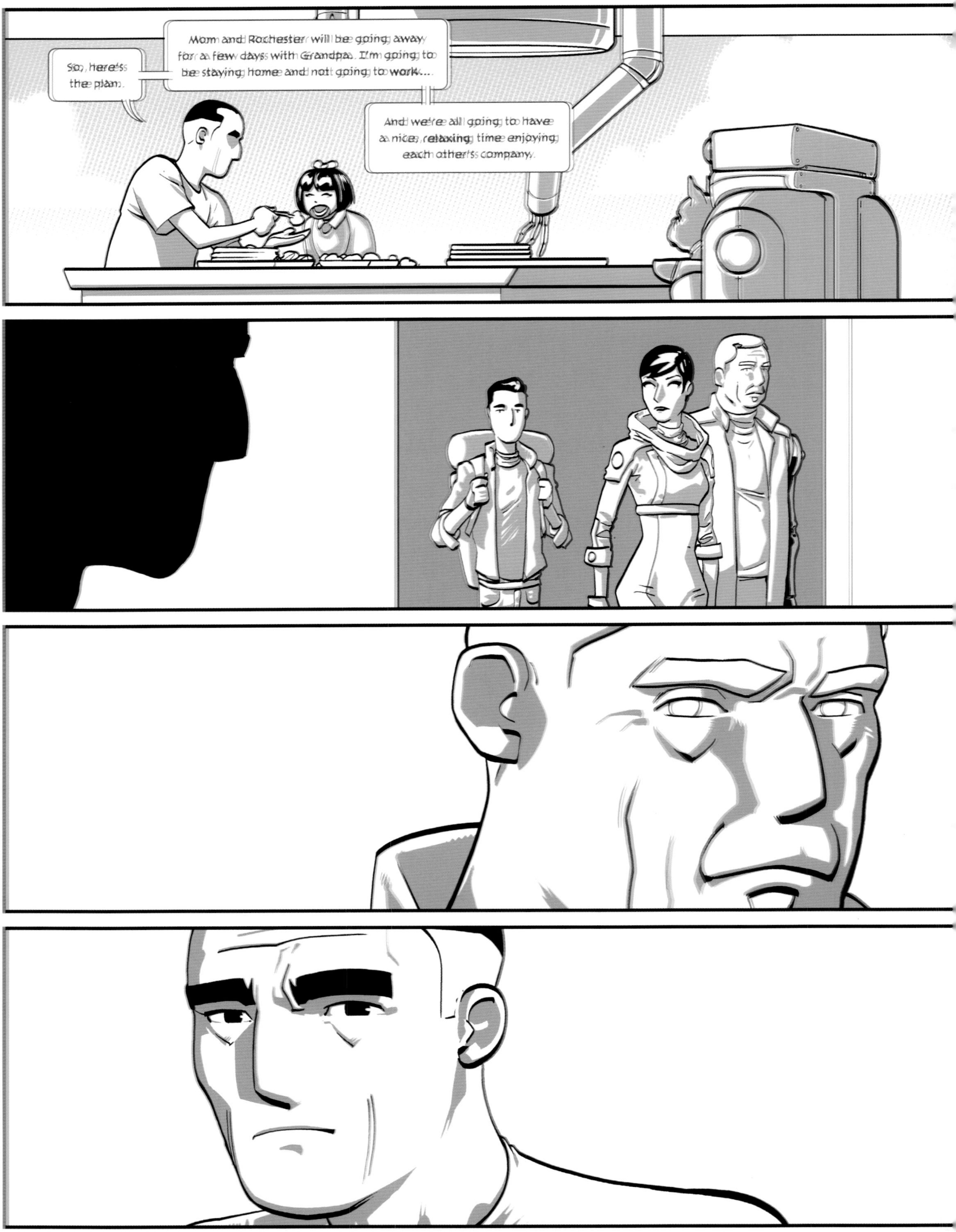
So, here's the plan.
Mom and Rochester will be going away for a few days with Grandpa. I'm going to be staying home and not going to work...
And we're all going to have a nice, **relaxing** time enjoying each other's company.

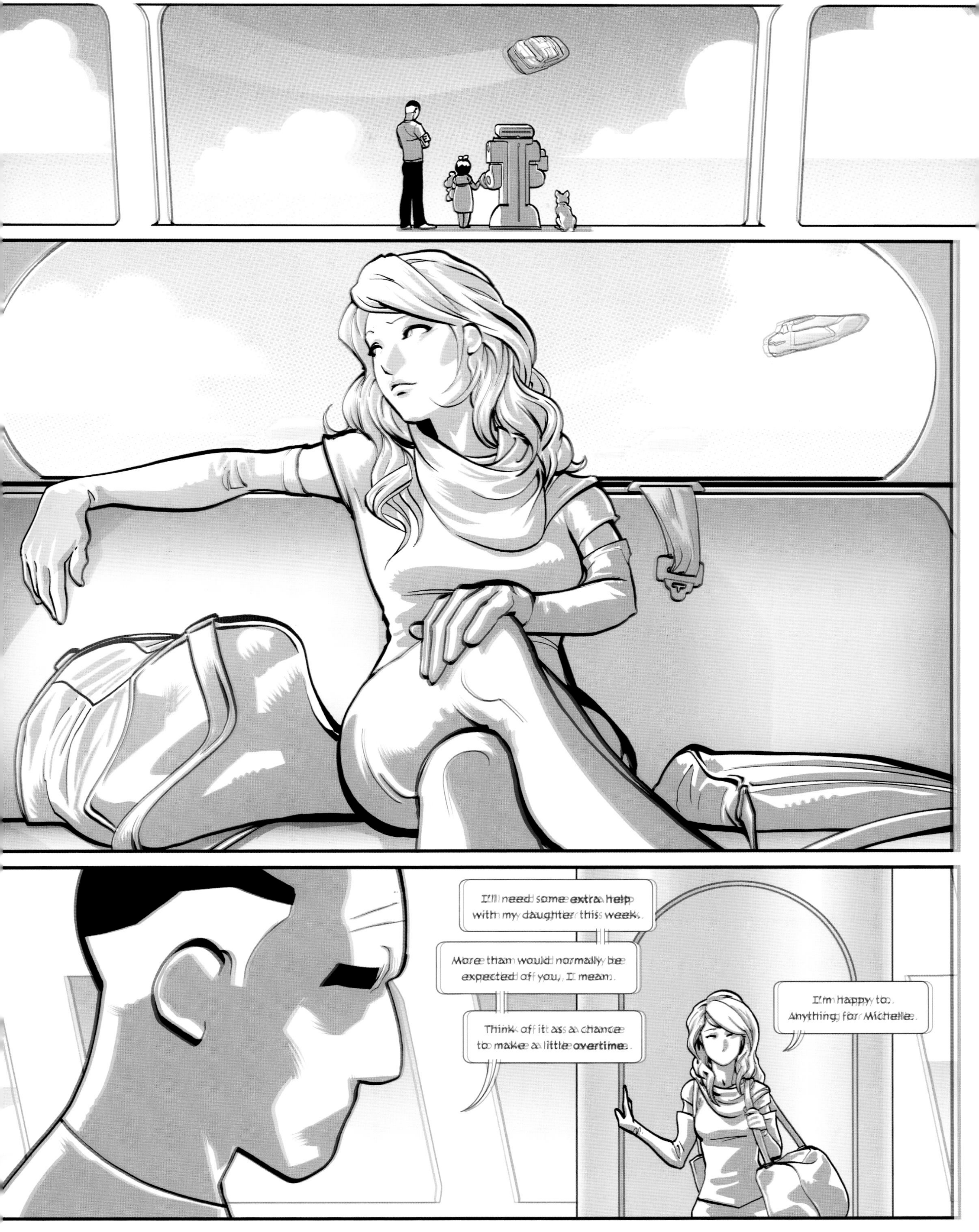
I'll need some extra help with my daughter this week.
More than would normally be expected of you, I mean.
Think of it as a chance to make a little overtime.
I'm happy to. Anything for Michelle.

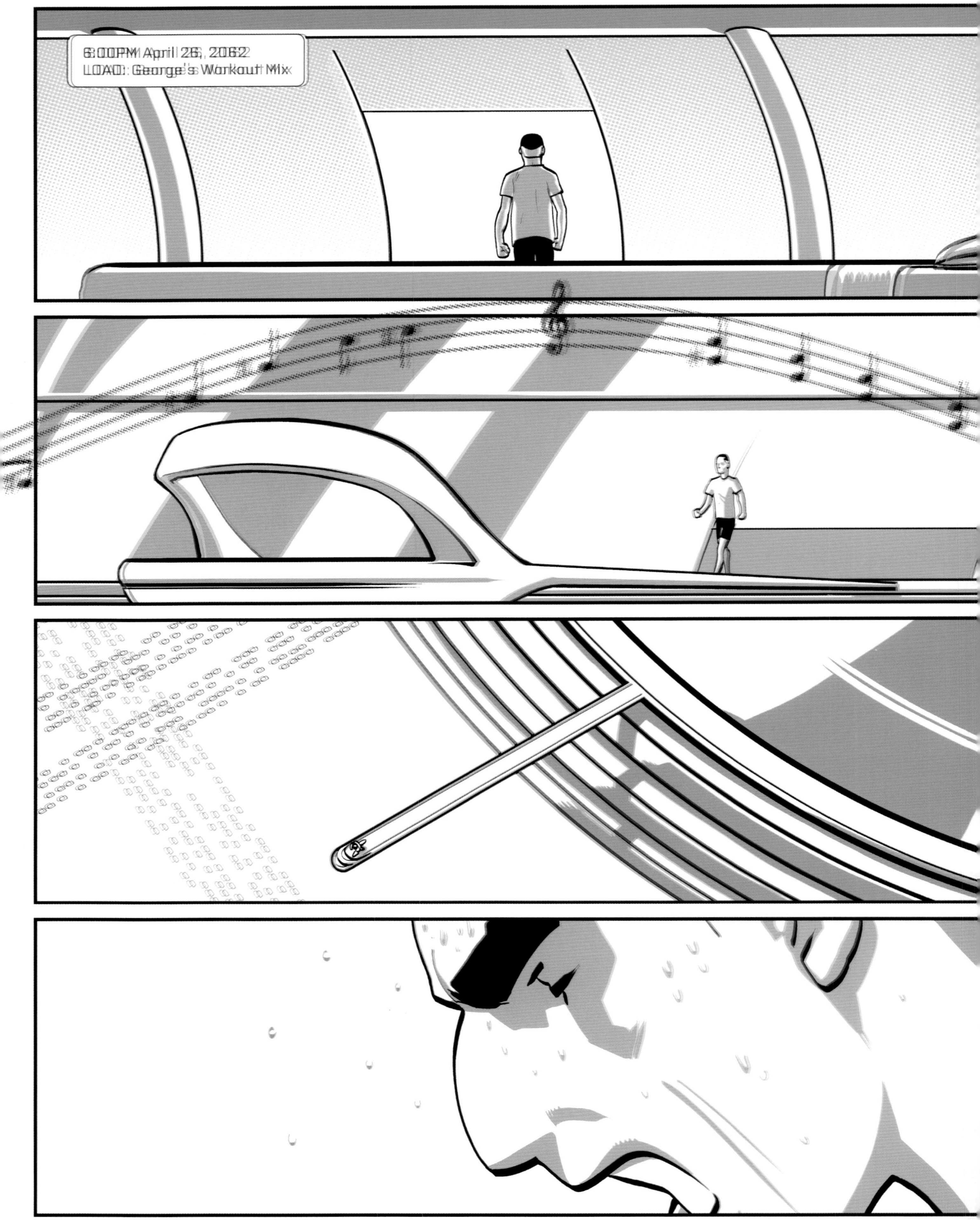
6:00PM April 26, 2062
LOAD: George's Workout Mix

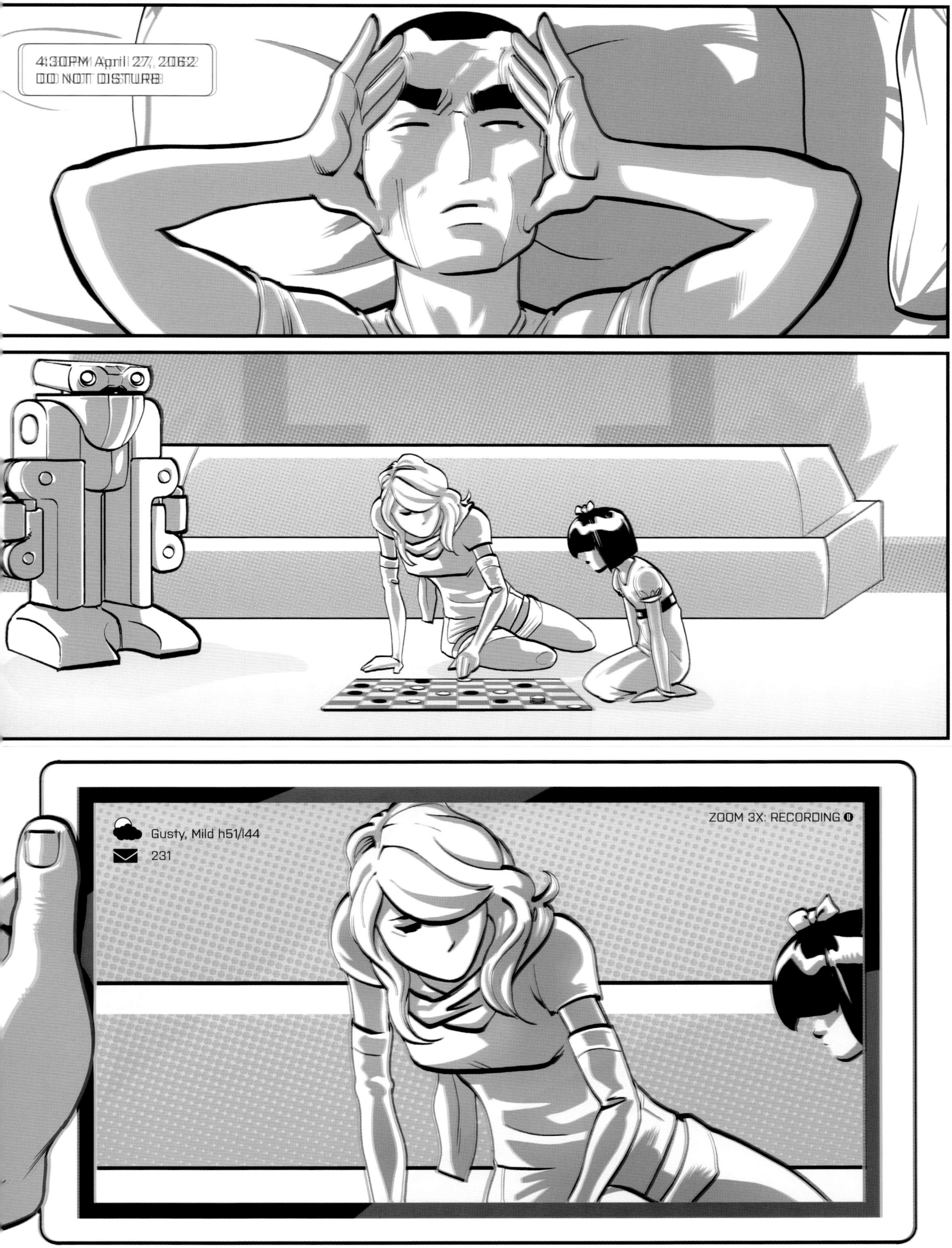
4:30PM April 27, 2062
DO NOT DISTURB
Gusty, Mild h51/l44
231
ZOOM 3X: RECORDING

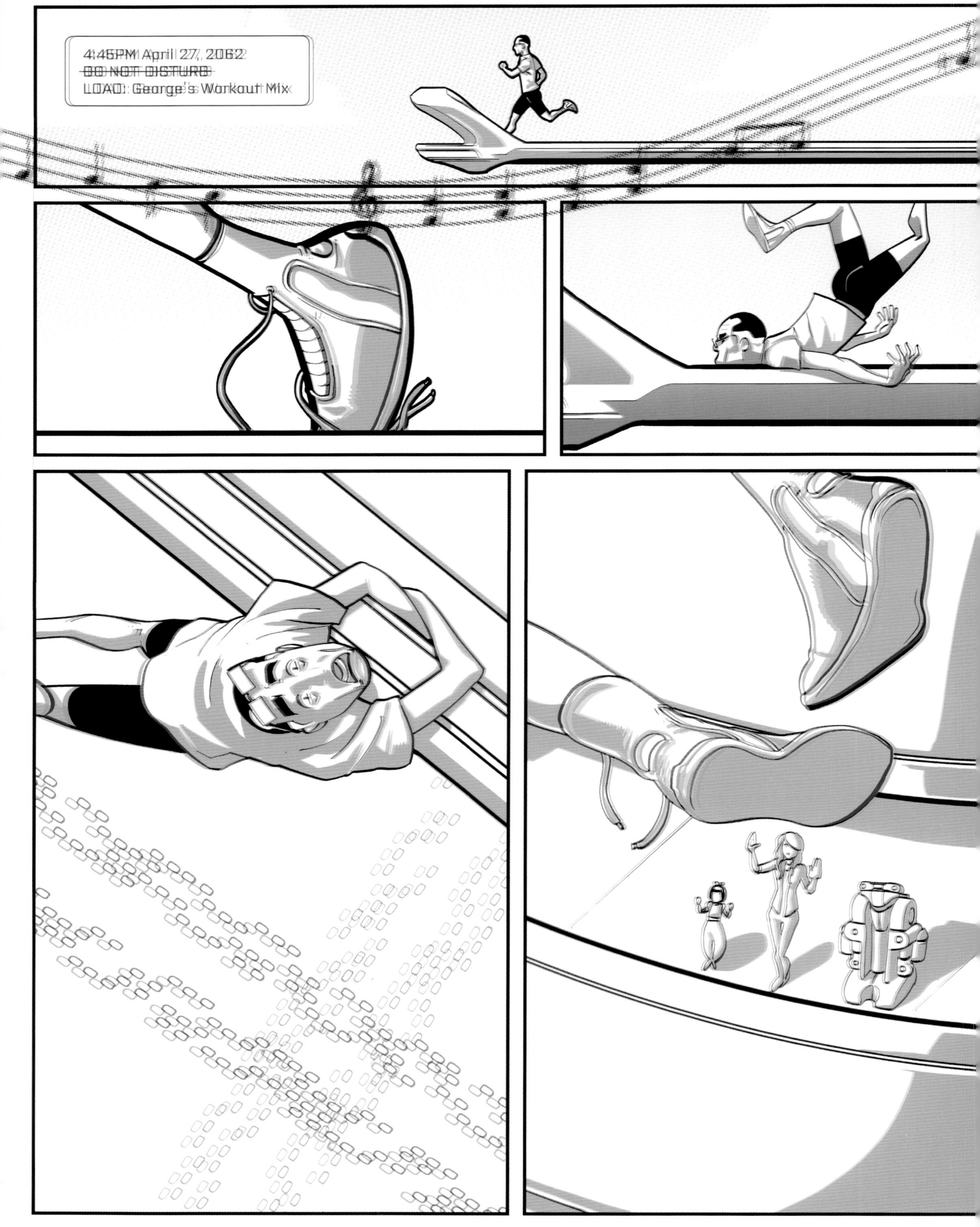
4:45PM April 27, 2062
DO NOT DISTURB
LOAD: George's Workout Mix

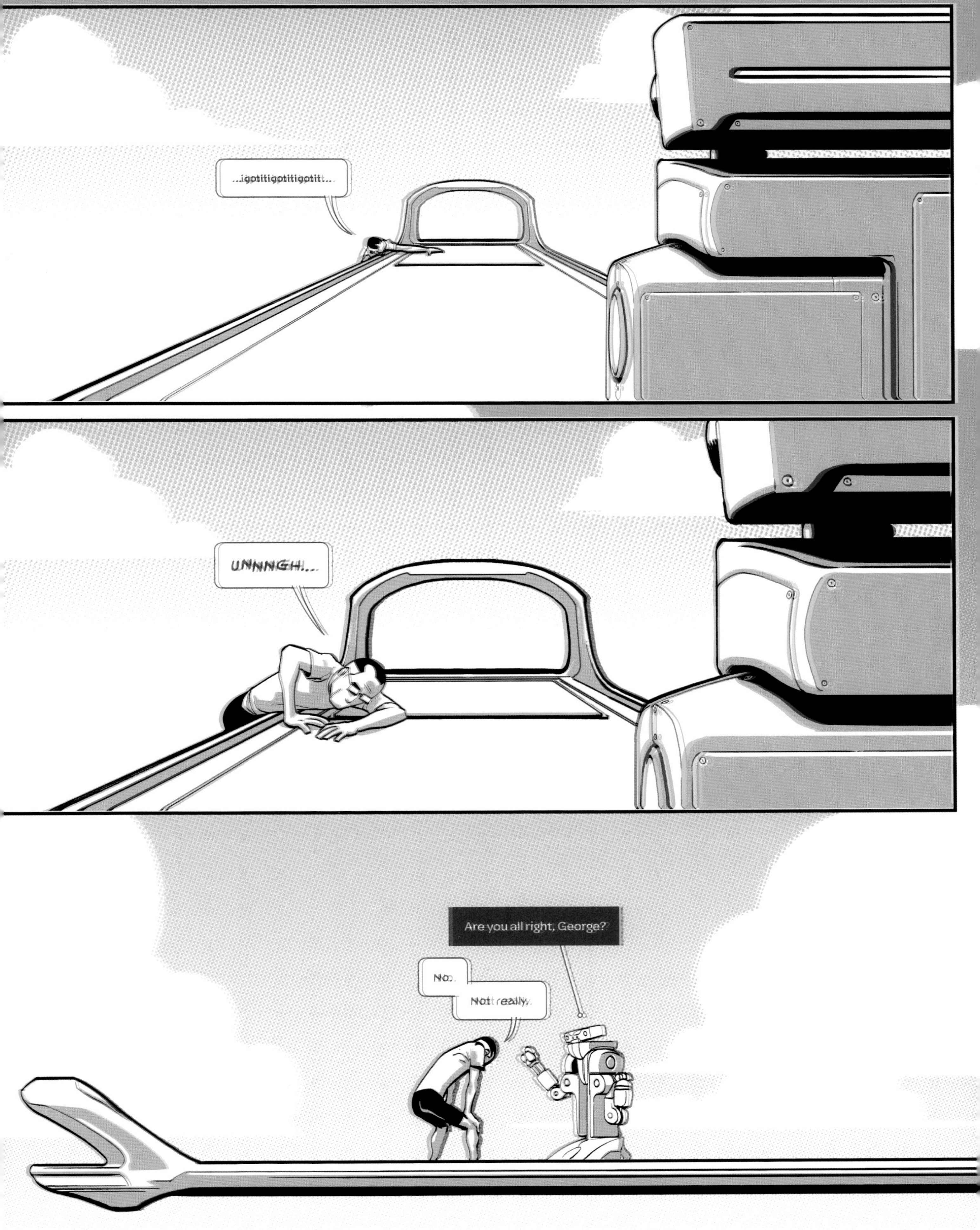
...igotitigotitigotit...
UNNNGH!...
Are you all right, George?
No.
Not really.

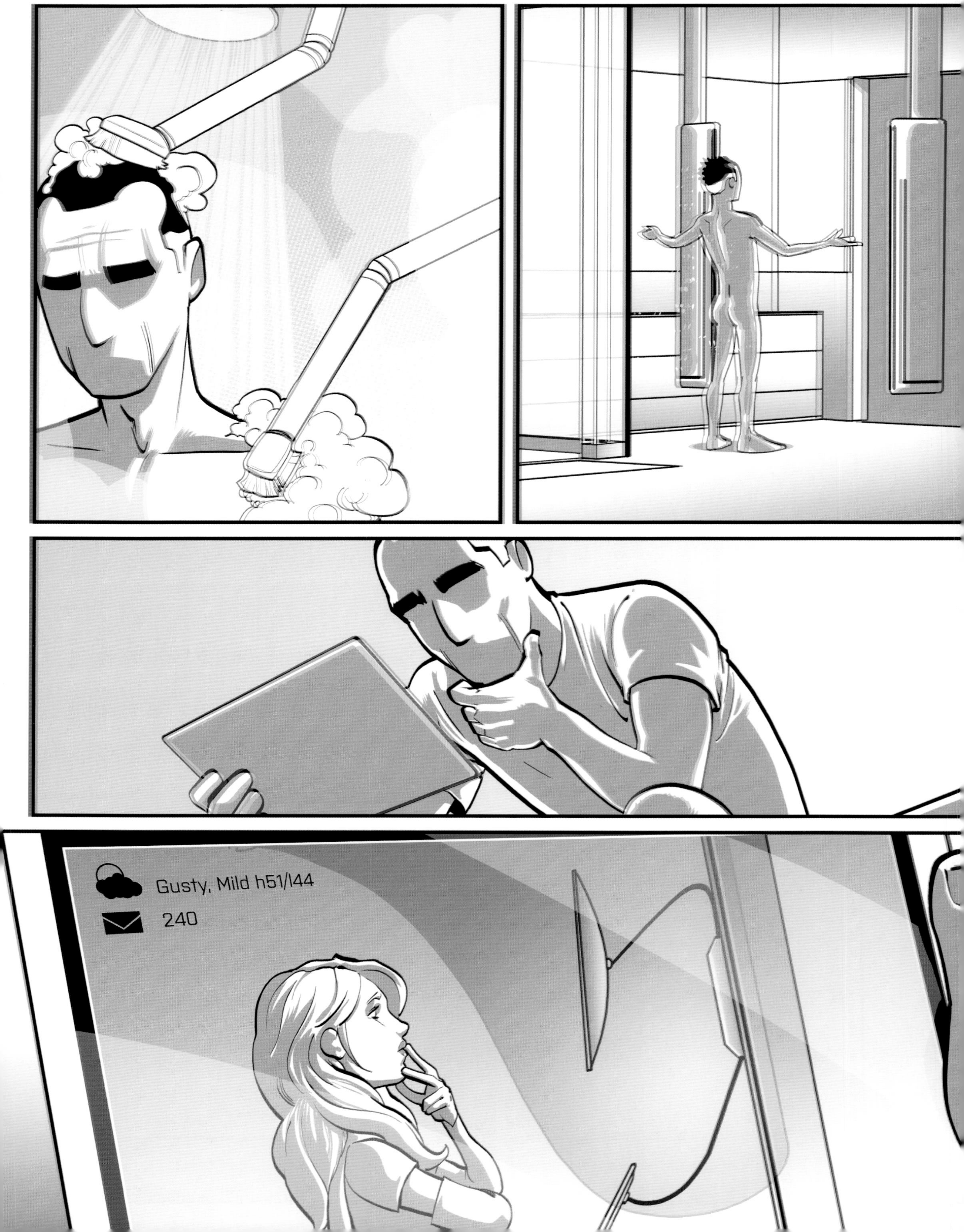
Gusty, Mild h51/144
240

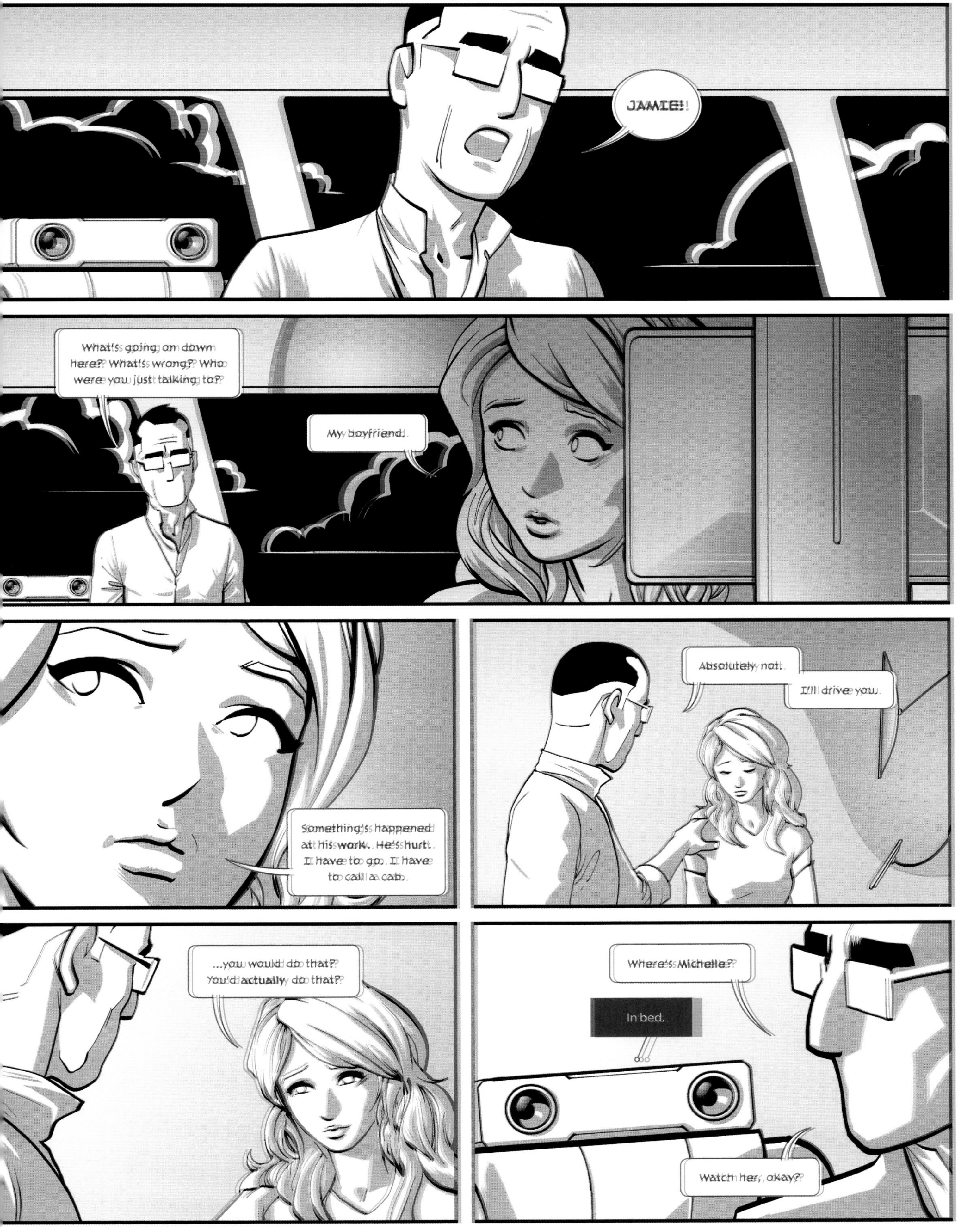
JAMIE!
What's going on down here? What's wrong? Who were you just talking to?
My boyfriend.
Something's happened at his work. He's hurt. I have to go. I have to call a cab.
Absolutely not.
I'll drive you.
...you would do that? You'd actually do that?
Where's Michelle?
In bed.
Watch her, okay?

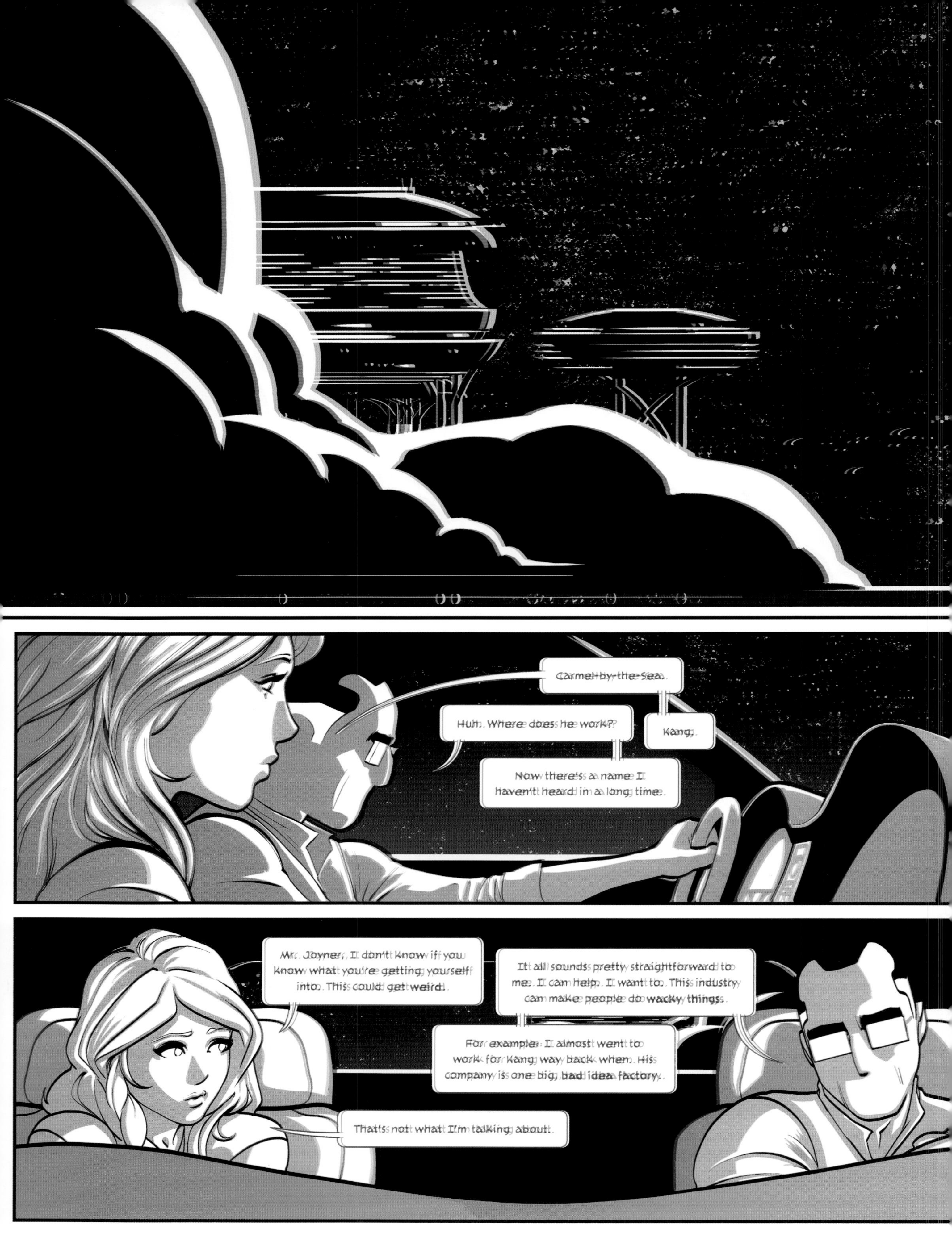
Carmel-by-the-Sea.
Huh. Where does he work?
Kang.
Now there's a name I haven't heard in a long time.
Mr. Joyner, I don't know if you know what you're getting yourself into. This could get weird.
It all sounds pretty straightforward to me. I can help. I want to. This industry can make people do wacky things.
For example: I almost went to work for Kang way back when. His company is one big, bad idea factory.
That's not what I'm talking about.

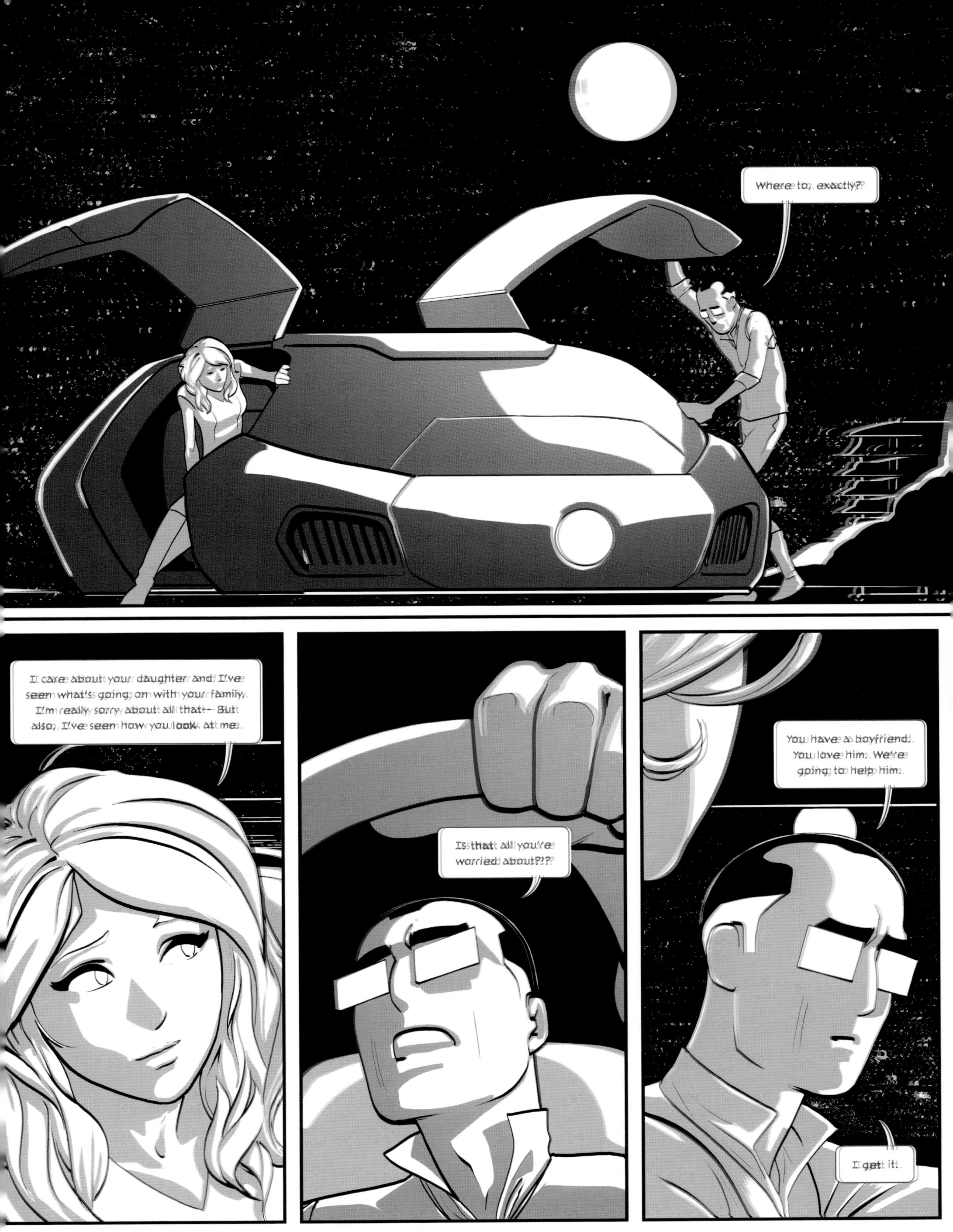
Where to, exactly?
I care about your daughter and I've seen what's going on with your family. I'm really sorry about all that-- But also, I've seen how you look at me.
Is that all you're worried about?!?
You have a boyfriend. You love him. We're going to help him.
I get it.

KANG
You can see why he loves it here.

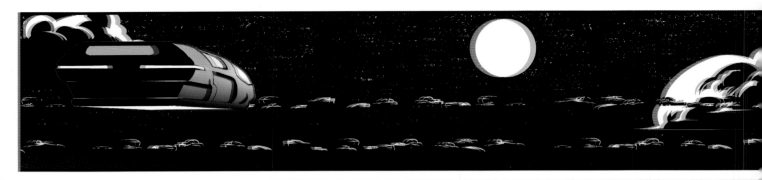

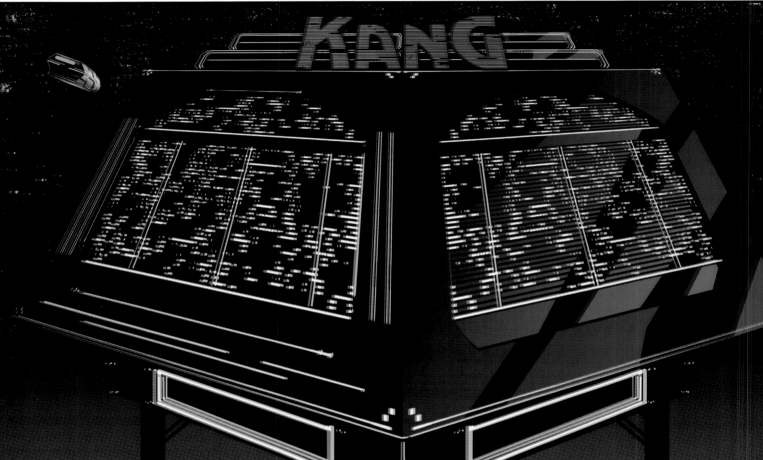

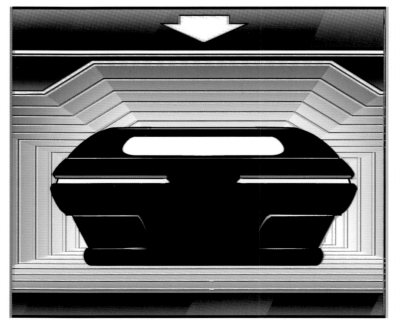

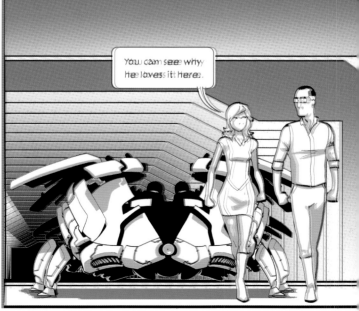

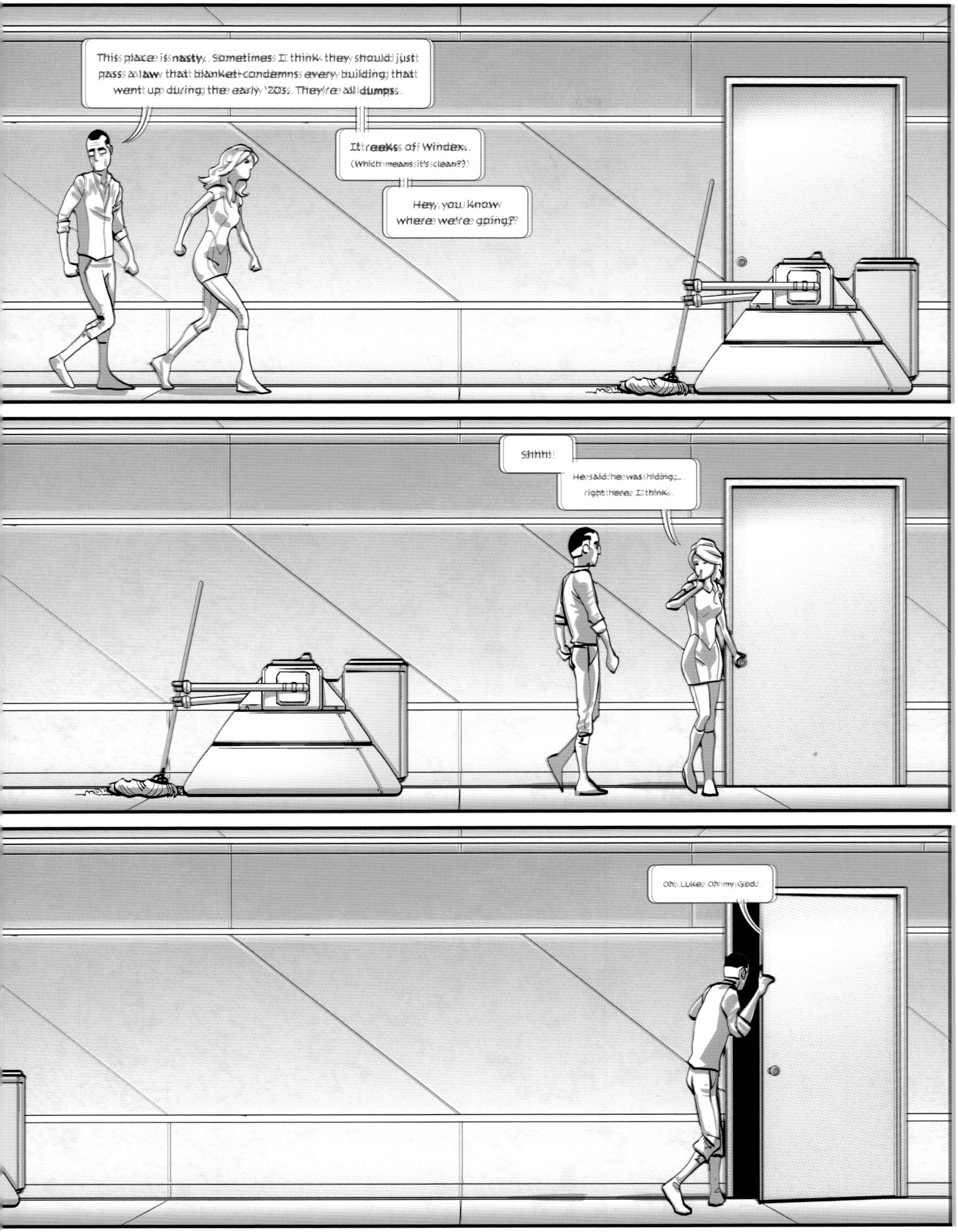
This place is nasty. Sometimes I think they should just pass a law that blanket-condemns every building that went up during the early '20s. They're all dumps.
It reeks of Windex. (Which means it's clean?)
Hey, you know where we're going?
Shhh!
He said he was hiding... right there, I think.
Oh, Luke. Oh my God.

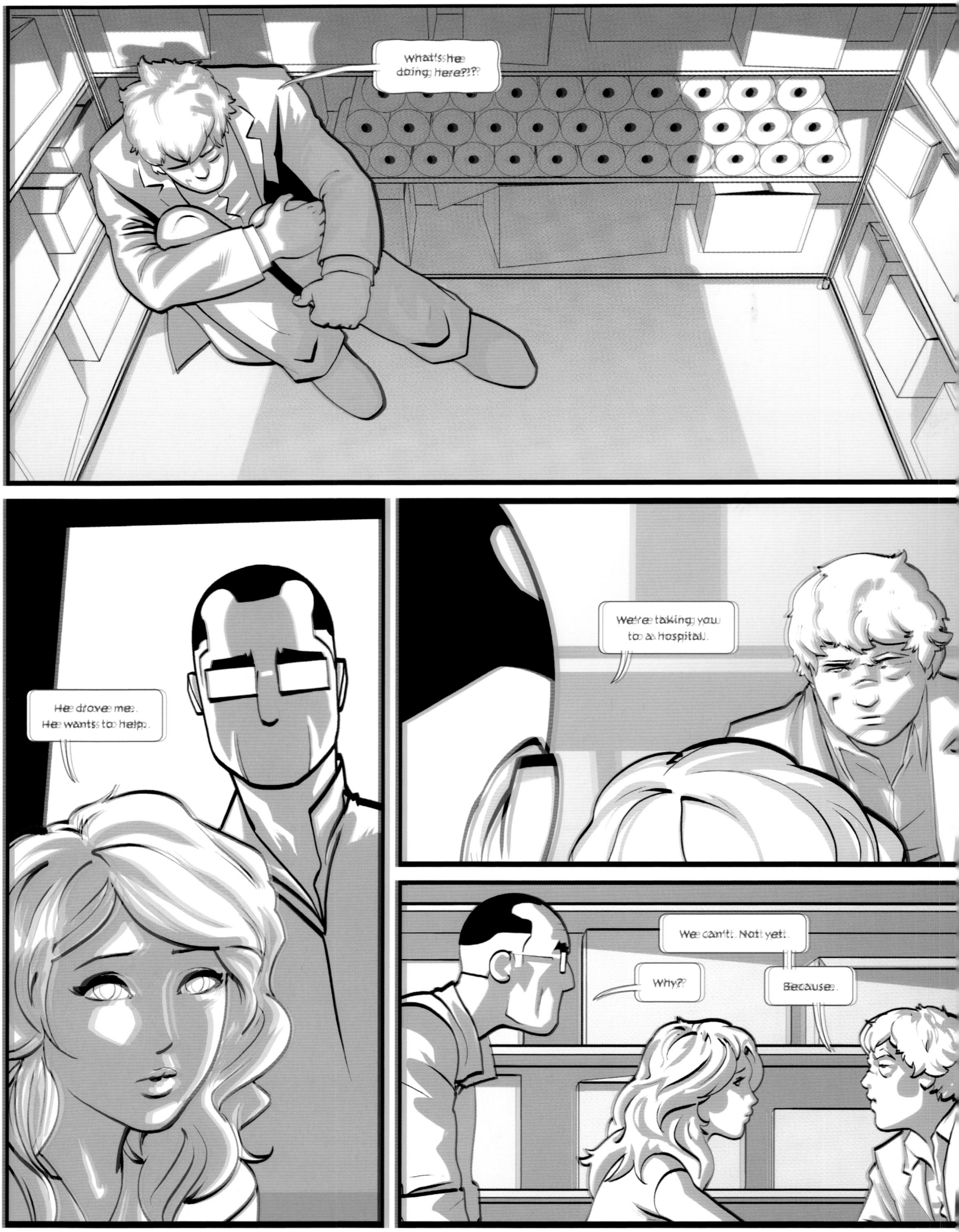
What's he doing here??
He drove me. He wants to help.
We're taking you to a hospital.
We can't. Not yet.
Why?
Because.

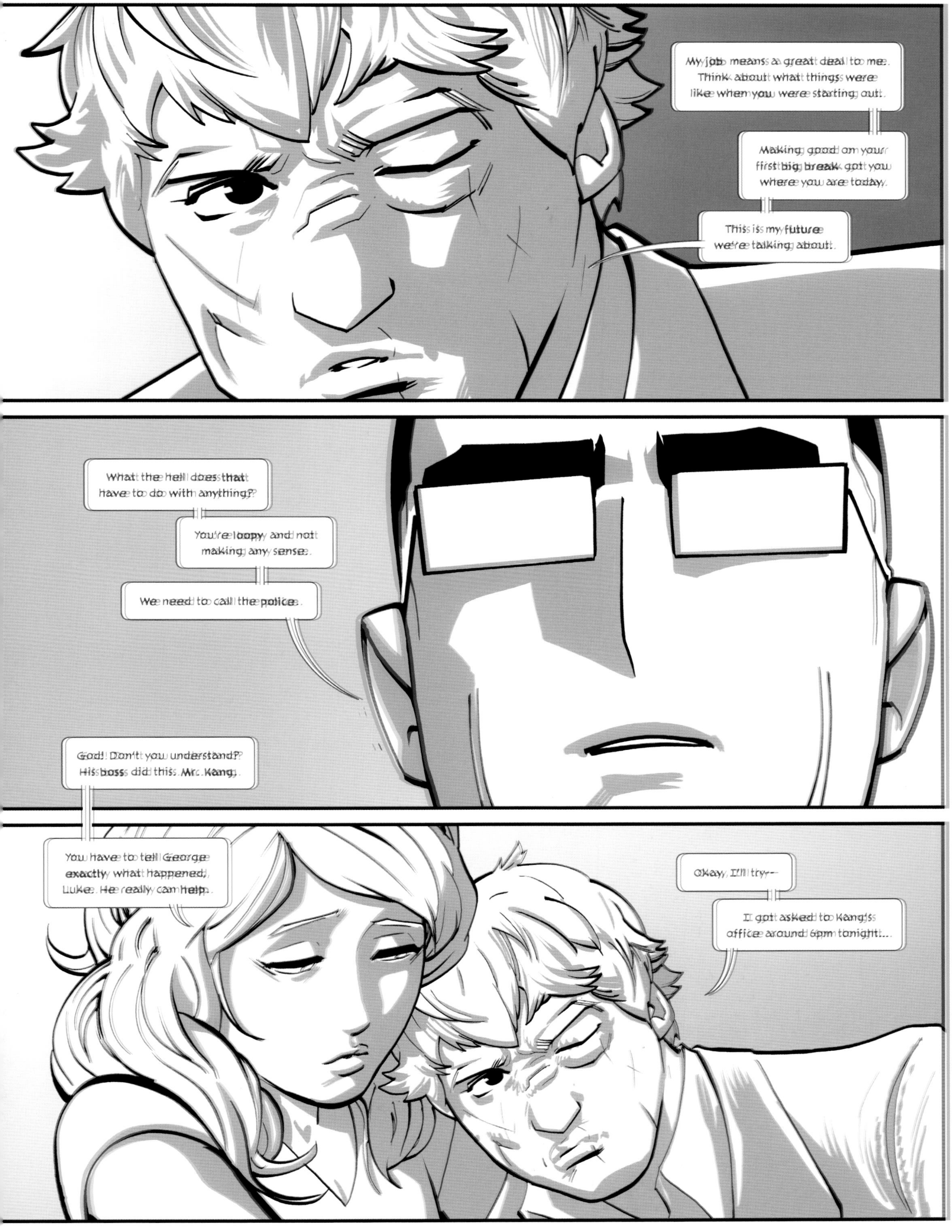
My job means a great deal to me. Think about what things were like when you were starting out.
Making good on your first big break got you where you are today.
This is my future we're talking about.
What the hell does that have to do with anything?
You're loopy and not making any sense.
We need to call the police.
God! Don't you understand? His boss did this. Mr. Kang.
You have to tell George exactly what happened, Luke. He really can help.
Okay, I'll try--
I got asked to Kang's office around 6pm tonight...

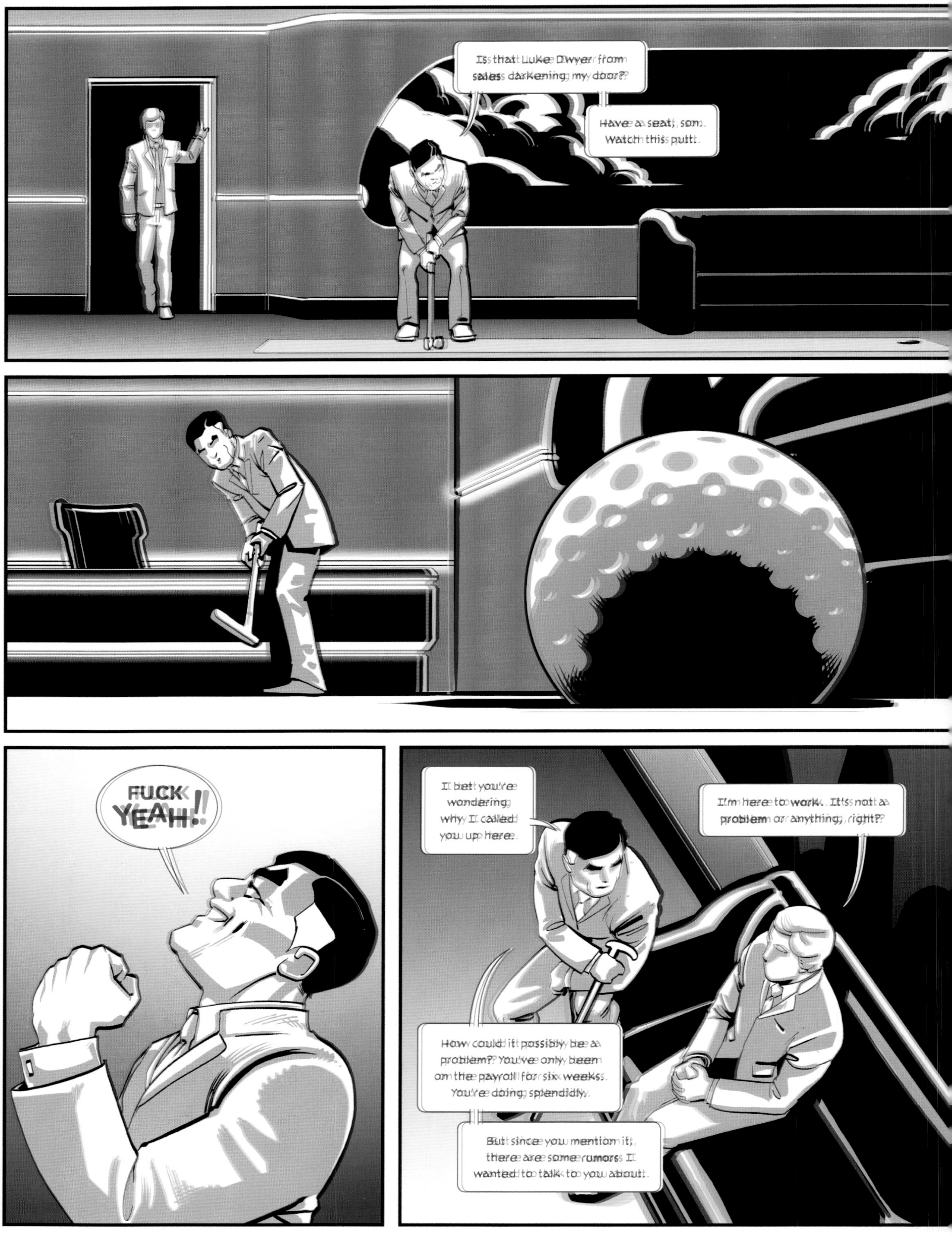
Is that Luke Dwyer from sales darkening my door?
Have a seat, son. Watch this putt.
FUCK YEAH!!
I bet you're wondering why I called you up here.
I'm here to work. It's not a problem or anything, right?
How could it possibly be a problem? You've only been on the payroll for six weeks. You're doing splendidly.
But since you mention it, there are some rumors I wanted to talk to you about.

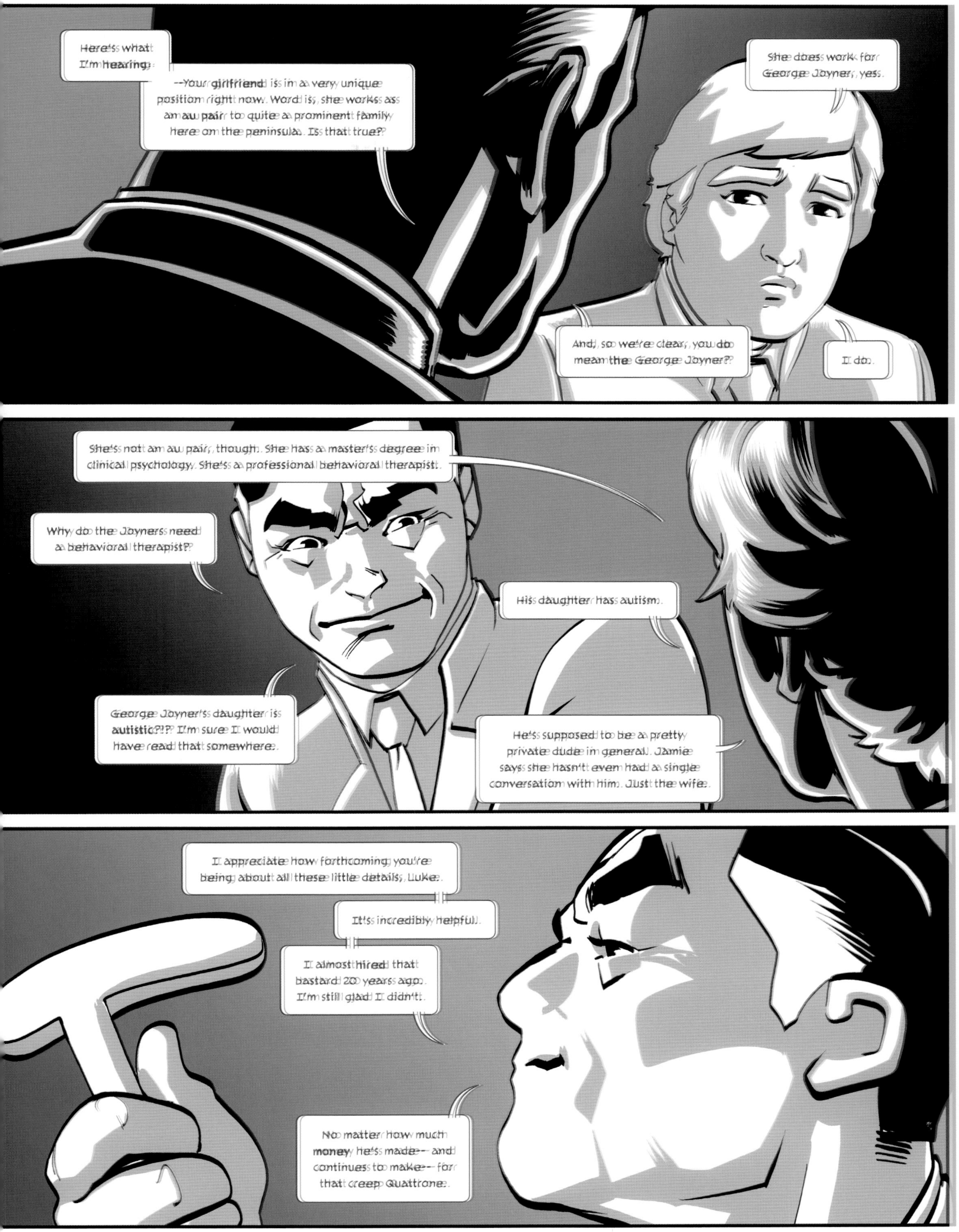
Here's what I'm hearing:
--Your girlfriend is in a very unique position right now. Word is, she works as an au pair to quite a prominent family here on the peninsula. Is that true?
She does work for George Joyner, yes.
And, so we're clear, you do mean the George Joyner?
I do.
She's not an au pair, though. She has a master's degree in clinical psychology. She's a professional behavioral therapist.
Why do the Joyners need a behavioral therapist?
His daughter has autism.
George Joyner's daughter is autistic?!? I'm sure I would have read that somewhere.
He's supposed to be a pretty private dude in general. Jamie says she hasn't even had a single conversation with him. Just the wife.
I appreciate how forthcoming you're being about all these little details, Luke.
It's incredibly helpful.
I almost hired that bastard 20 years ago. I'm still glad I didn't.
No matter how much money he's made-- and continues to make-- for that creep Quattrone.

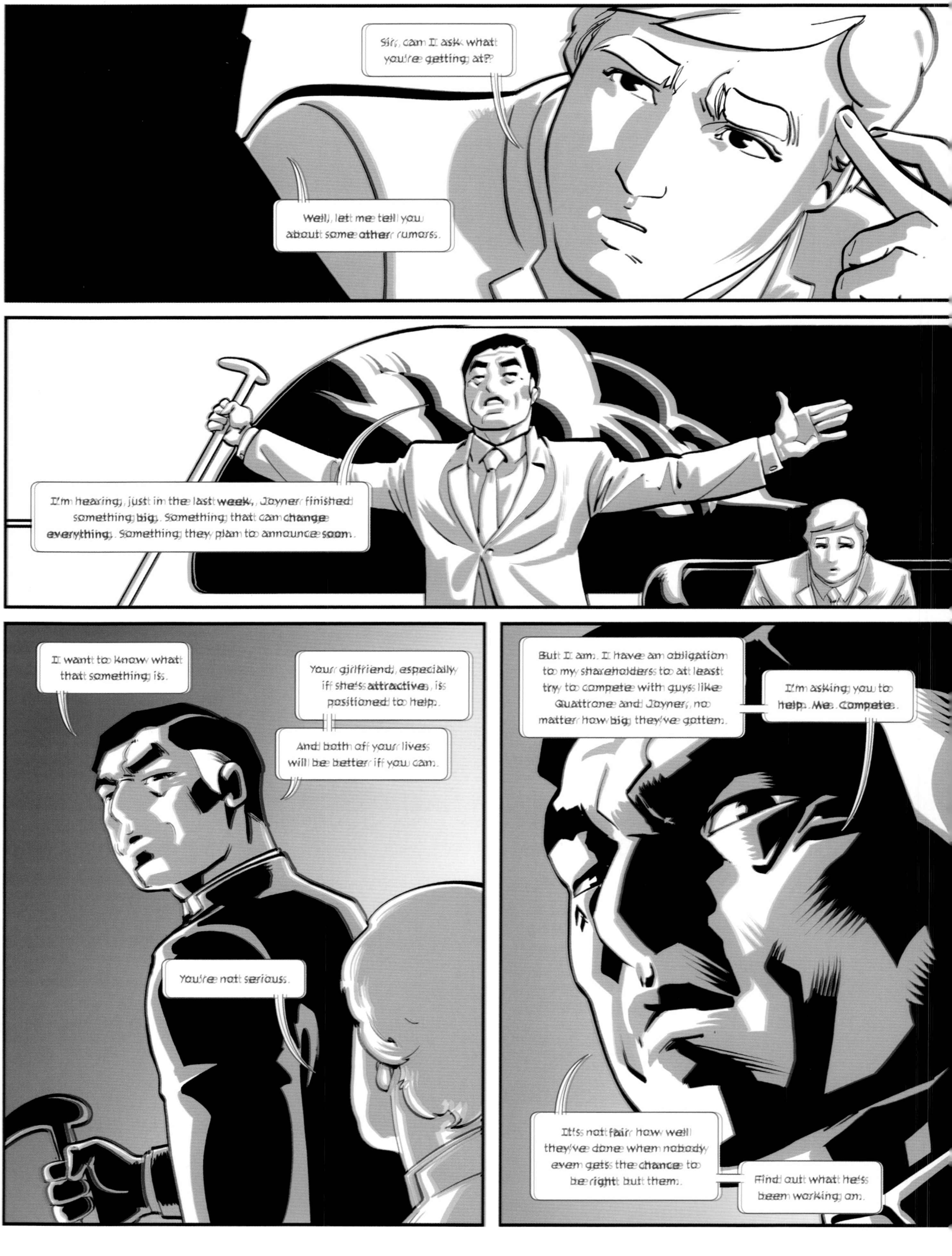
Sir, can I ask what you're getting at?
Well, let me tell you about some other rumors.
I'm hearing, just in the last week, Joyner finished something big. Something that can change everything. Something they plan to announce soon.
I want to know what that something is.
Your girlfriend, especially if she's attractive, is positioned to help.
And both of your lives will be better if you can.
You're not serious.
But I am. I have an obligation to my shareholders to at least try to compete with guys like Quattrone and Joyner, no matter how big they've gotten.
I'm asking you to help. Me. Compete.
It's not fair how well they've done when nobody even gets the chance to be right but them.
Find out what he's been working on.

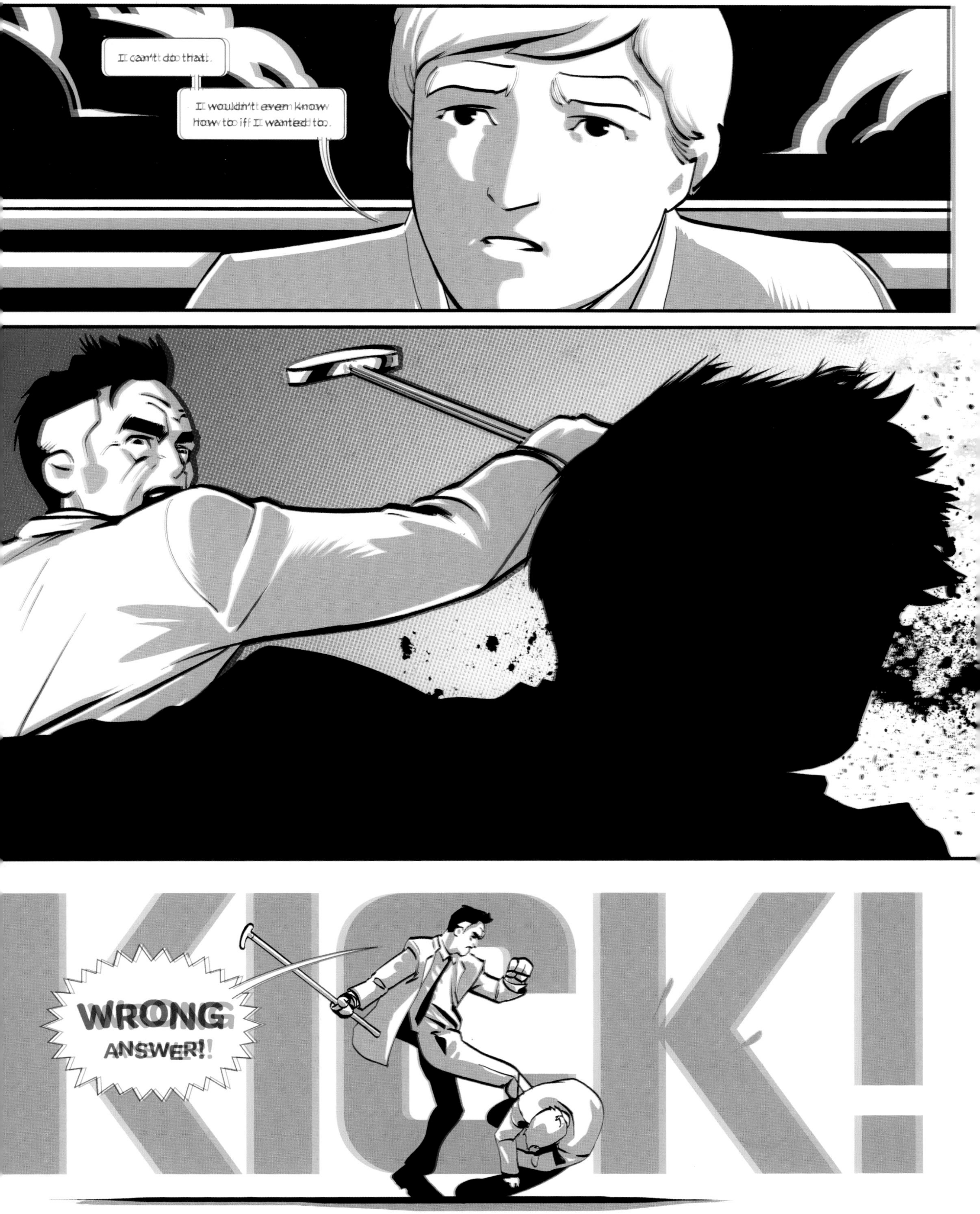
I can't do that.
I wouldn't even know how to if I wanted to.
KICK!
WRONG ANSWER!

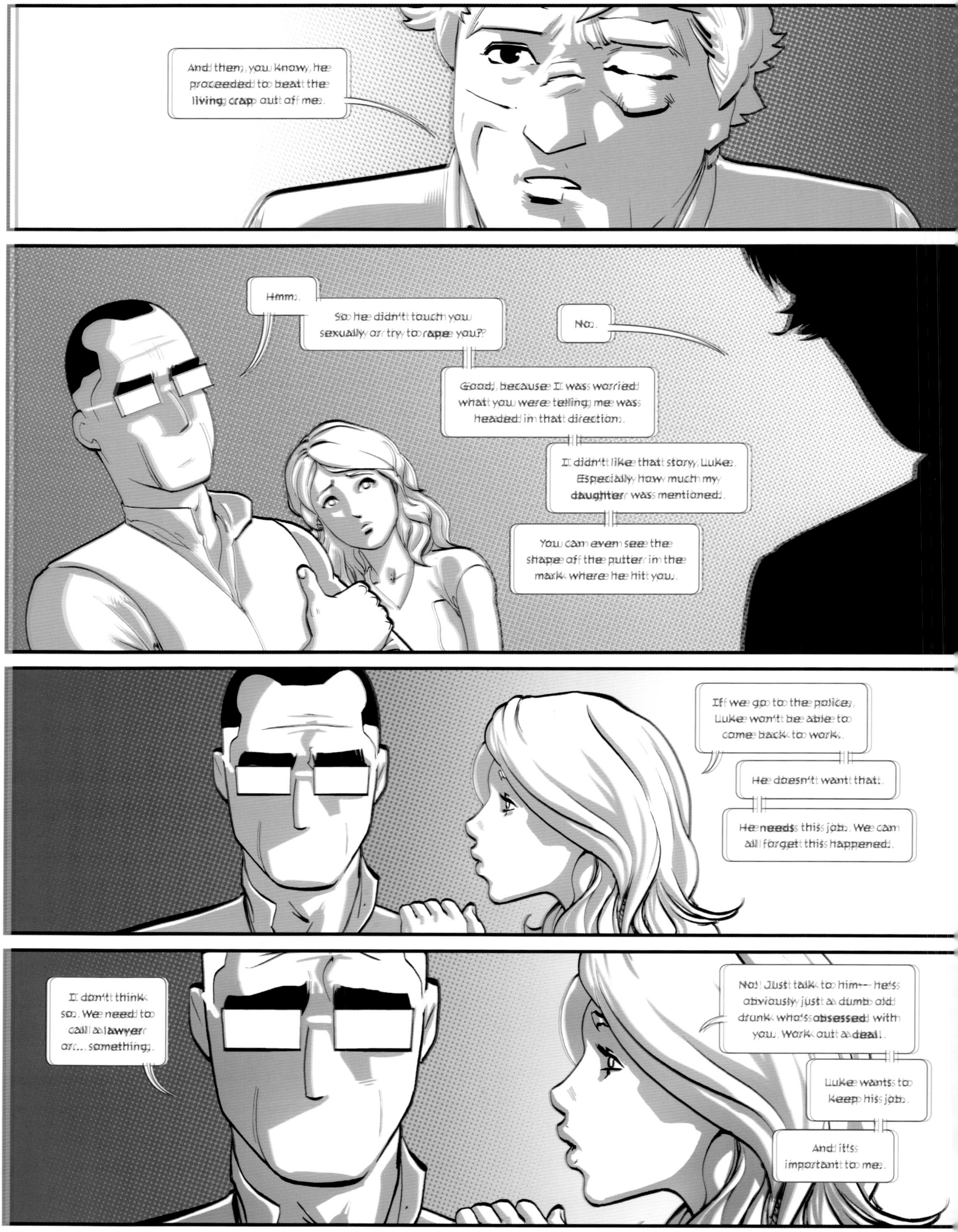
And then, you know, he proceeded to beat the **living crap** out of me.
Hmm.
So he didn't touch you sexually or try to **rape** you?
No.
Good, because I was worried what you were telling me was headed in that direction.
I didn't like that story, Luke. Especially how much my **daughter** was mentioned.
You can **even see** the shape of the putter in the mark where he hit you.
If we go to the police, Luke won't be able to come back to work.
He doesn't want that.
He **needs** this job. We can all forget this happened.
I don't think so. We need to call a **lawyer** or... something.
No! Just talk to him-- he's obviously just a dumb old drunk who's **obsessed** with you. Work out a **deal**.
Luke wants to **keep** his job.
And it's important to me.

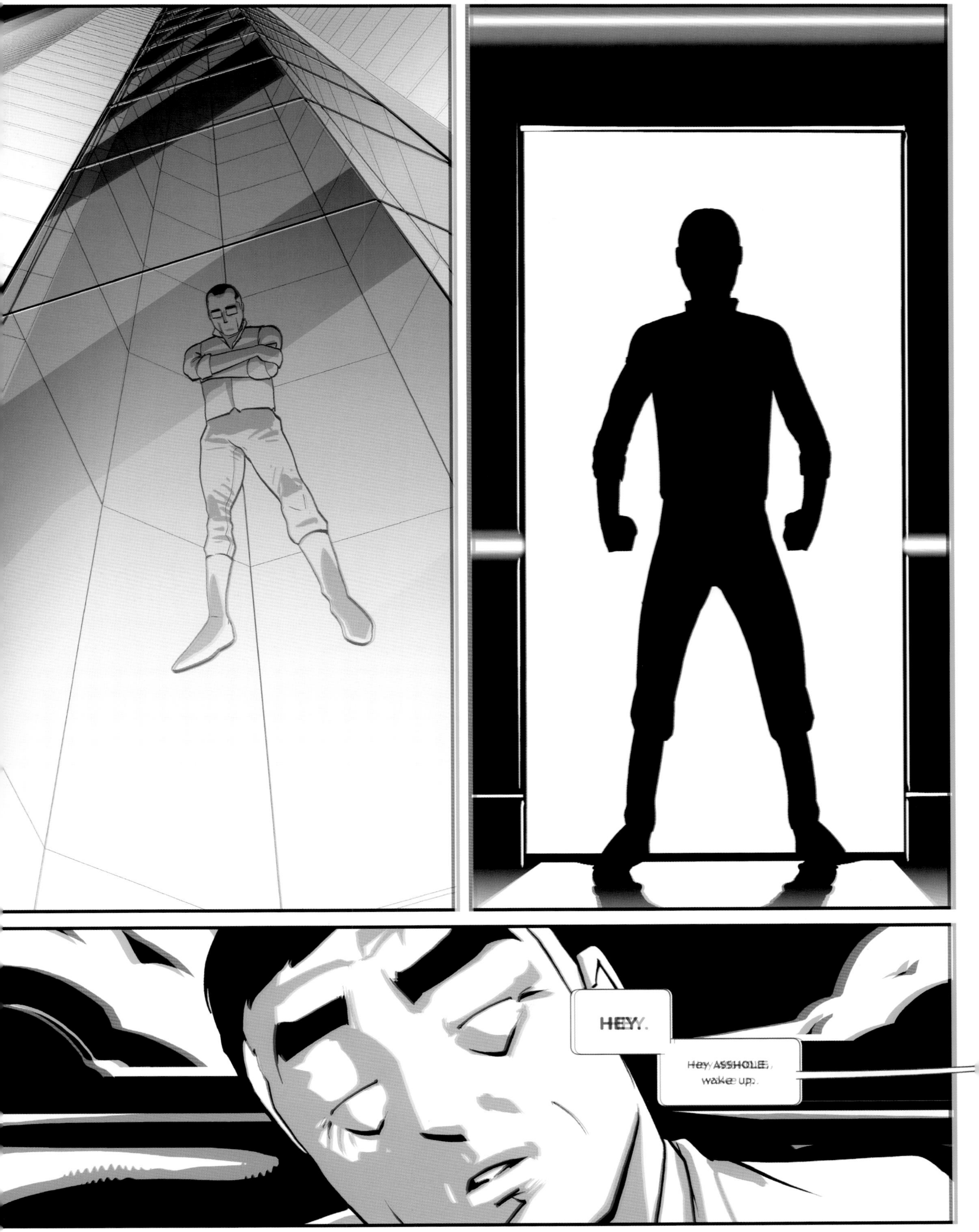
HEY.
Hey, ASSHOLE, wake up.

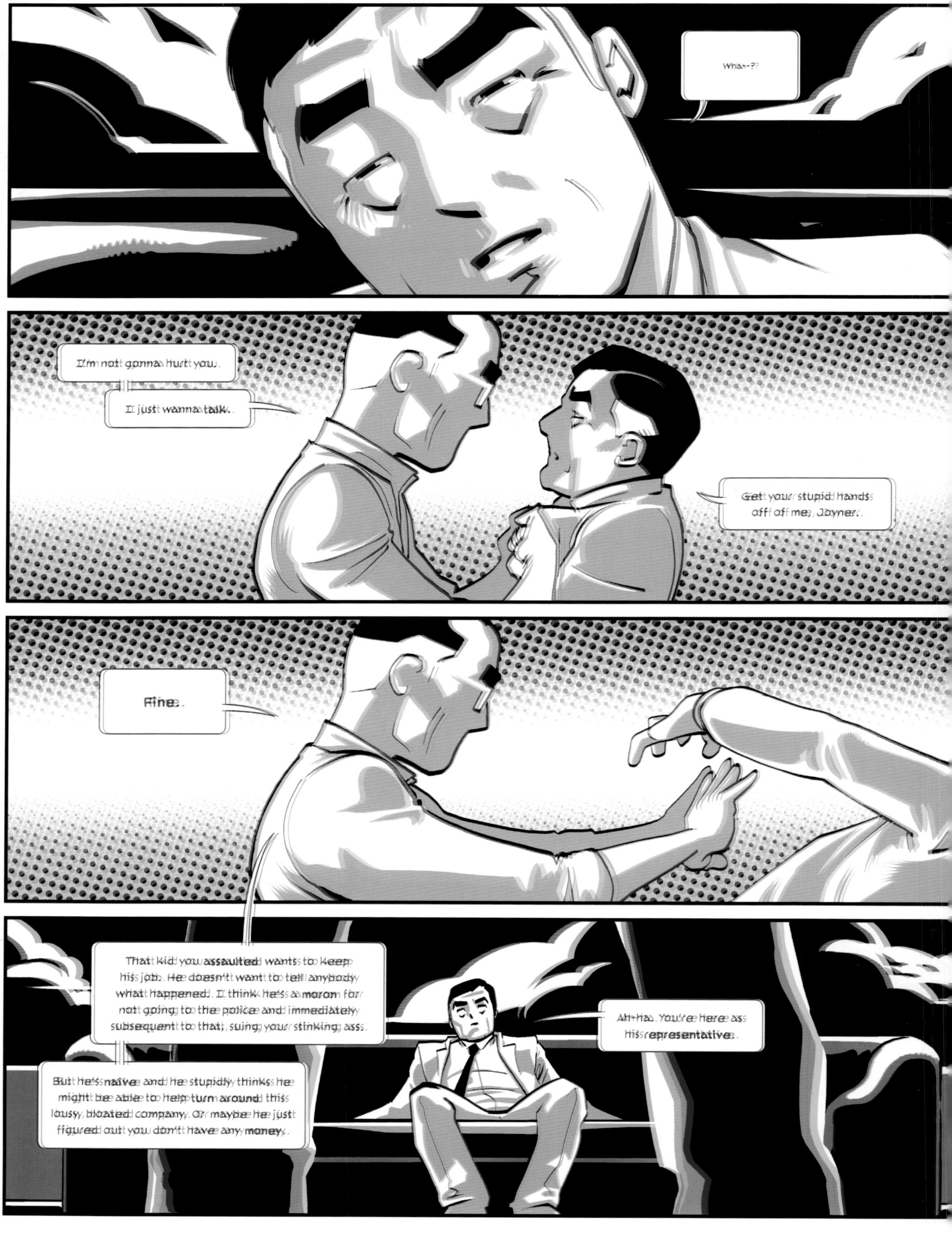

Wha-?
I'm not gonna hurt you.
I just wanna talk.
Get your stupid hands off of me, Joyner.
Fine.
That kid you assaulted wants to keep his job. He doesn't want to tell anybody what happened. I think he's a moron for not going to the police and immediately subsequent to that, suing your stinking ass.
But he's naive and he stupidly thinks he might be able to help turn around this lousy, bloated company. Or maybe he just figured out you don't have any money.
Ah-ha. You're here as his representative.

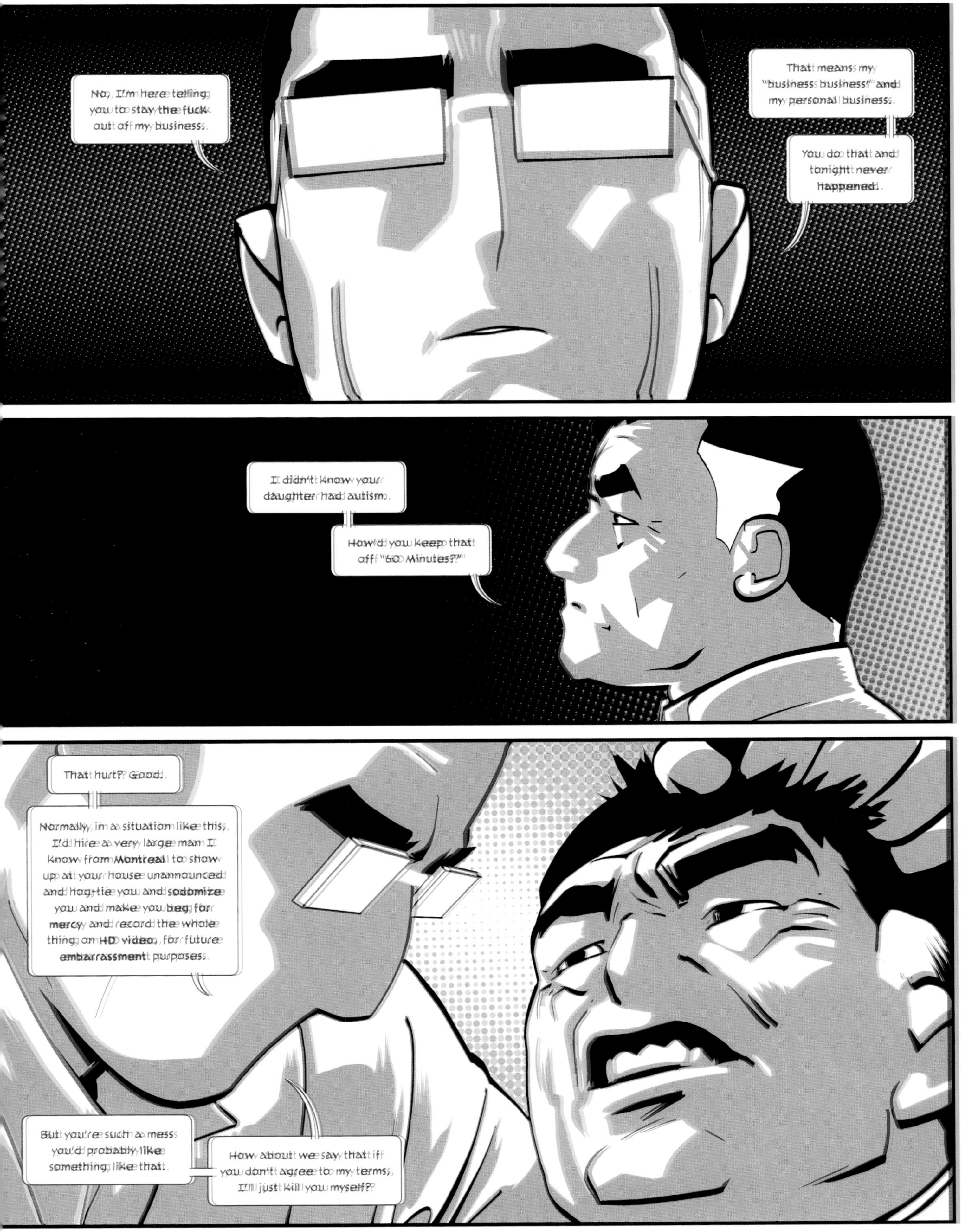
No, I'm here telling you to stay the fuck out of my business.
That means my "business business" and my personal business.
You do that and tonight never happened.
I didn't know your daughter had autism.
How'd you keep that off "60 Minutes?"
That hurt? Good.
Normally, in a situation like this, I'd hire a very large man I know from Montreal to show up at your house unannounced and hog-tie you and sodomize you and make you beg for mercy and record the whole thing on HD video, for future embarrassment purposes.
But you're such a mess you'd probably like something like that.
How about we say that if you don't agree to my terms, I'll just kill you myself?

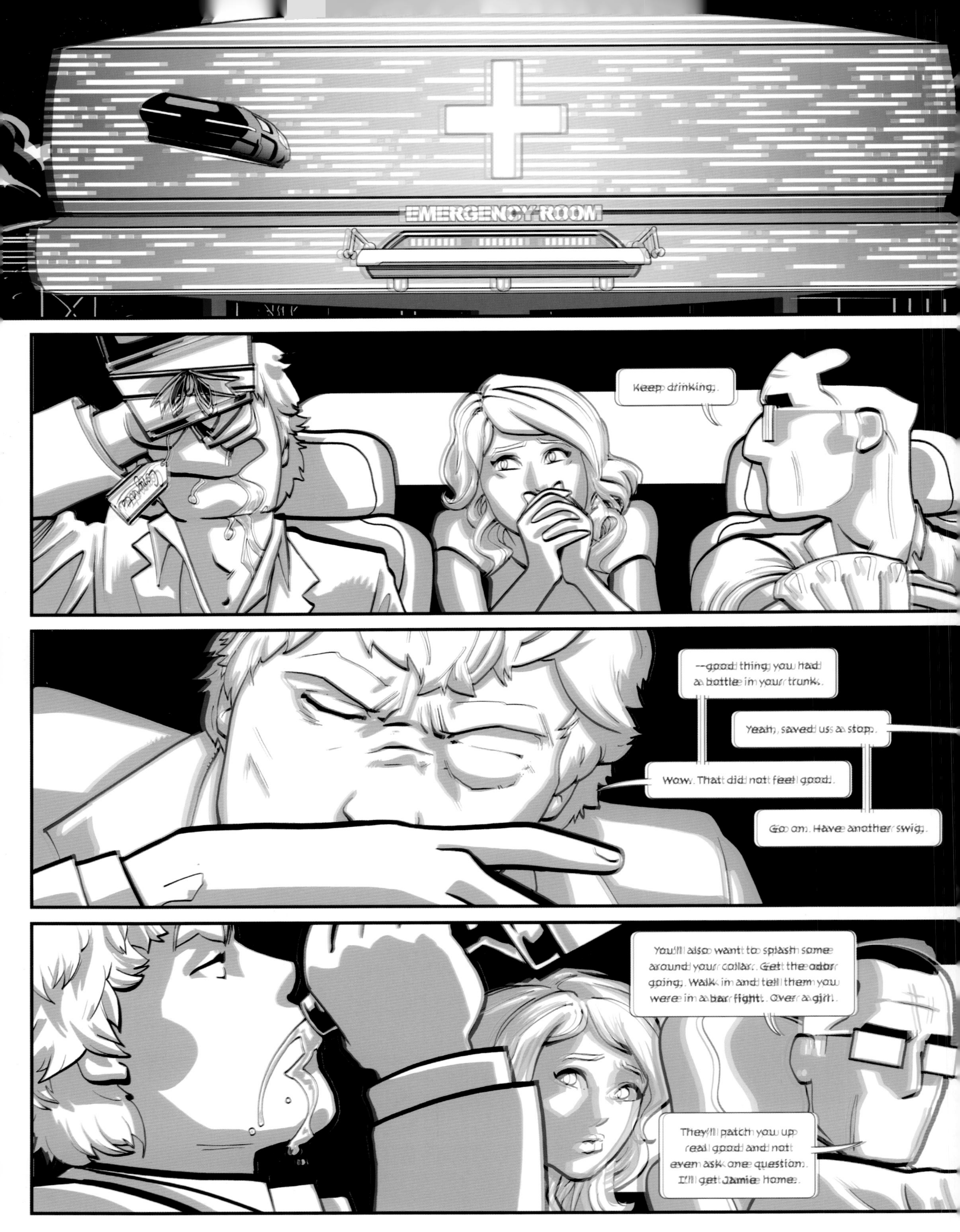
EMERGENCY ROOM
Keep drinking.
--good thing you had a bottle in your trunk.
Yeah, saved us a stop.
Wow. That did not feel good.
Go on. Have another swig.
You'll also want to splash some around your collar. Get the odor going. Walk in and tell them you were in a bar fight. Over a girl.
They'll patch you up real good and not even ask one question. I'll get Jamie home.

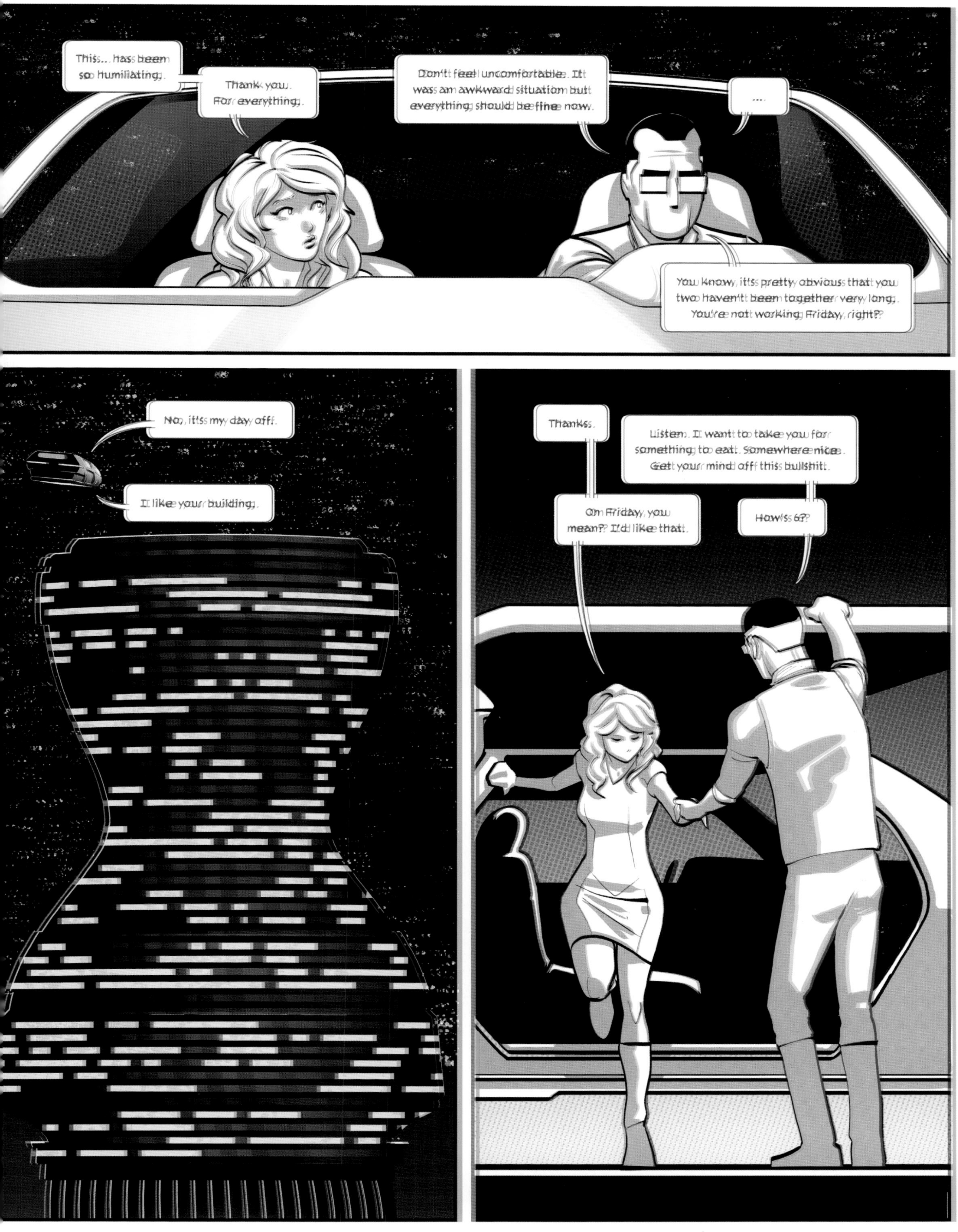
This... has been so humiliating.
Thank you. For everything.
Don't feel uncomfortable. It was an awkward situation but everything should be fine now.
....
You know, it's pretty obvious that you two haven't been together very long. You're not working Friday, right?
No, it's my day off.
I like your building.
Thanks.
Listen. I want to take you for something to eat. Somewhere nice. Get your mind off this bullshit.
On Friday, you mean? I'd like that.
How's 6?

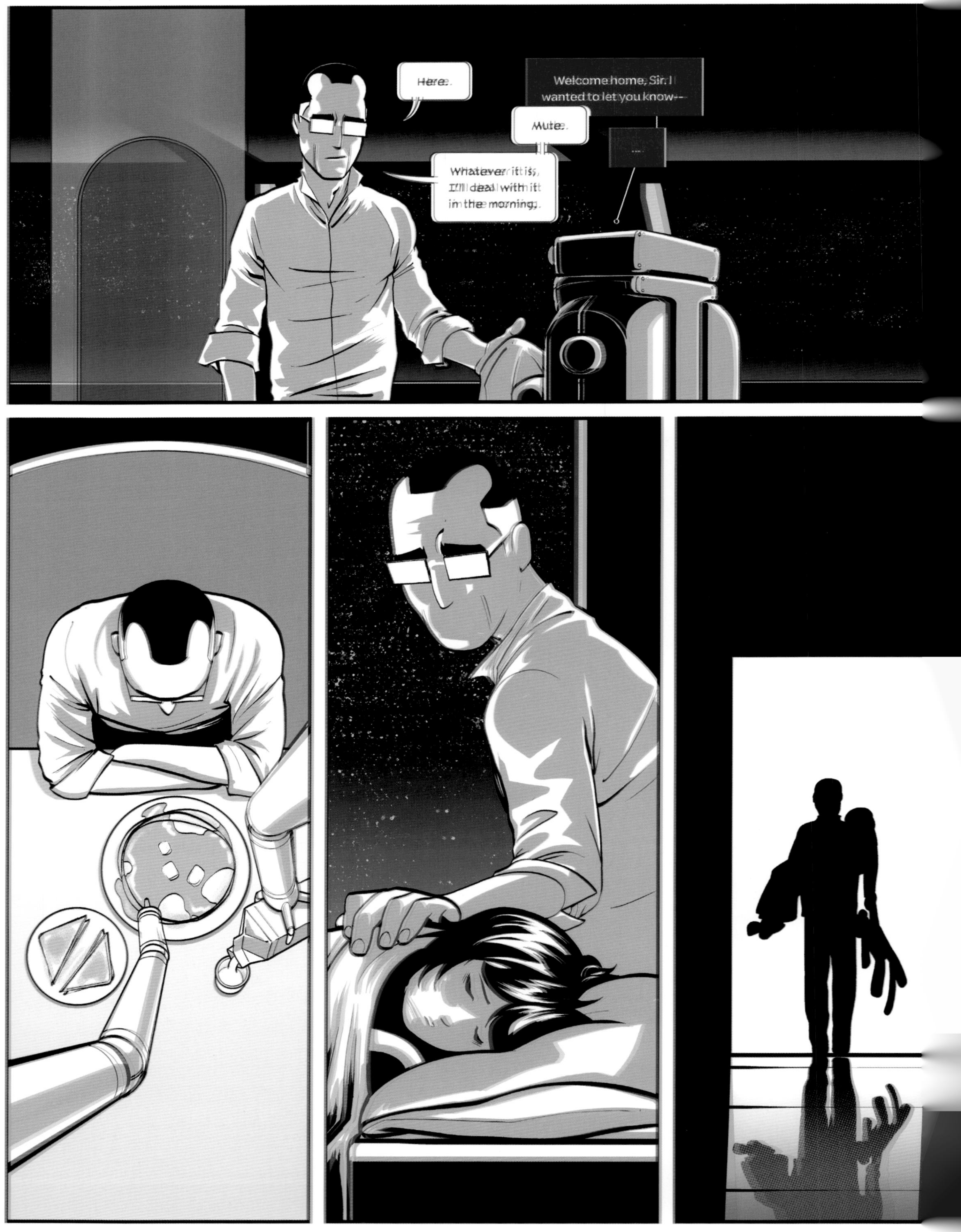
Here.
Welcome home, Sir. I wanted to let you know--
Mute.
...
Whatever it is, I'll deal with it in the morning.

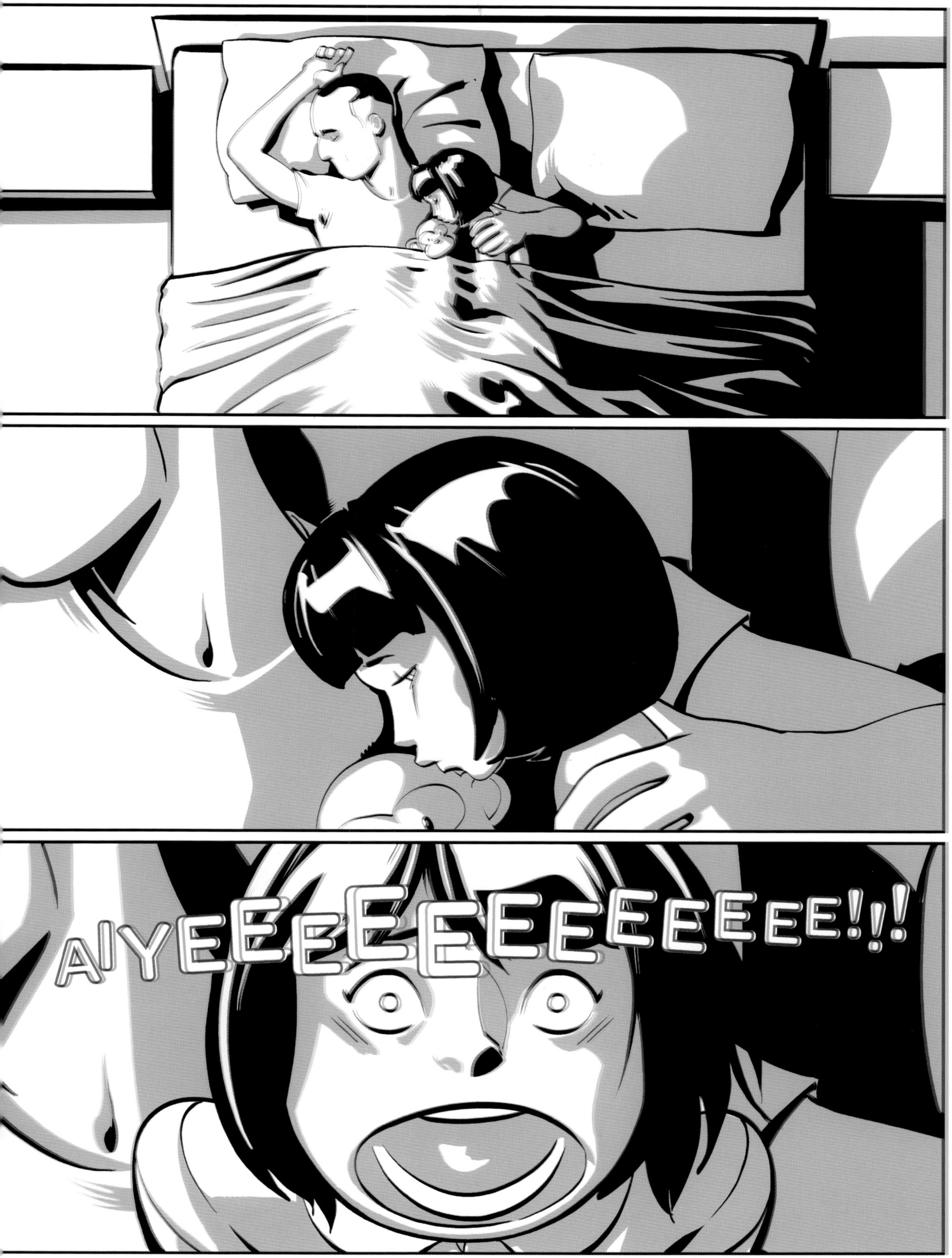
AIYEEEEEEEEEEEEE!!!

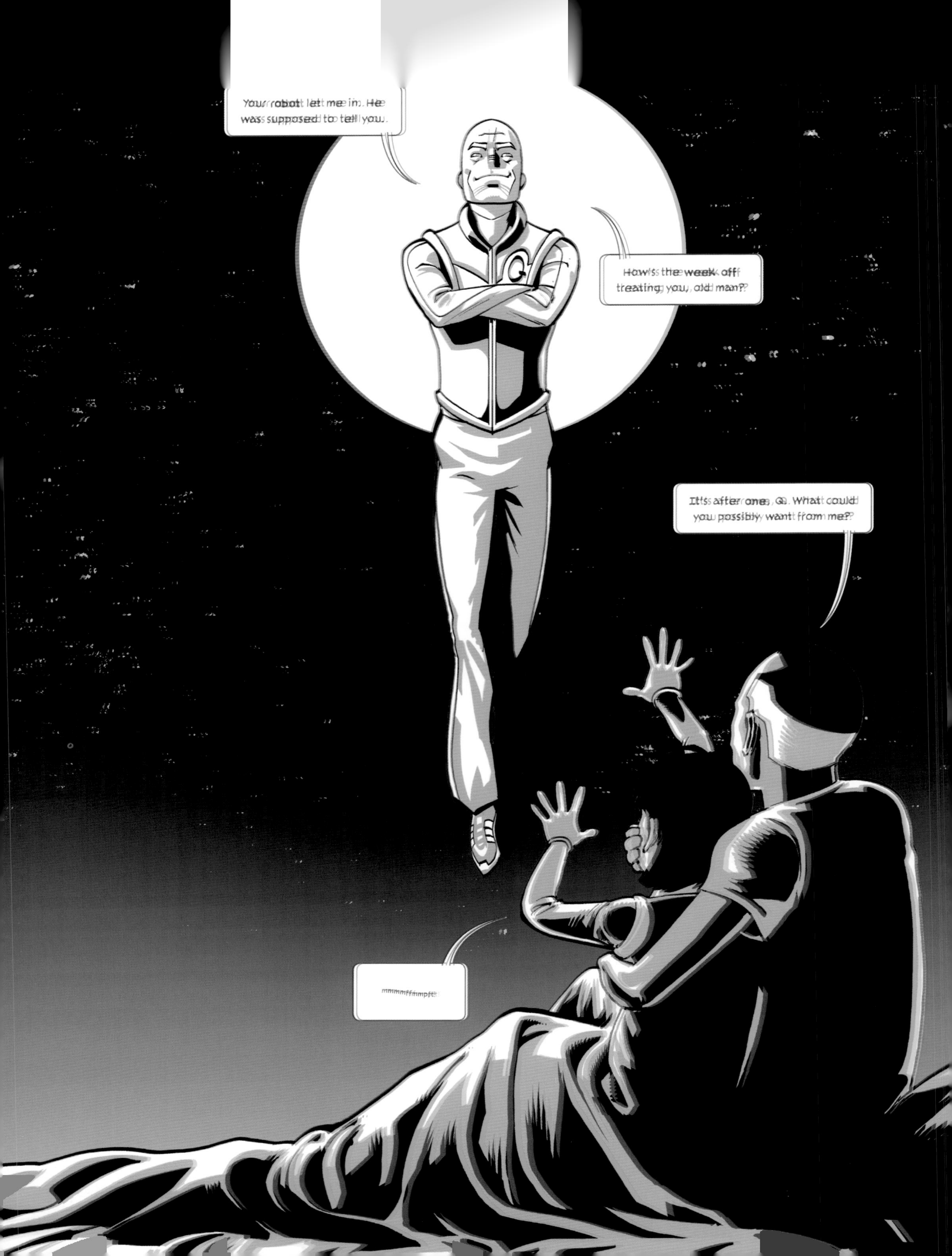
Your robot let me in. He was supposed to tell you.
How's the week off treating you, old man?
It's after one, Q. What could you possibly want from me?
mmmmffmmpft!

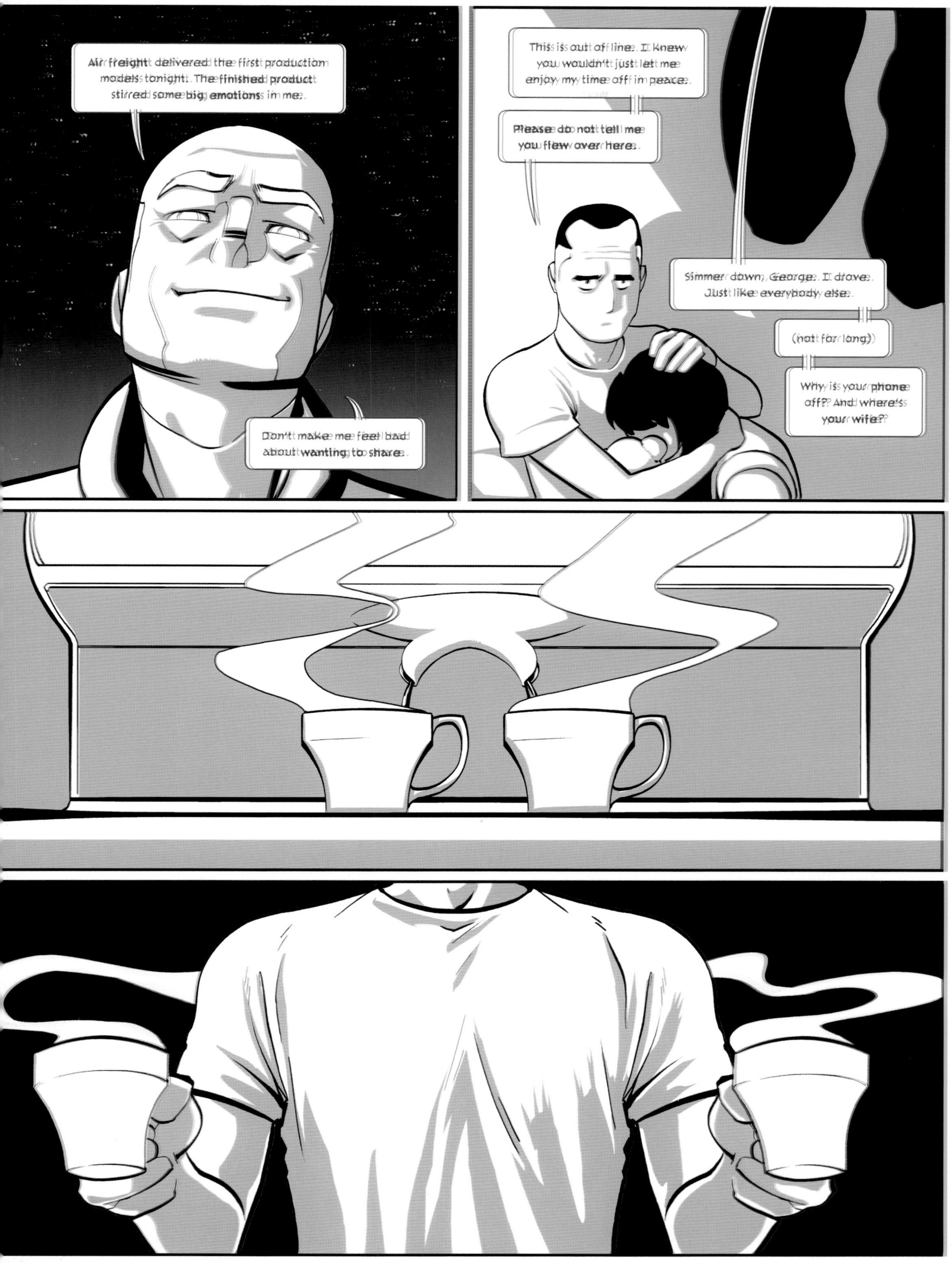
Air freight delivered the first production models tonight. The finished product stirred some big emotions in me.
Don't make me feel bad about wanting to share.
This is out of line. I knew you wouldn't just let me enjoy my time off in peace.
Please do not tell me you flew over here.
Simmer down, George. I drove. Just like everybody else.
(not for long)
Why is your phone off? And where's your wife?

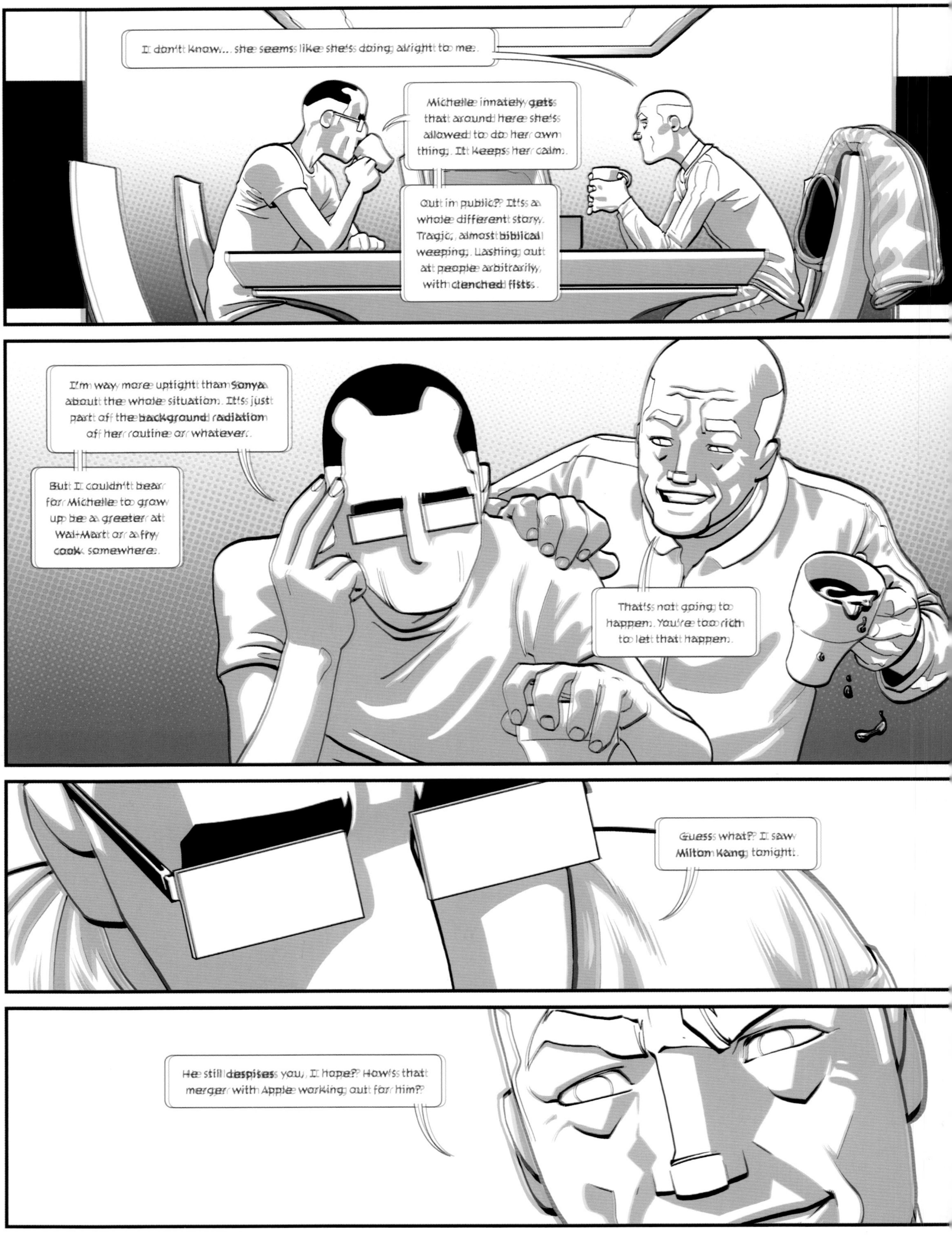
I don't know... she seems like she's doing alright to me.
Michelle innately gets that around here she's allowed to do her own thing. It keeps her calm.
Out in public? It's a whole different story. Tragic, almost biblical weeping. Lashing out at people arbitrarily, with clenched fists.
I'm way more uptight than Sonya about the whole situation. It's just part of the background radiation of her routine or whatever.
But I couldn't bear for Michelle to grow up be a greeter at Wal-Mart or a fry cook somewhere.
That's not going to happen. You're too rich to let that happen.
Guess what? I saw Milton Kang tonight.
He still despises you, I hope? How's that merger with Apple working out for him?

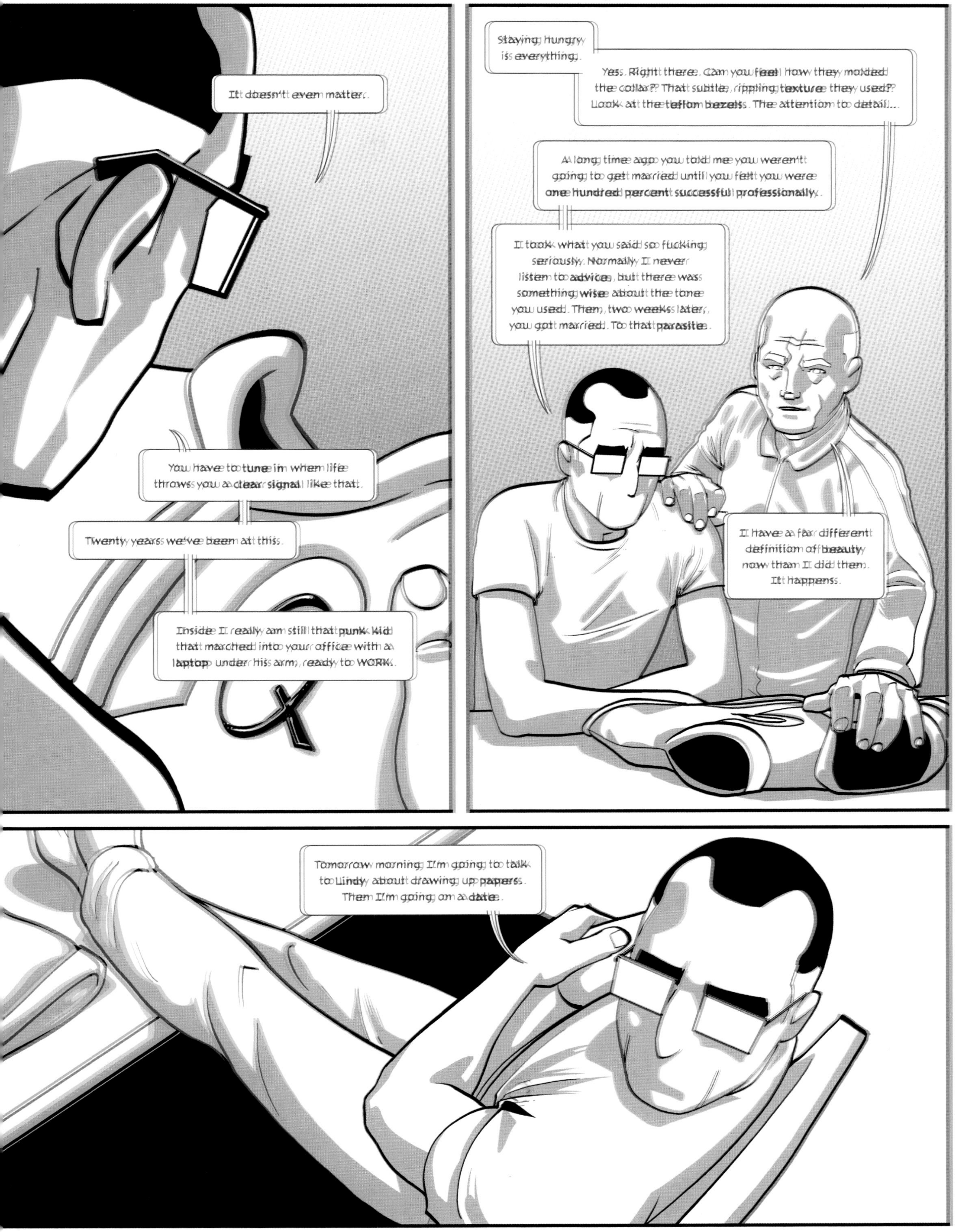
It doesn't even matter.
You have to tune in when life throws you a clear signal like that.
Twenty years we've been at this.
Inside I really am still that punk kid that marched into your office with a laptop under his arm, ready to WORK.
Staying hungry is everything.
Yes. Right there. Can you feel how they molded the collar? That subtle, rippling texture they used? Look at the teflon bezels. The attention to detail...
A long time ago you told me you weren't going to get married until you felt you were one hundred percent successful professionally.
I took what you said so fucking seriously. Normally I never listen to advice, but there was something wise about the tone you used. Then, two weeks later, you got married. To that parasite.
I have a far different definition of beauty now than I did then. It happens.
Tomorrow morning I'm going to talk to Lindy about drawing up papers. Then I'm going on a date.

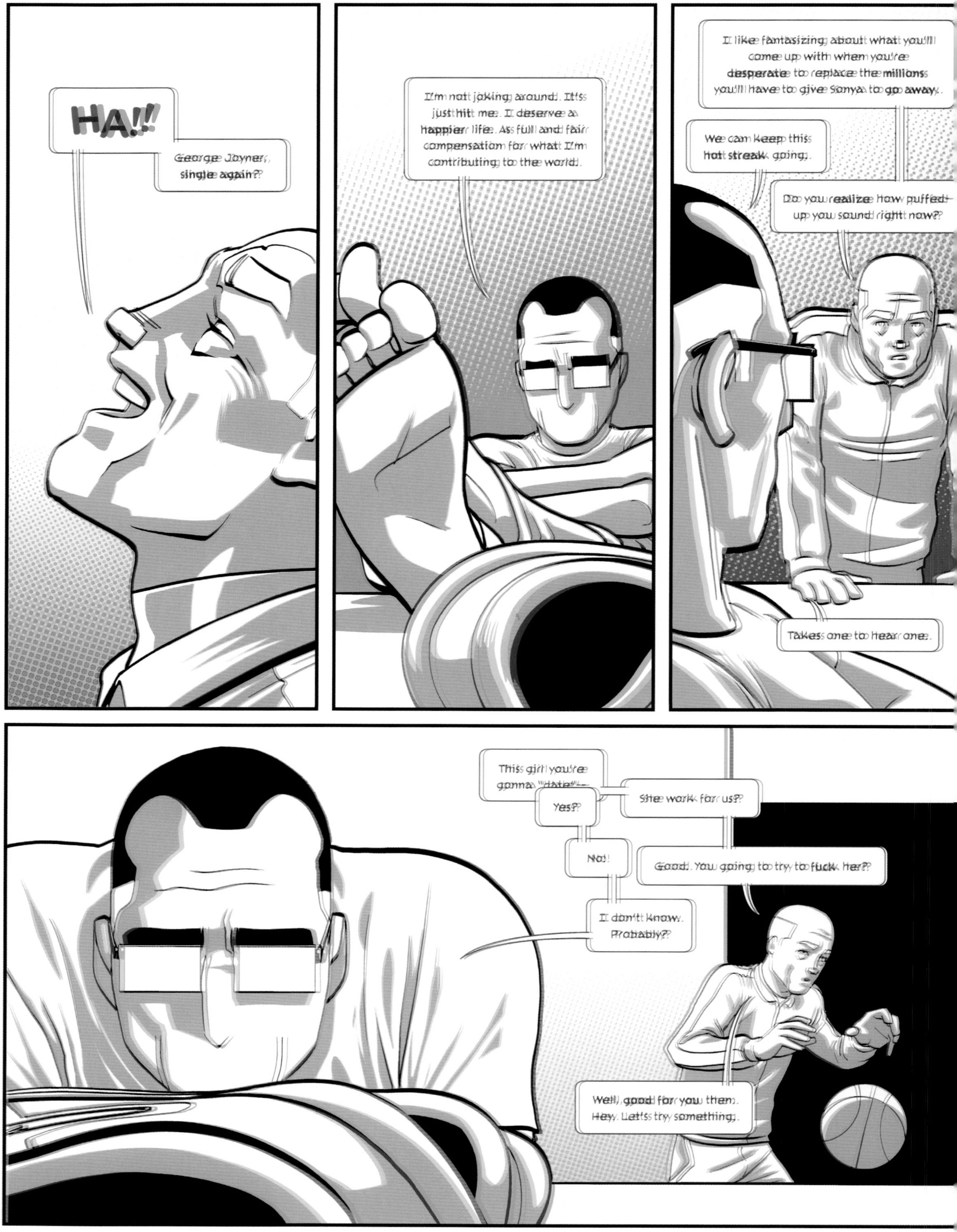
HA!!
George Joyner, single again?
I'm not joking around. It's just hit me. I deserve a happier life. As full and fair compensation for what I'm contributing to the world.
I like fantasizing about what you'll come up with when you're desperate to replace the millions you'll have to give Sonya to go away.
We can keep this hot streak going.
Do you realize how puffed-up you sound right now?
Takes one to hear one.
This girl you're gonna "date"--
Yes?
She work for us?
No!
Good. You going to try to fuck her?
I don't know. Probably?
Well, good for you then. Hey. Let's try something.

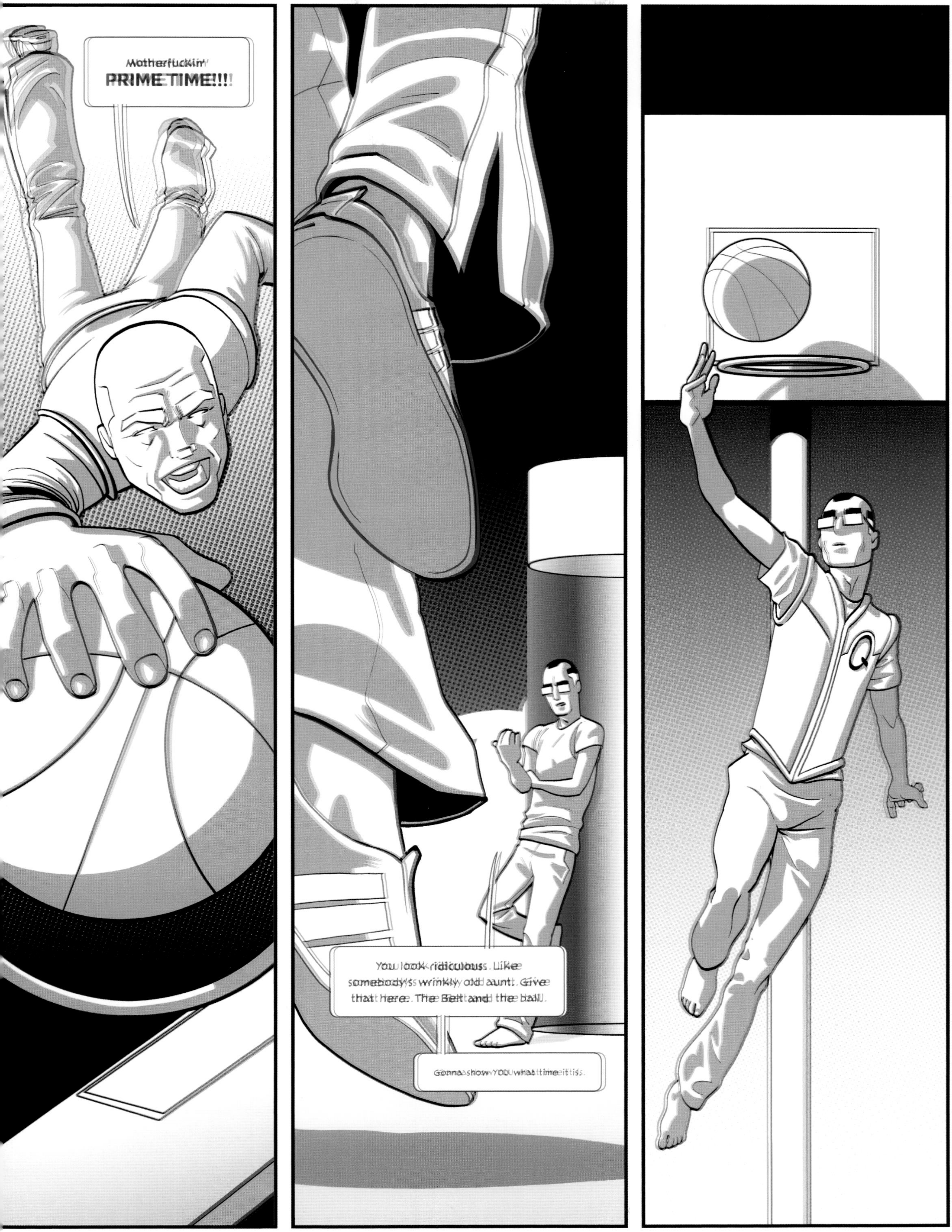
Motherfuckin'
PRIME TIME!!!!
You look ridiculous. Like somebody's wrinkly old aunt. Give that here. The Belt and the ball.
Gonna show YOU what time it is.

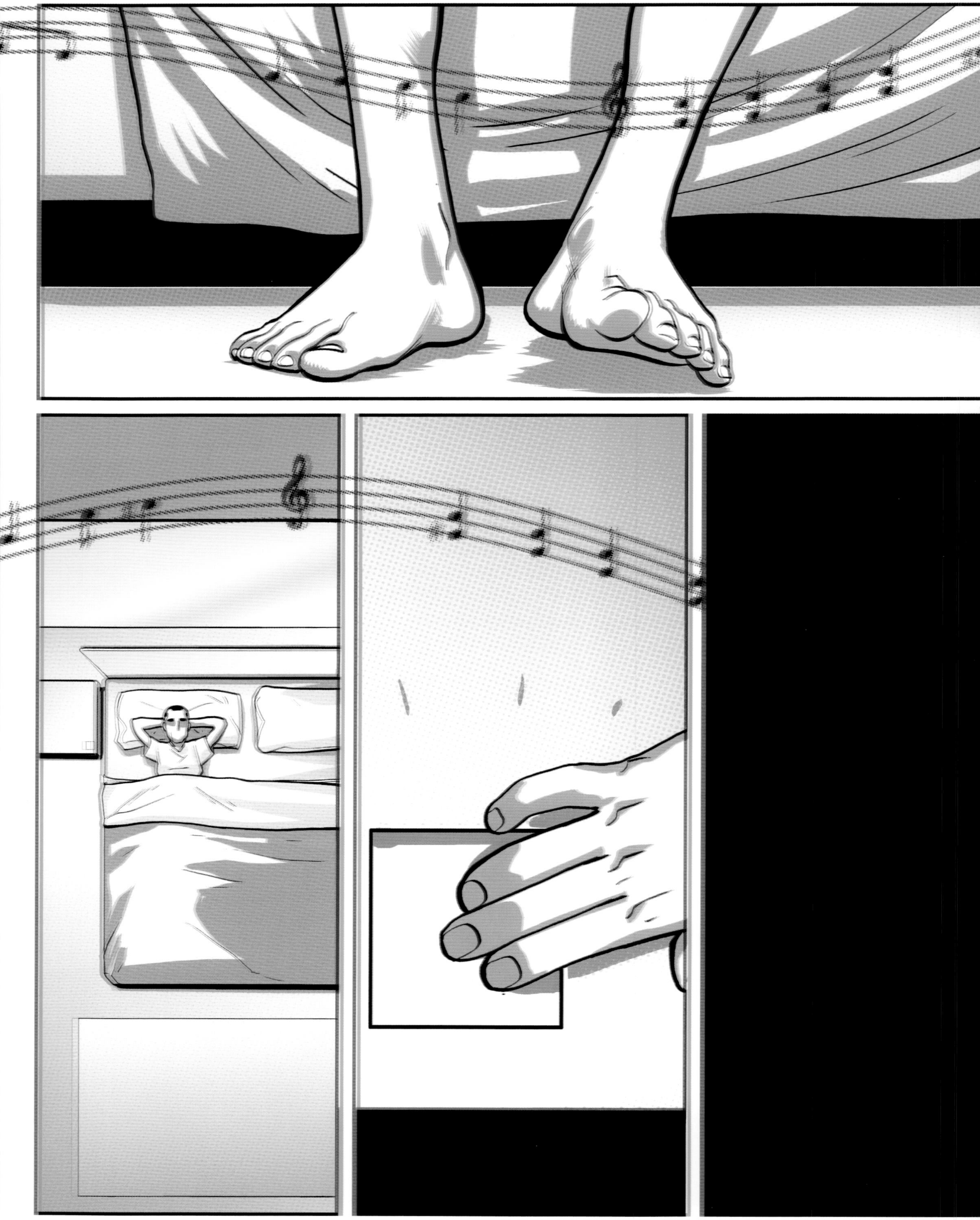

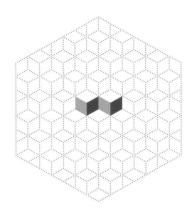

CHAPTER TWO

HAPPY LANDING

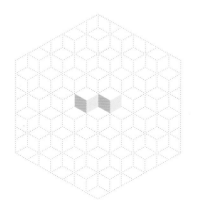

CHAPTER TWO
HAPPY LANDING

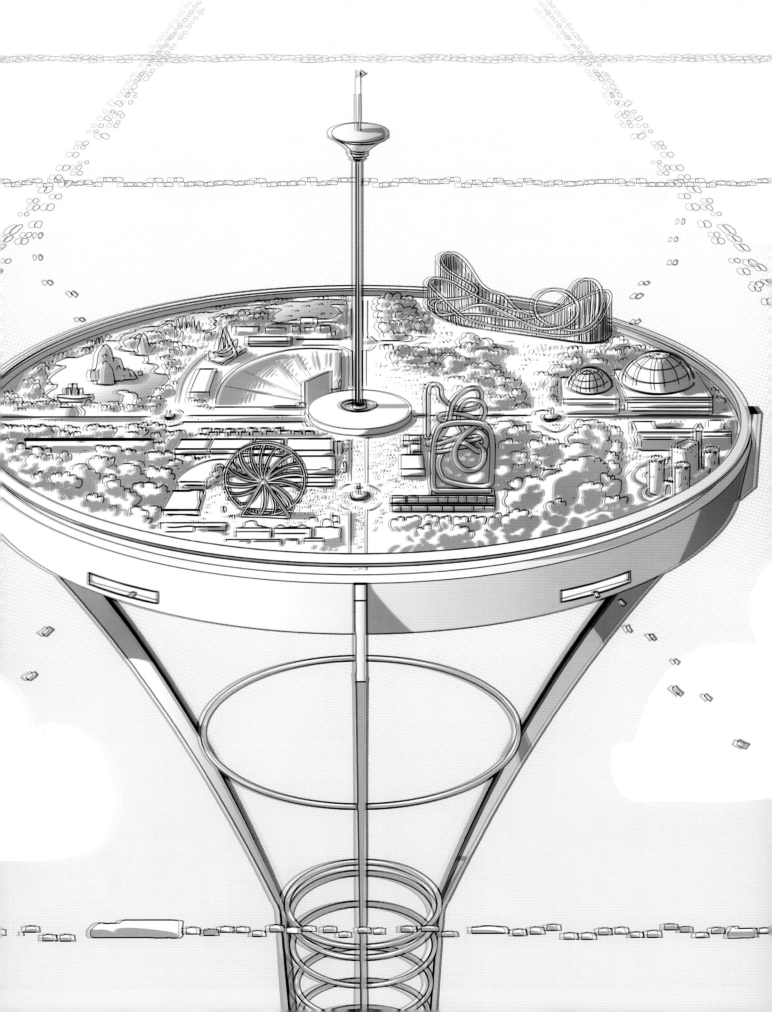

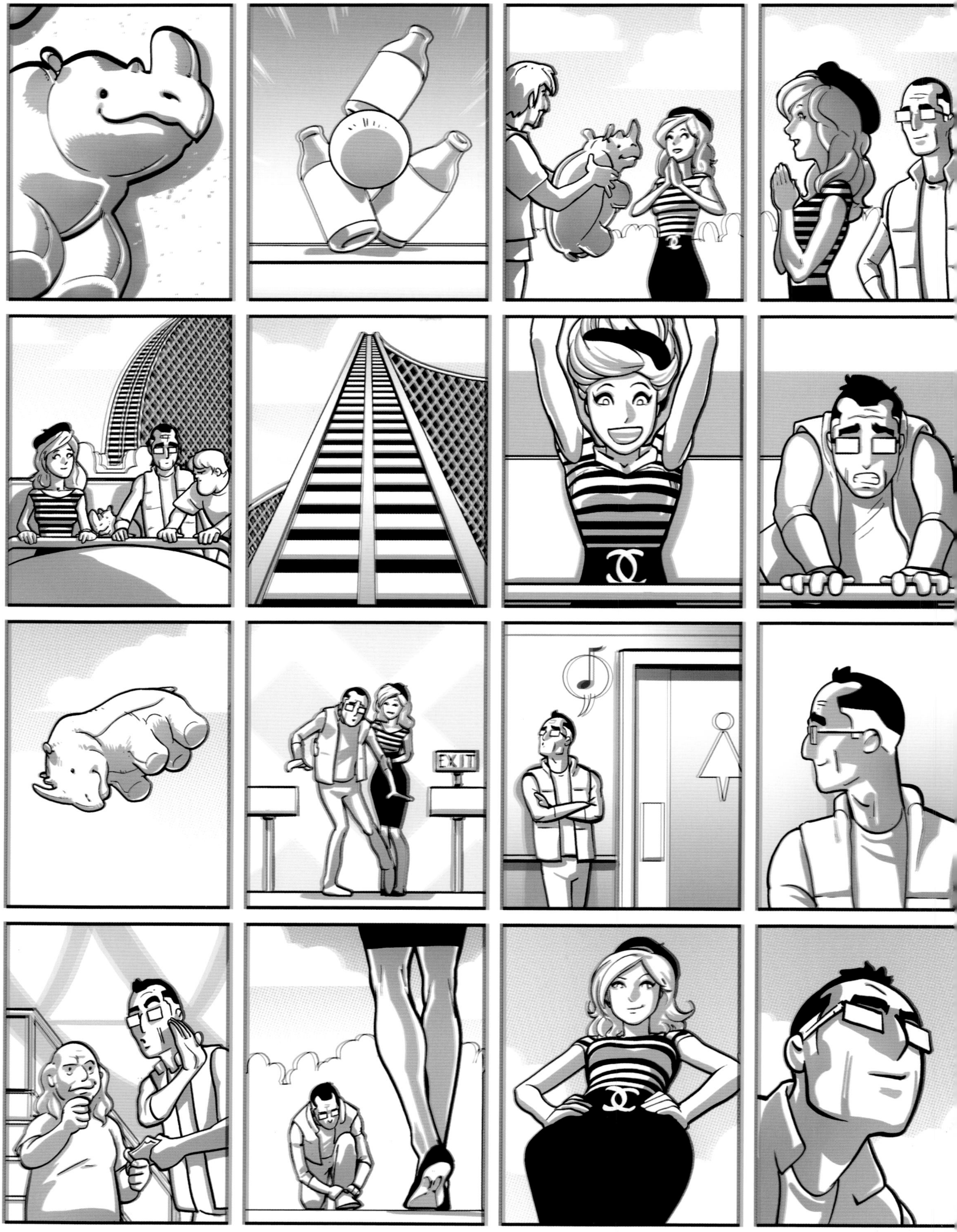
EXIT

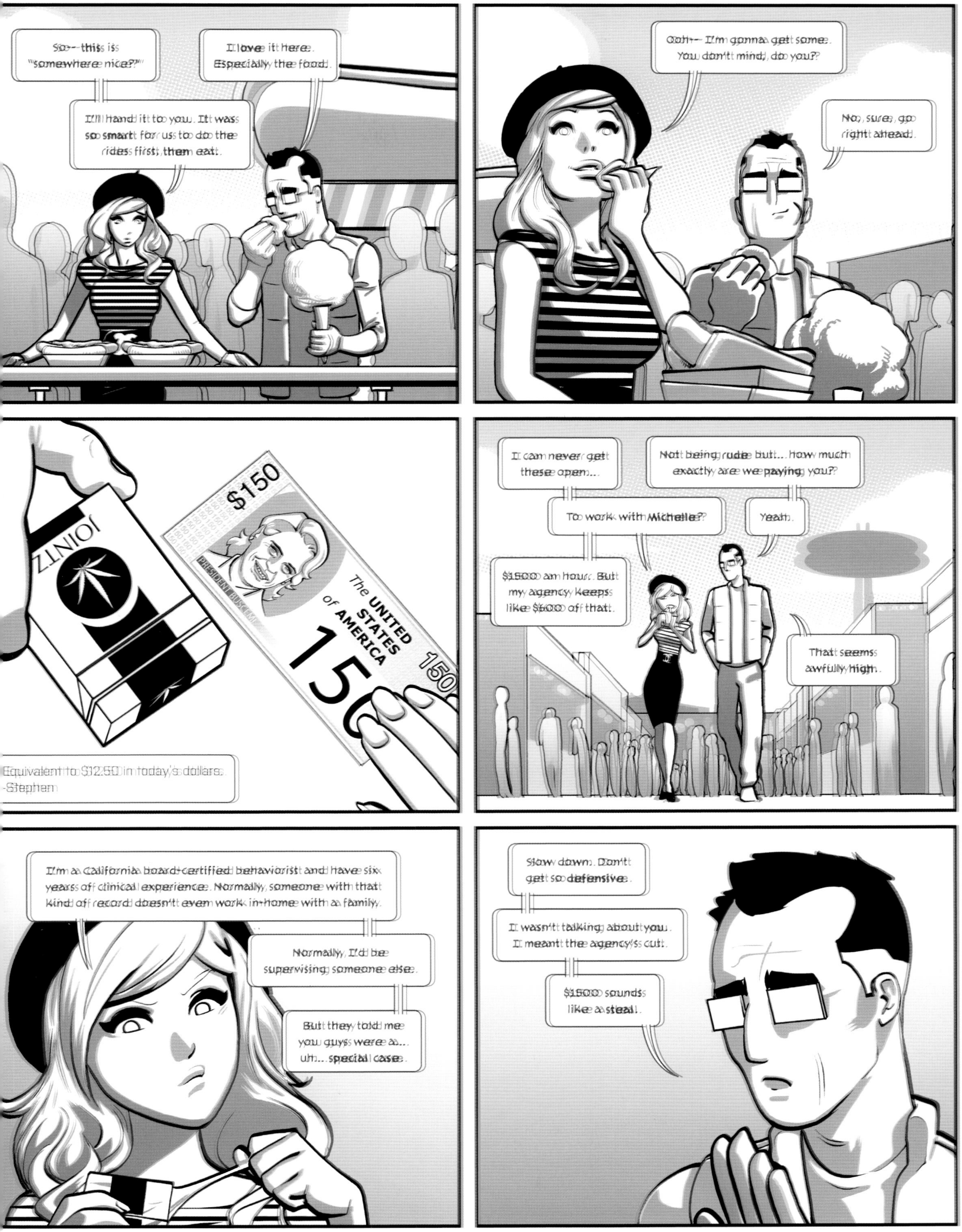
So—this is "somewhere nice?"
I love it here. Especially the food.
I'll hand it to you. It was so smart for us to do the rides first, then eat.
Ooh— I'm gonna get some. You don't mind, do you?
No, sure, go right ahead.
$150
The UNITED STATES of AMERICA
150
Equivalent to $12.50 in today's dollars. -Stephen
I can never get these open...
Not being rude but... how much exactly are we paying you?
To work with Michelle?
Yeah.
$1500 an hour. But my agency keeps like $600 of that.
That seems awfully high.
I'm a California board-certified behaviorist and have six years of clinical experience. Normally, someone with that kind of record doesn't even work in-home with a family.
Normally, I'd be supervising someone else.
But they told me you guys were a... uh... special case.
Slow down. Don't get so defensive.
I wasn't talking about you. I meant the agency's cut.
$1500 sounds like a steal.

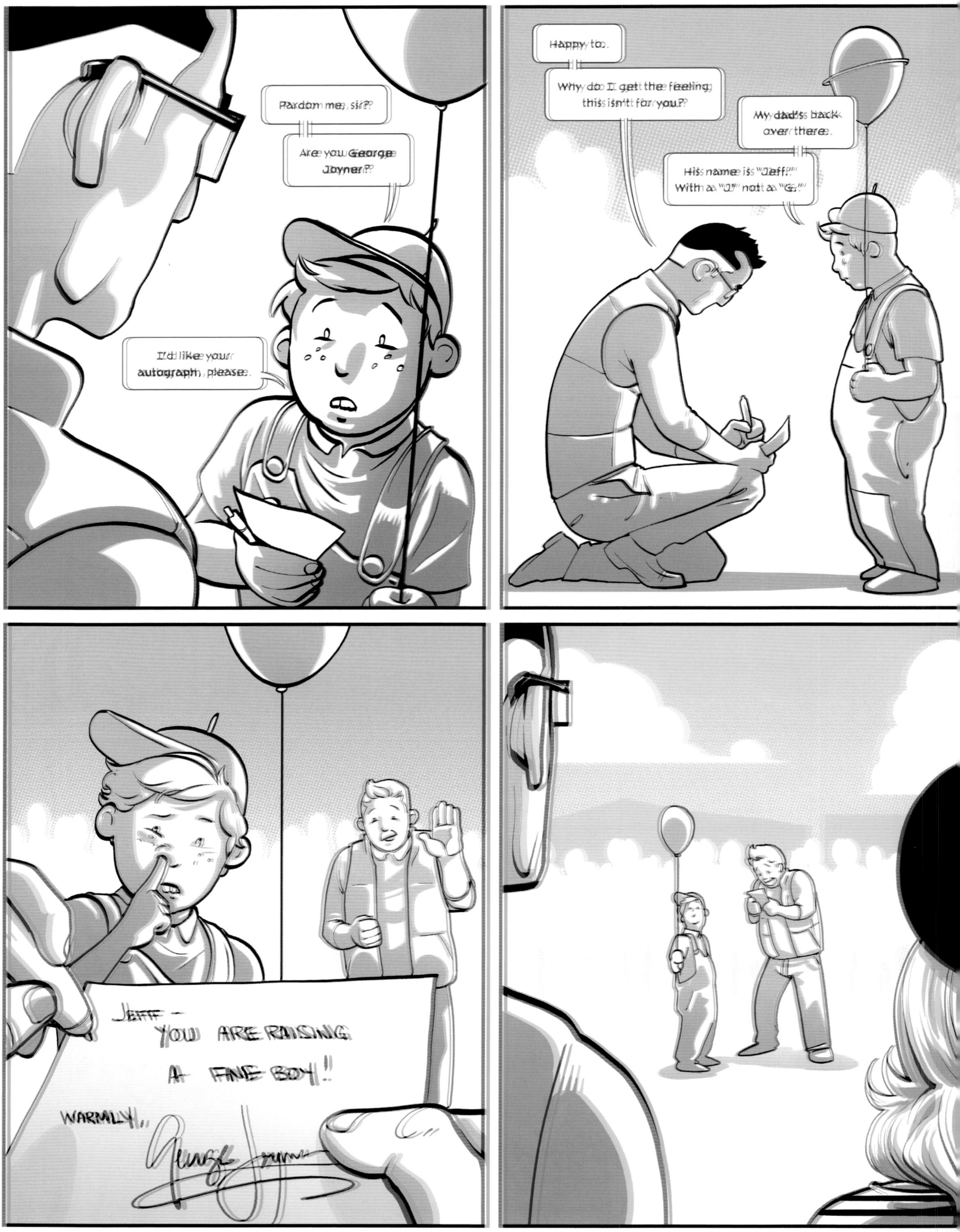

Pardon me, sir?
Are you George Joyner?
I'd like your autograph, please.
Happy to.
Why do I get the feeling this isn't for you?
My dad's back over there.
His name is "Jeff." With a "J" not a "G."
JEFF -
YOU ARE RAISING A FINE BOY!!
WARMLY,

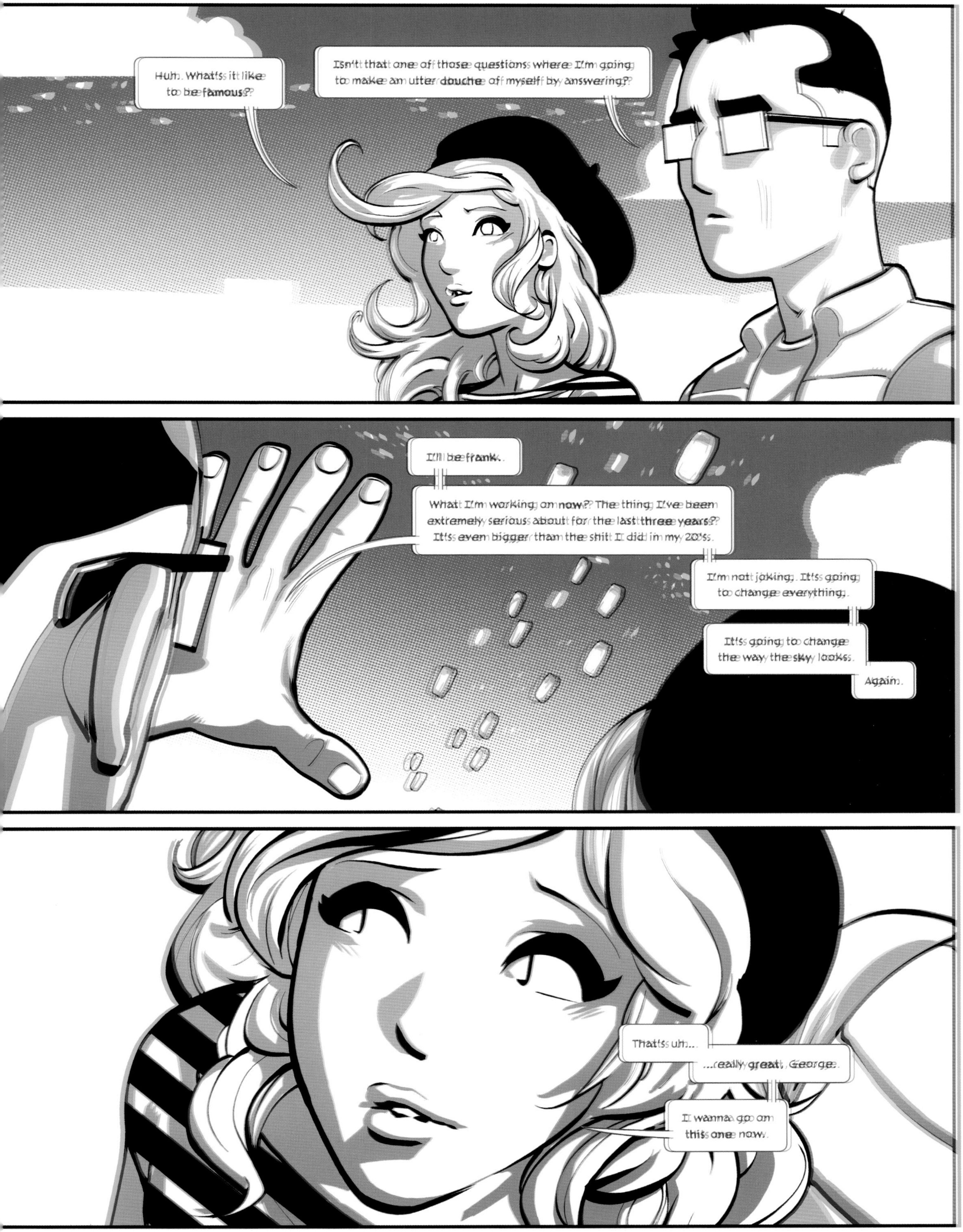
Huh. What's it like to be famous?
Isn't that one of those questions where I'm going to make an utter douche of myself by answering?
I'll be frank.
What I'm working on now? The thing I've been extremely serious about for the last three years? It's even bigger than the shit I did in my 20's.
I'm not joking. It's going to change everything.
It's going to change the way the sky looks.
Again.
That's uh...
...really great, George.
I wanna go on this one now.

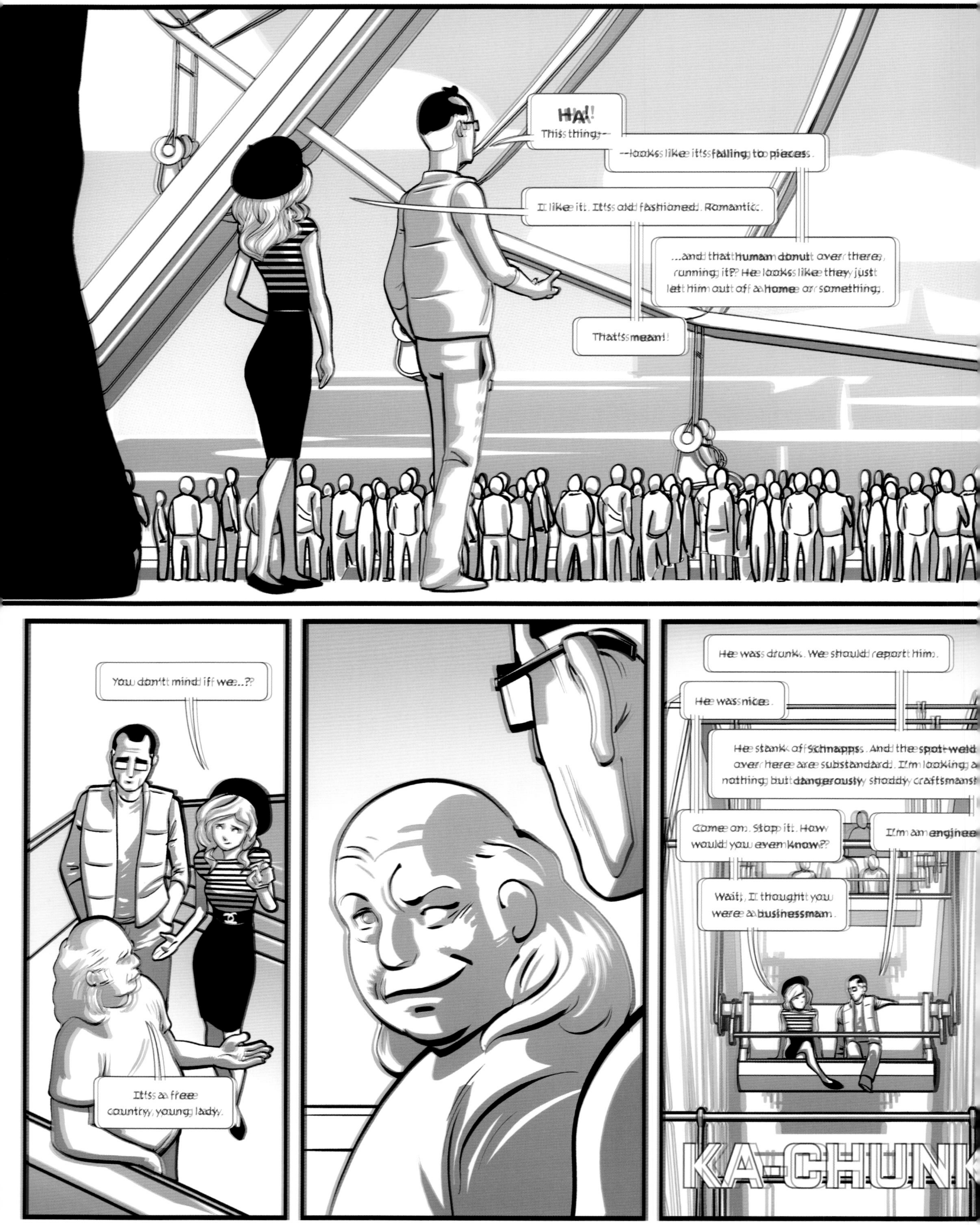
HA!
This thing--
--looks like it's falling to pieces.
I like it. It's old fashioned. Romantic.
...and that human donut over there, running it? He looks like they just let him out of a home or something.
That's mean!
You don't mind if we...?
It's a free country, young lady.
He was drunk. We should report him.
He was nice.
He stank of Schnapps. And the spot-weld over here are substandard. I'm looking a nothing but dangerously shoddy craftsmansh
Come on. Stop it. How would you even know?
I'm an enginee
Wait, I thought you were a businessman.
KA-CHUNK

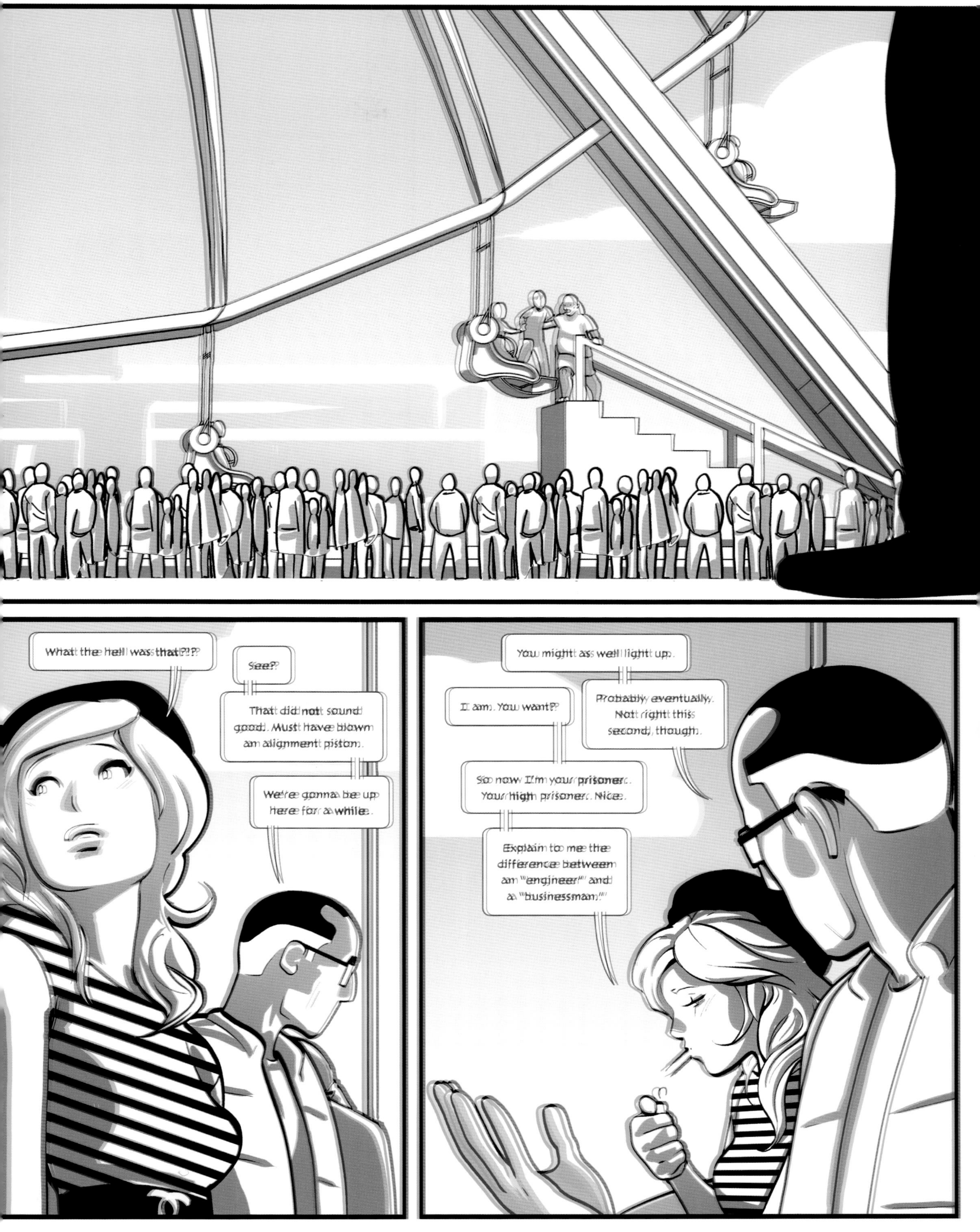
What the hell was that?!?
See?
That did not sound good. Must have blown an alignment piston.
We're gonna be up here for a while.
You might as well light up.
I am. You want?
Probably eventually. Not right this second, though.
So now I'm your prisoner. Your high prisoner. Nice.
Explain to me the difference between an "engineer" and a "businessman."

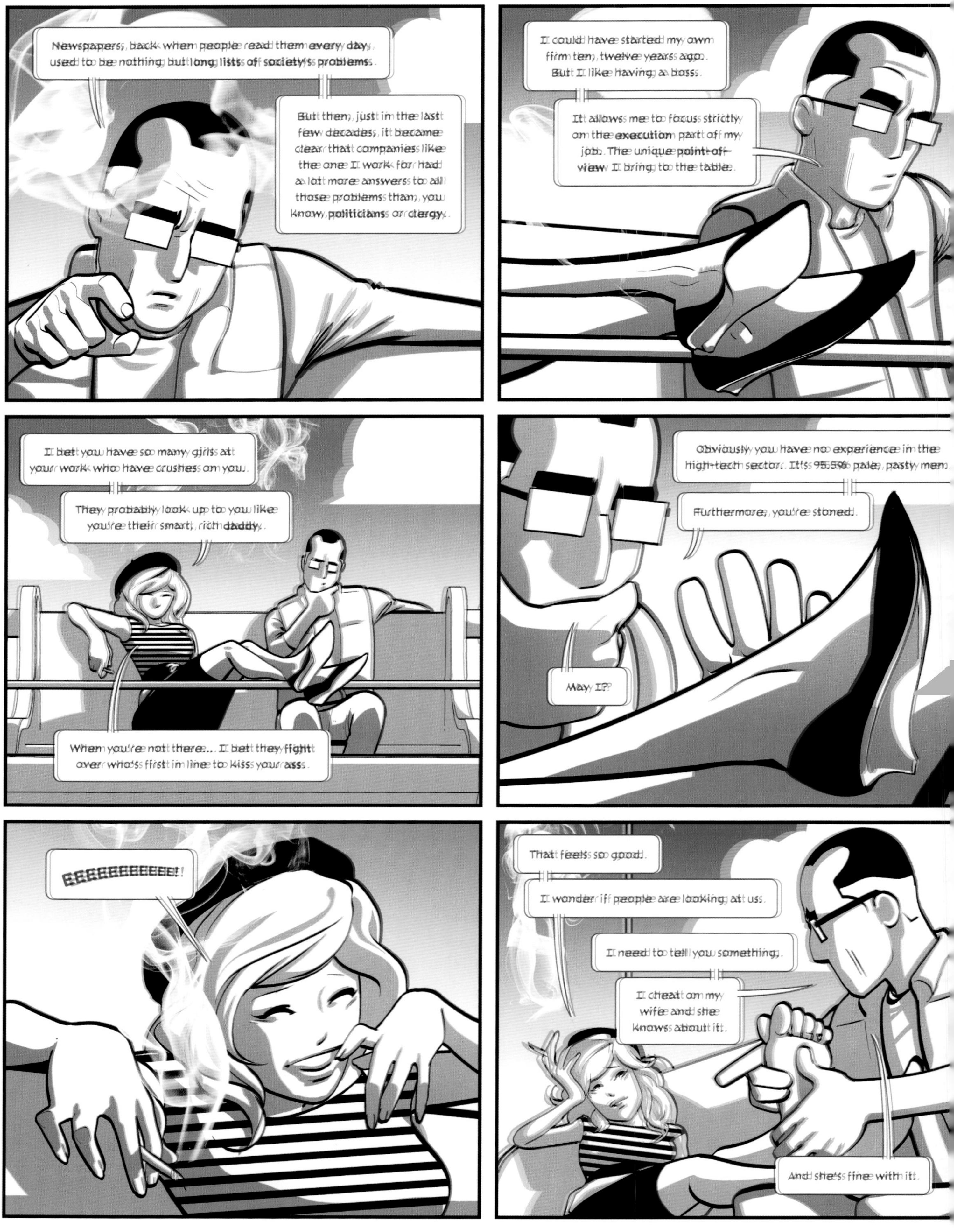

Newspapers, back when people read them every day, used to be nothing but long lists of society's problems.
But then, just in the last few decades, it became clear that companies like the one I work for had a lot more answers to all those problems than, you know, politicians or clergy.
I could have started my own firm ten, twelve years ago. But I like having a boss.
It allows me to focus strictly on the execution part of my job. The unique point-of-view I bring to the table.
I bet you have so many girls at your work who have crushes on you.
They probably look up to you like you're their smart, rich daddy.
When you're not there... I bet they fight over who's first in line to kiss your ass.
Obviously you have no experience in the high-tech sector. It's 95.5% pale, pasty men.
Furthermore, you're stoned.
May I?
EEEEEEEEEEEE!
That feels so good.
I wonder if people are looking at us.
I need to tell you something.
I cheat on my wife and she knows about it.
And she's fine with it.

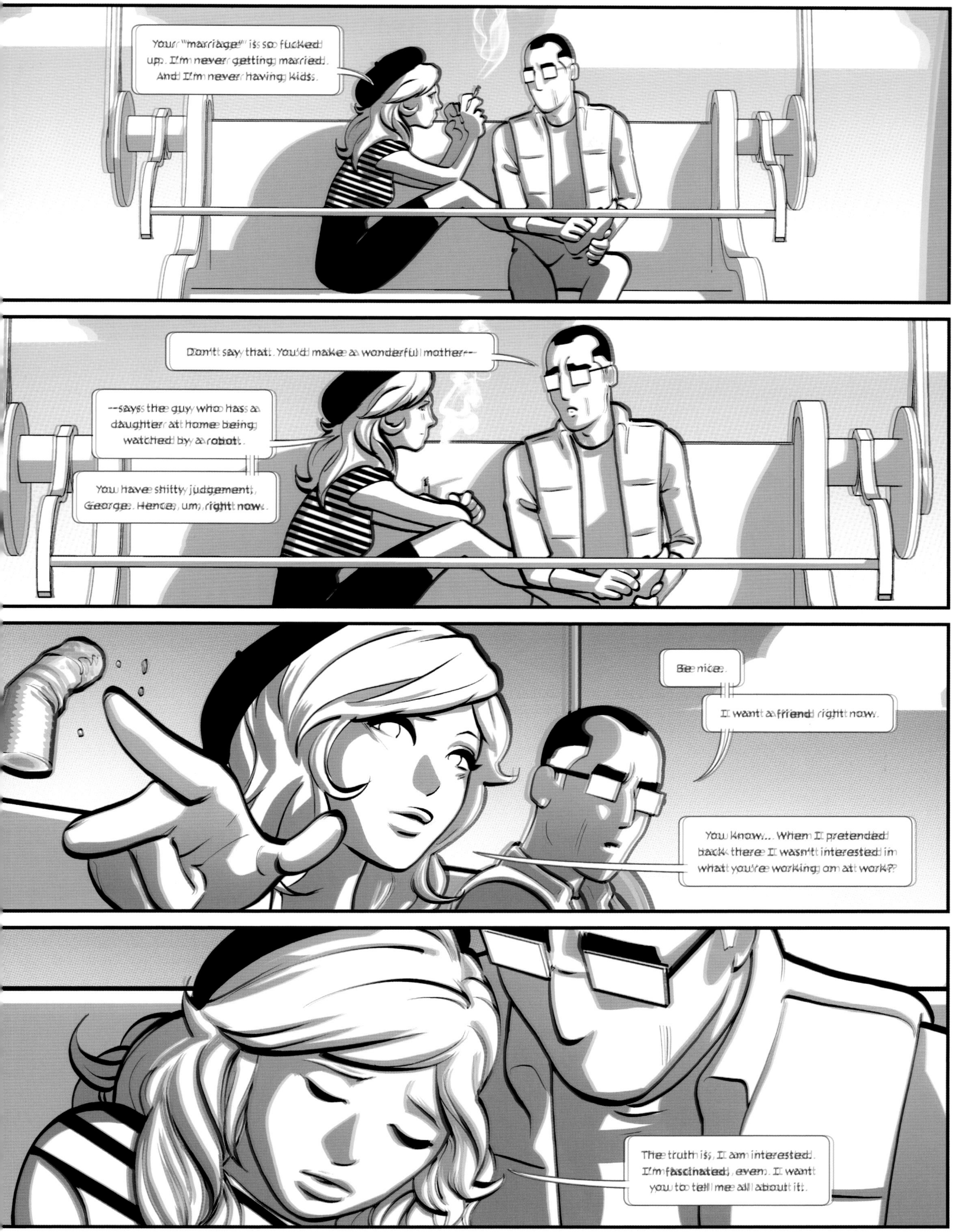
Your "marriage" is so fucked up. I'm never getting married. And I'm never having kids.
Don't say that. You'd make a wonderful mother--
--says the guy who has a daughter at home being watched by a robot.
You have shitty judgement, George. Hence, um, right now.
Be nice.
I want a friend right now.
You know... When I pretended back there I wasn't interested in what you're working on at work?
The truth is, I am interested. I'm fascinated, even. I want you to tell me all about it.

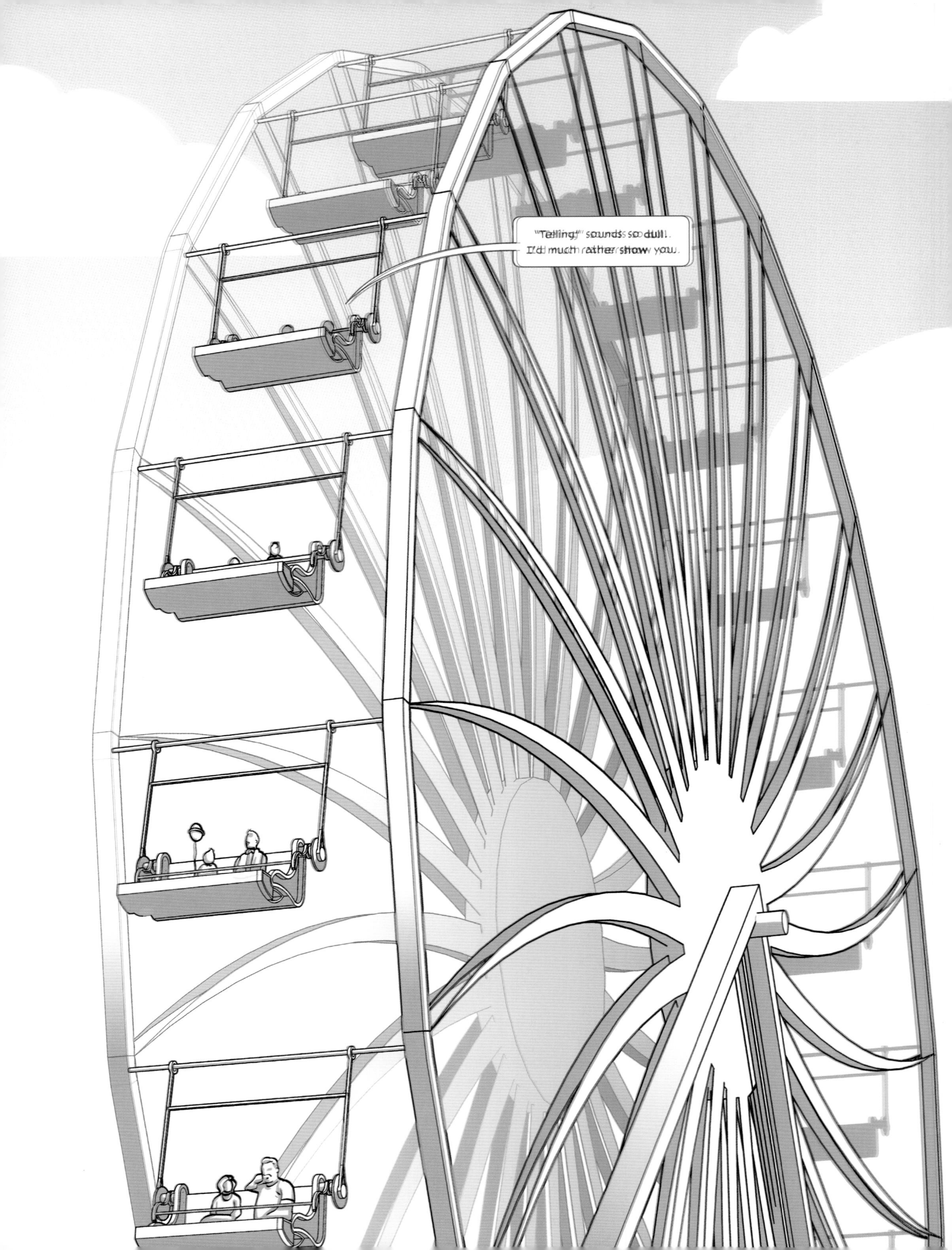
"Telling" sounds so dull.
I'd much rather show you.

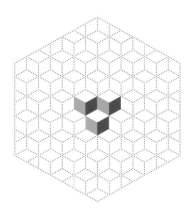

CHAPTER THREE

30 IS THE NEW 90

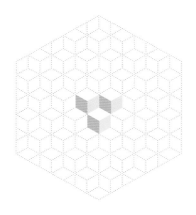

30 IS THE NEW 90

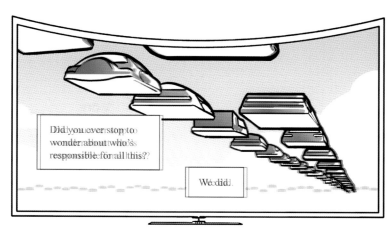

The Vertical Migration.

Flying cars. Cities in the sky. It all happened so fast.

Did you ever stop to wonder about who's responsible for all this?

We did.

We started out in a garage. Like a lot of other folks do.

There was no seed money. Nobody would give us a dime.

He doesn't do a lot of interviews, but he believed in me, in my ideas.

Even when everybody else thought we were insane.

Luckily, I turned out to be exactly right about everything.

He'll tell you the same thing if you can manage to get him on the phone.

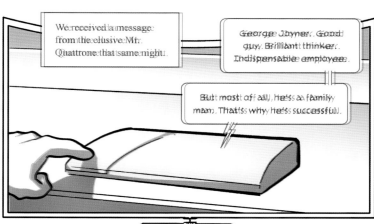

We received a message from the elusive Mr. Quattrone that same night.

George Joyner. Good guy. Brilliant thinker. Indispensable employee.

But most of all, he's a family man. That's why he's successful.

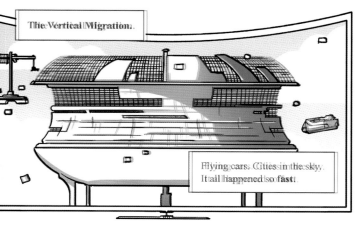

George Joyner provided us with a single picture of that family, lending strong support to his longtime boss' contention.

REMOVE 3D GLASSES NOW

*READER: Do NOT remove your glasses. -Stephen

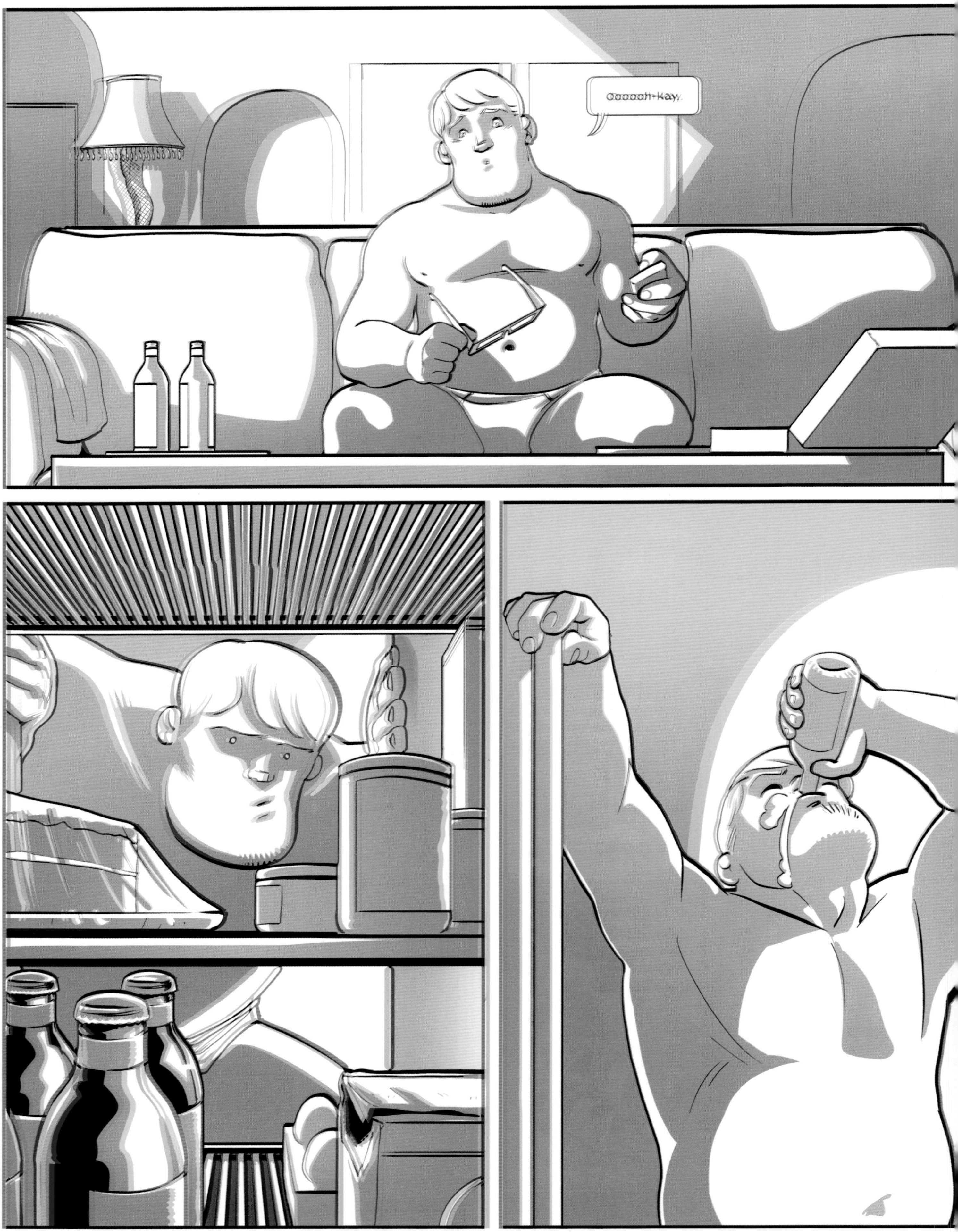
Oooooh-Kay.

NNGGGGHHH...
...69
SNNNOOOOORRRT!

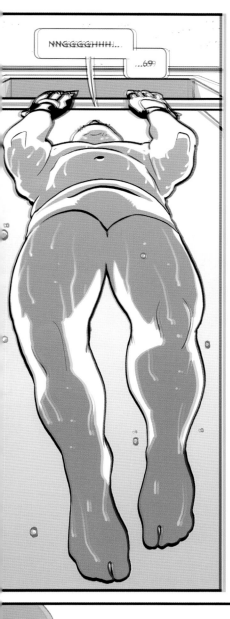

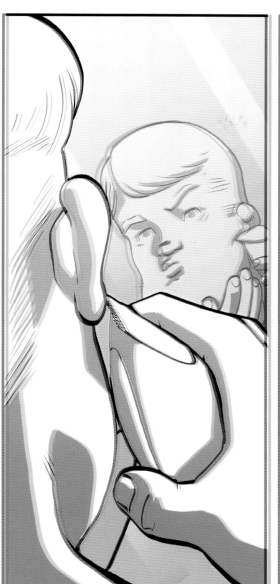

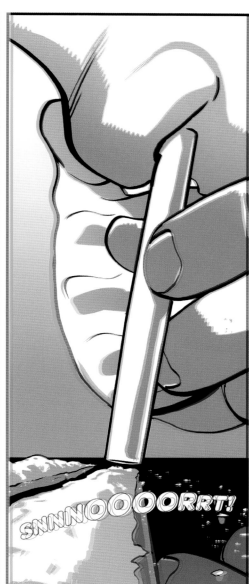

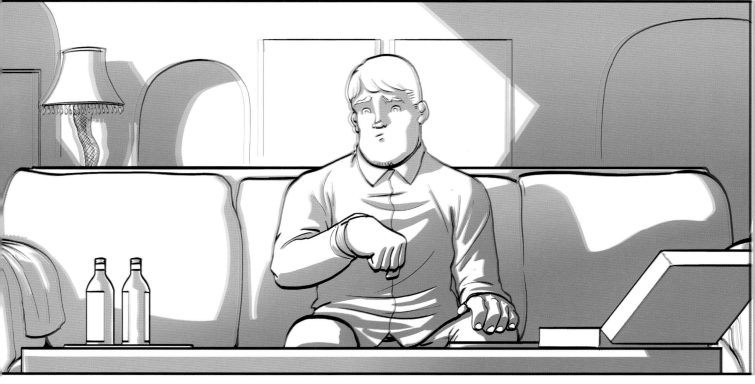

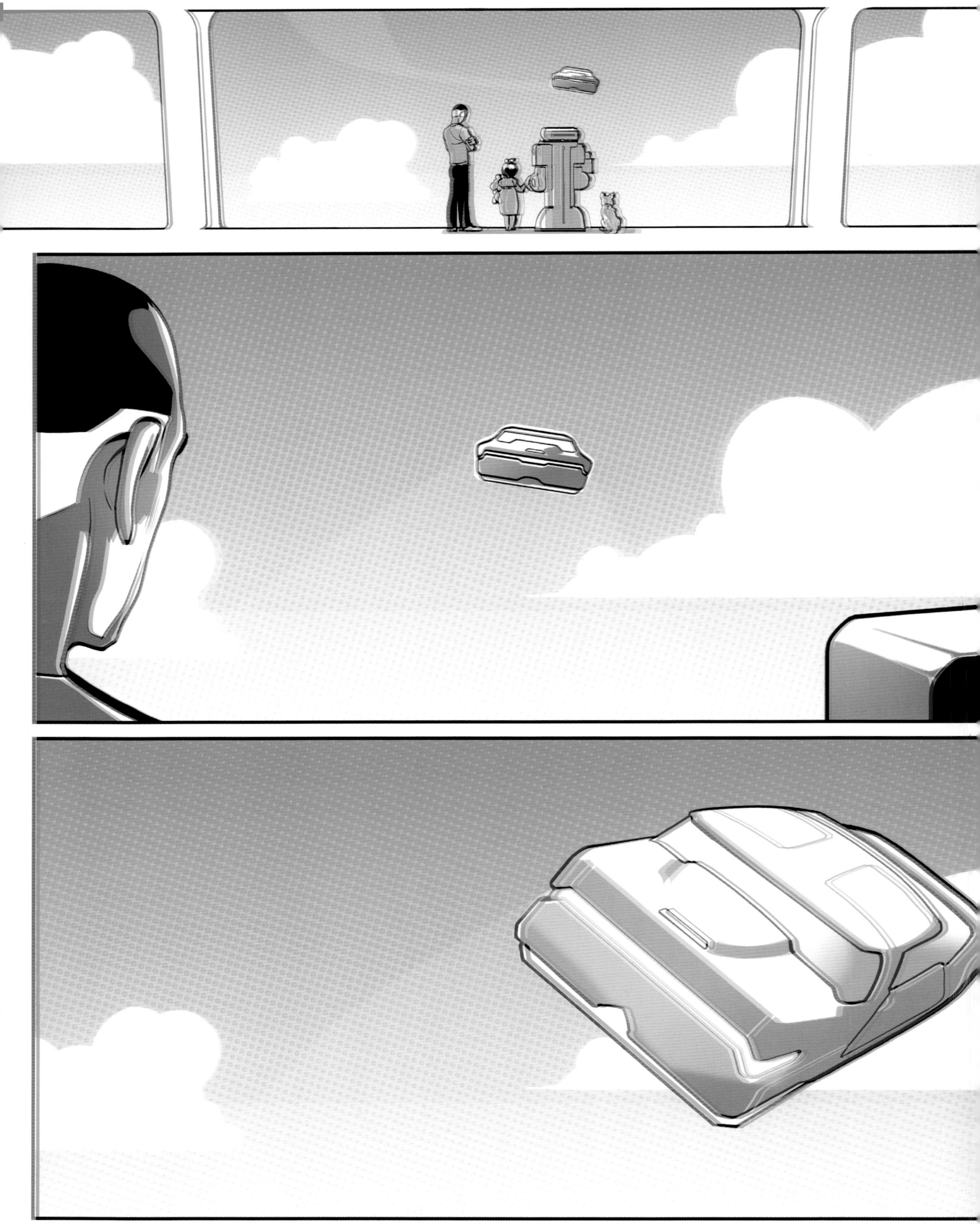

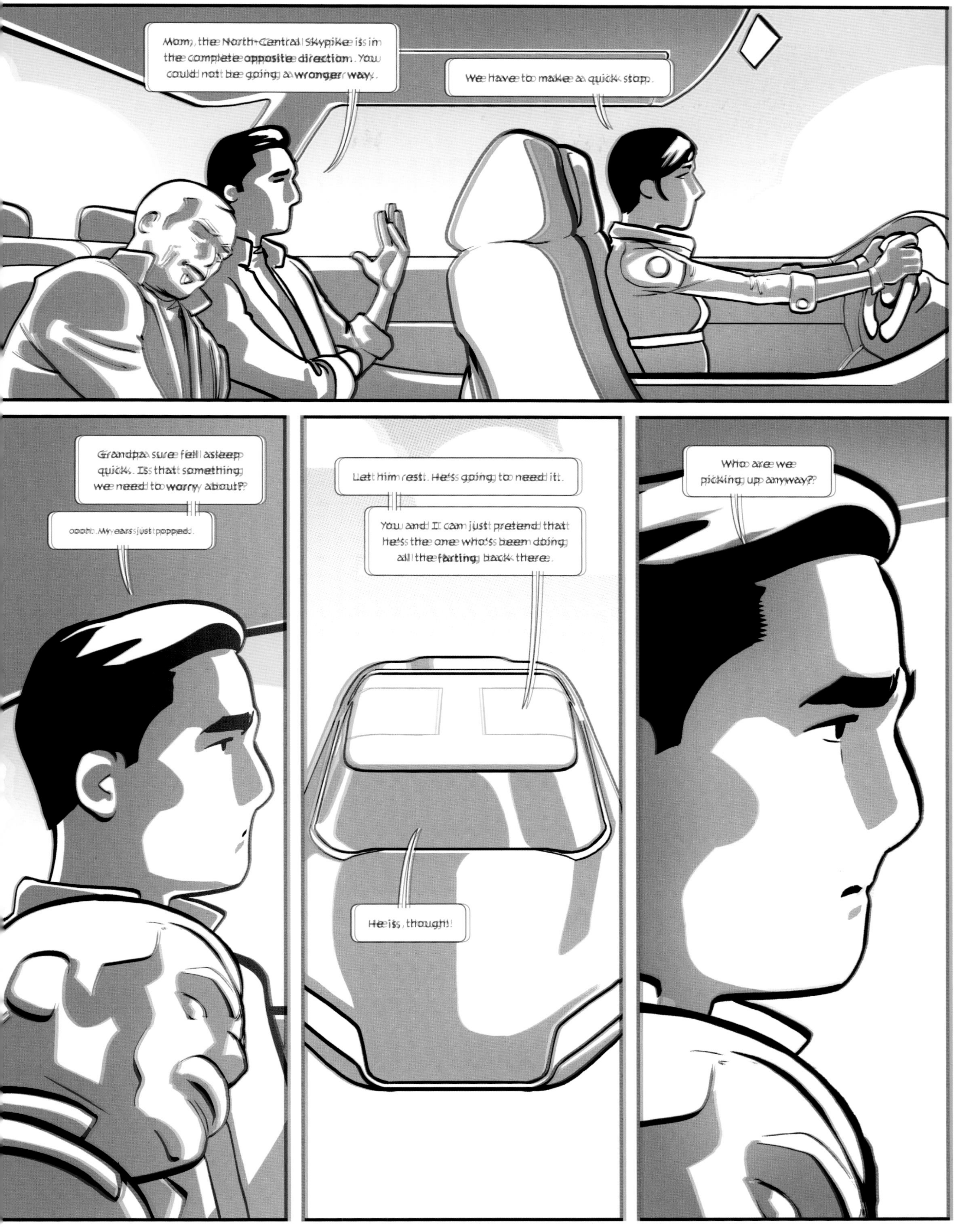

Mom, the North-Central Skypike is in the complete opposite direction. You could not be going a wronger way.
We have to make a quick stop.
Grandpa sure fell asleep quick. Is that something we need to worry about?
oooh. My ears just popped.
Let him rest. He's going to need it.
You and I can just pretend that he's the one who's been doing all the farting back there.
He is, though!
Who are we picking up anyway?

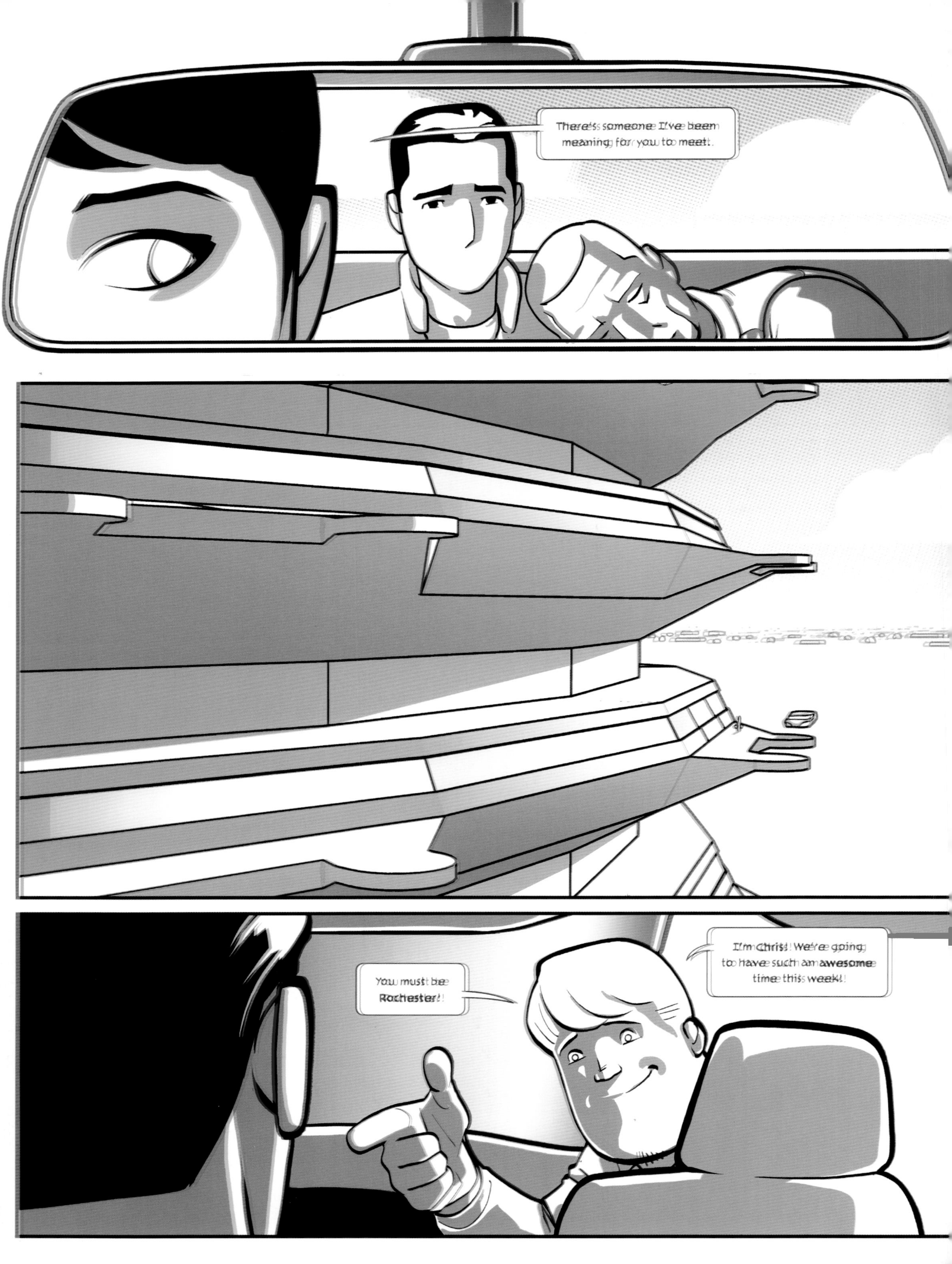
There's someone I've been meaning for you to meet.
You must be Rochester!
I'm Chris! We're going to have such an awesome time this week!

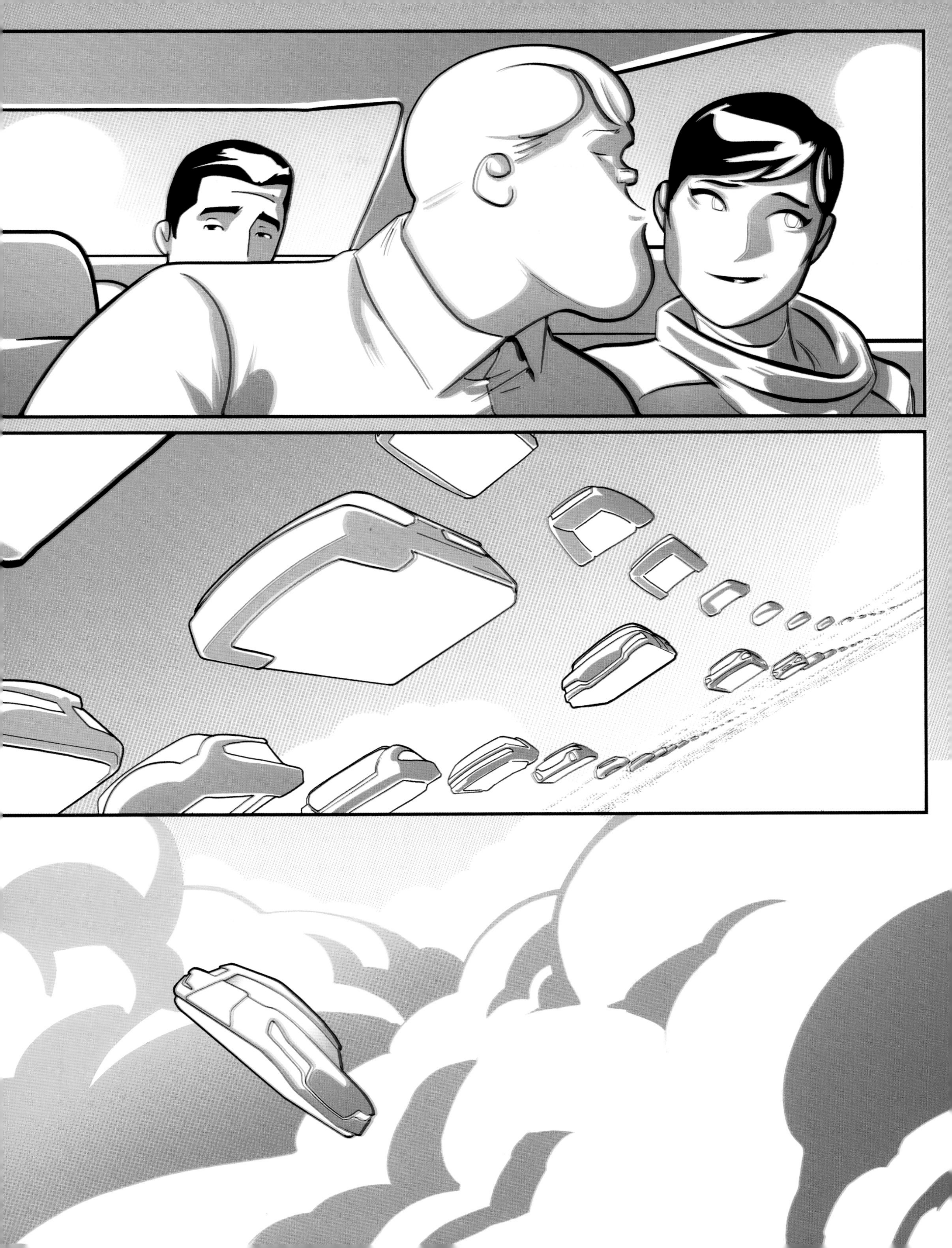

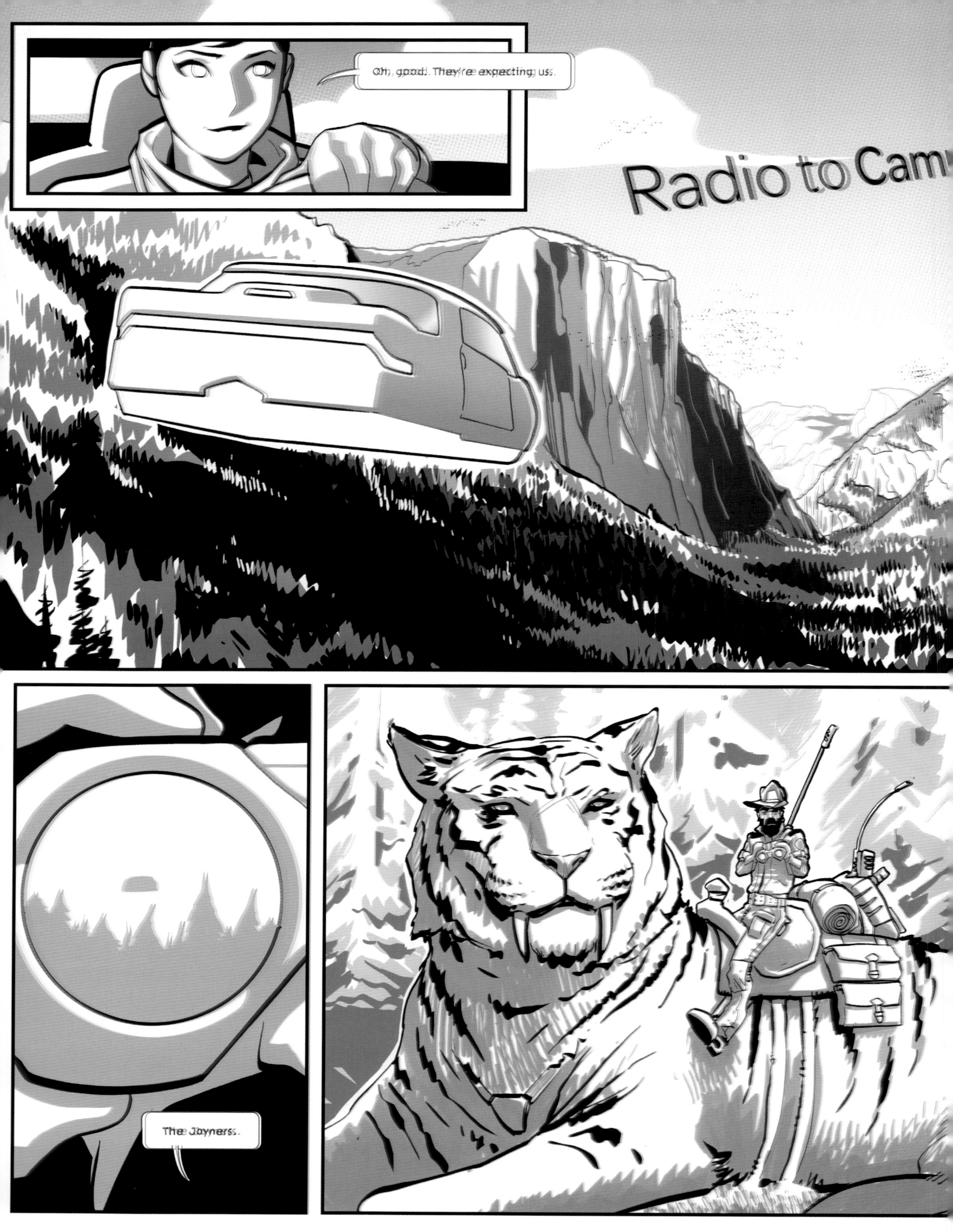
Oh, good. They're expecting us.
Radio to Cam
The Joyners.

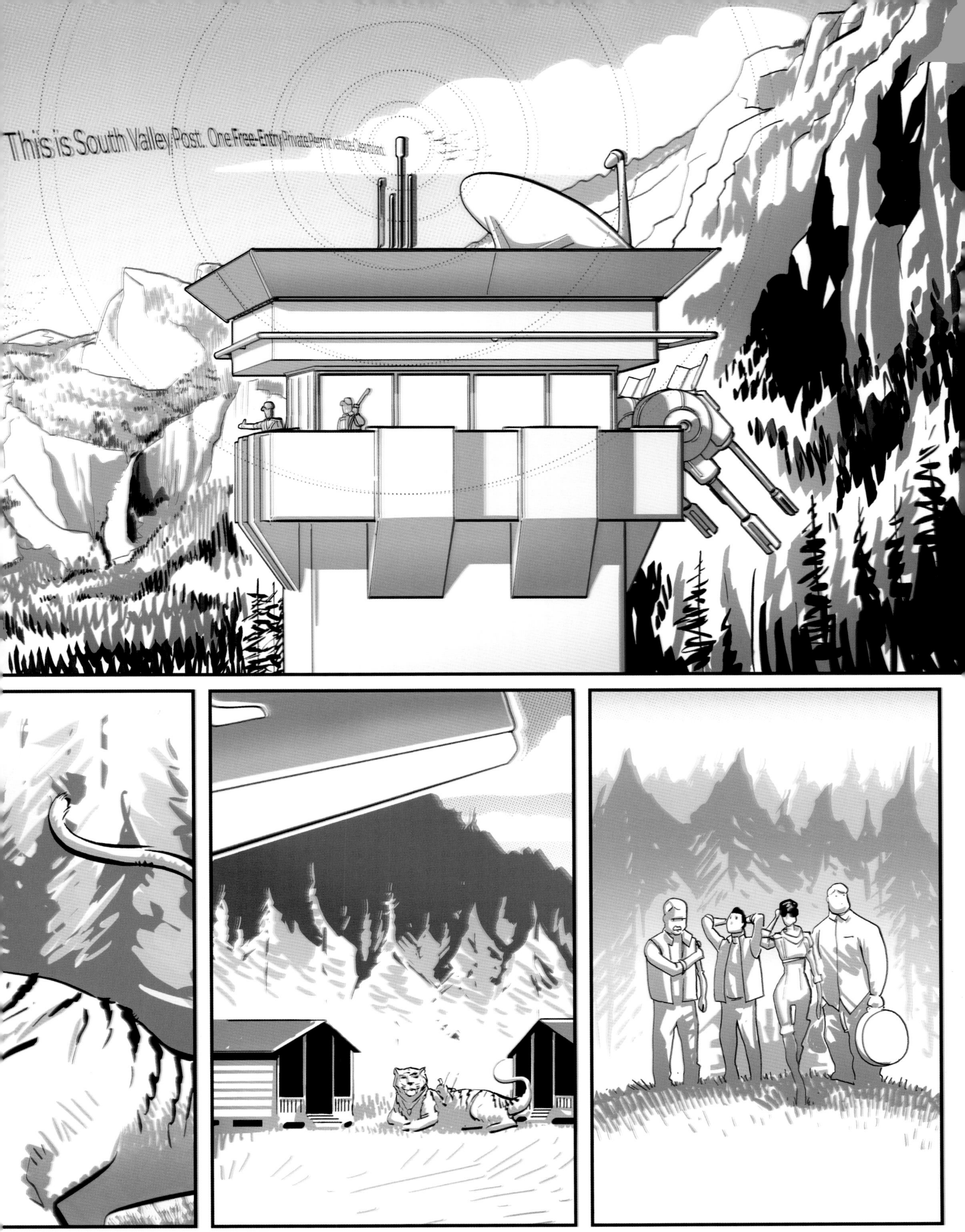
This is South Valley Post. One Free-Entry Private Permit Vehicle Clear to land.

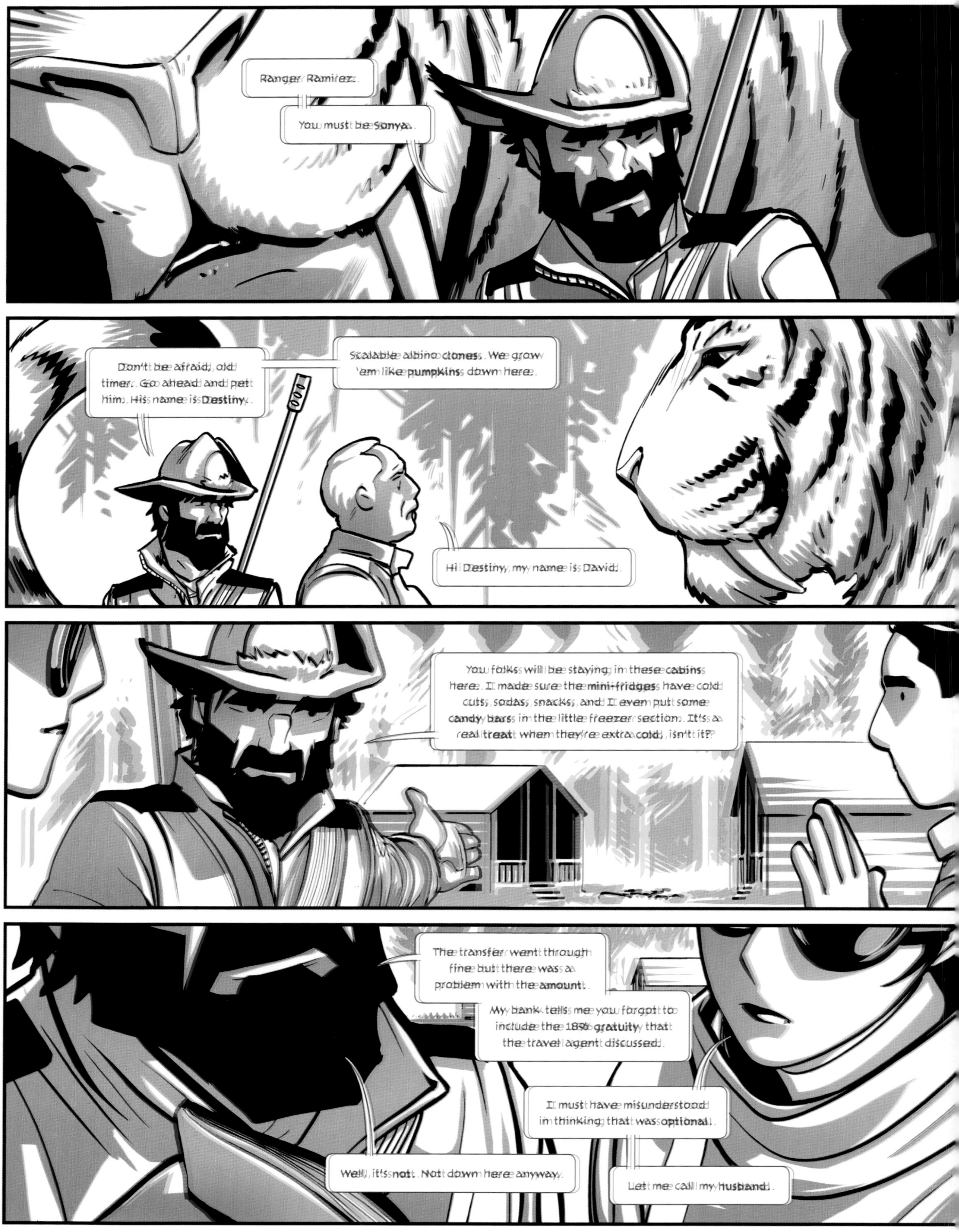
Ranger Ramirez.
You must be Sonya.
Don't be afraid, old timer. Go ahead and pet him. His name is Destiny.
Scalable albino clones. We grow 'em like pumpkins down here.
Hi Destiny, my name is David.
You folks will be staying in these cabins here. I made sure the mini-fridges have cold cuts, sodas, snacks, and I even put some candy bars in the little freezer section. It's a real treat when they're extra cold, isn't it?
The transfer went through fine but there was a problem with the amount.
My bank tells me you forgot to include the 18% gratuity that the travel agent discussed.
I must have misunderstood in thinking that was optional.
Well, it's not. Not down here anyway.
Let me call my husband.

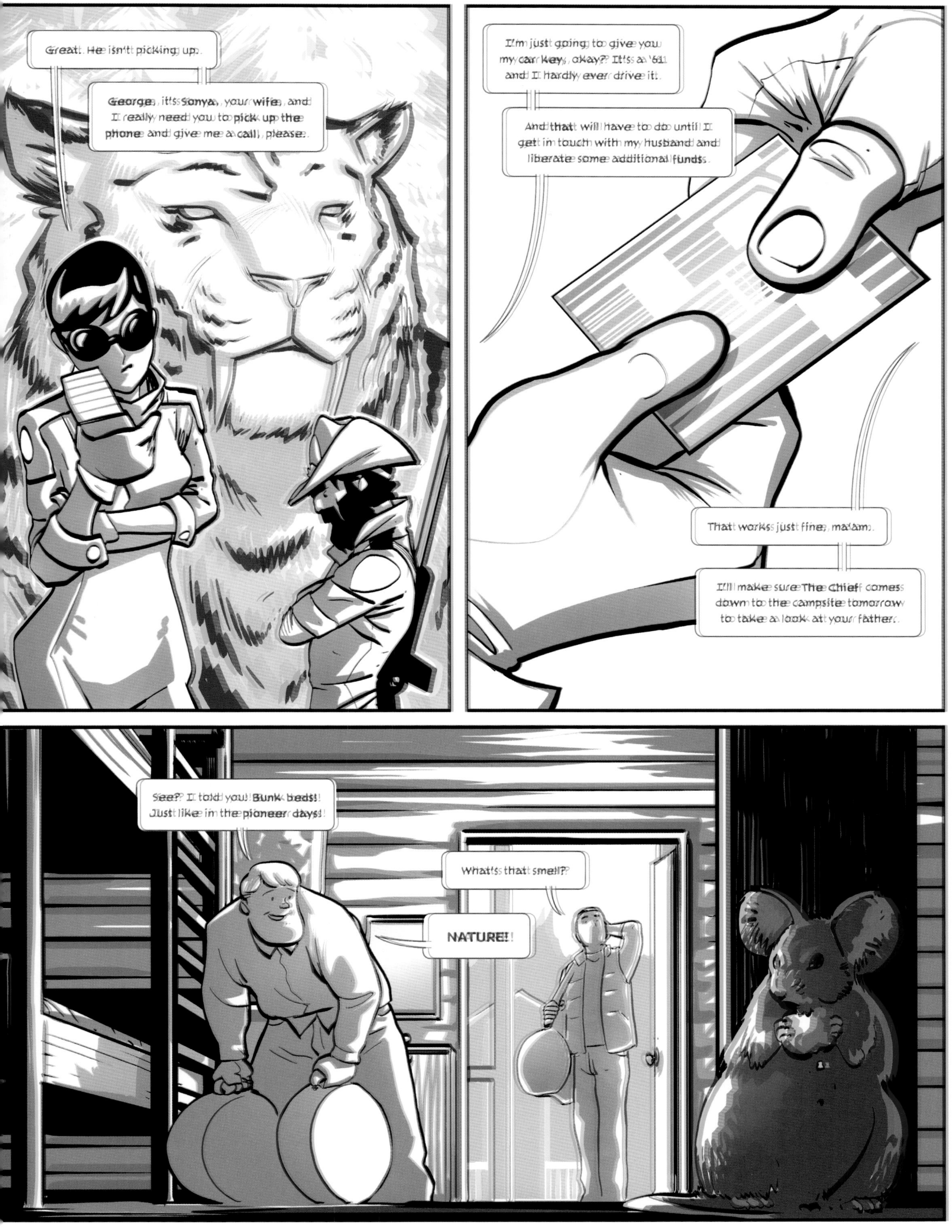
Great. He isn't picking up.
George, it's Sonya, your wife, and I really need you to pick up the phone and give me a call, please.
I'm just going to give you my car key, okay? It's a '61 and I hardly ever drive it.
And that will have to do until I get in touch with my husband and liberate some additional funds.
That works just fine, ma'am.
I'll make sure The Chief comes down to the campsite tomorrow to take a look at your father.
See? I told you! Bunk beds! Just like in the pioneer days!
What's that smell?
NATURE!

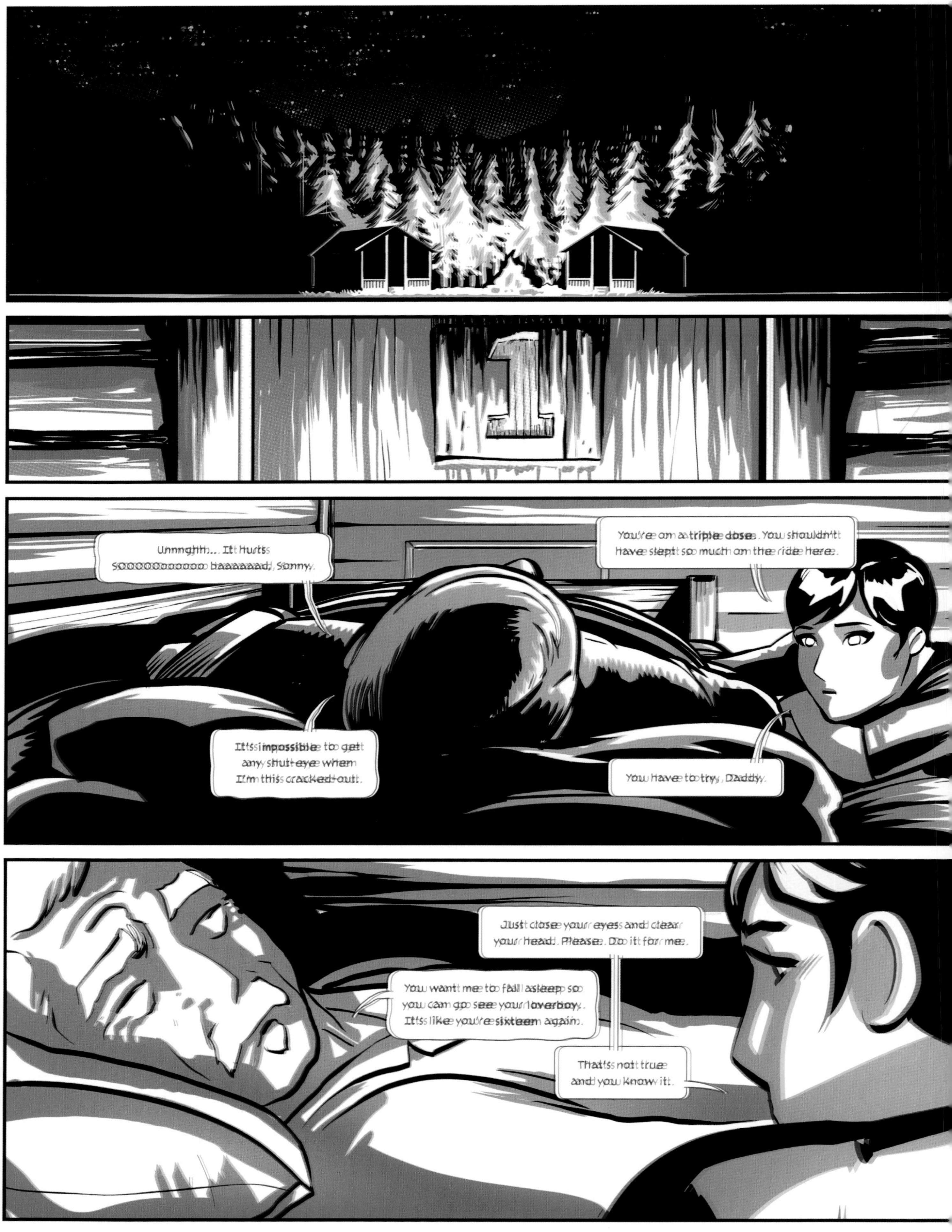

Unnngh... It hurts SOOOOOOoooooo baaaaaad, Sonny.
You're on a triple dose. You shouldn't have slept so much on the ride here.
It's impossible to get any shut-eye when I'm this cracked-out.
You have to try, Daddy.
Just close your eyes and clear your head. Please. Do it for me.
You want me to fall asleep so you can go see your loverboy. It's like you're sixteen again.
That's not true and you know it.

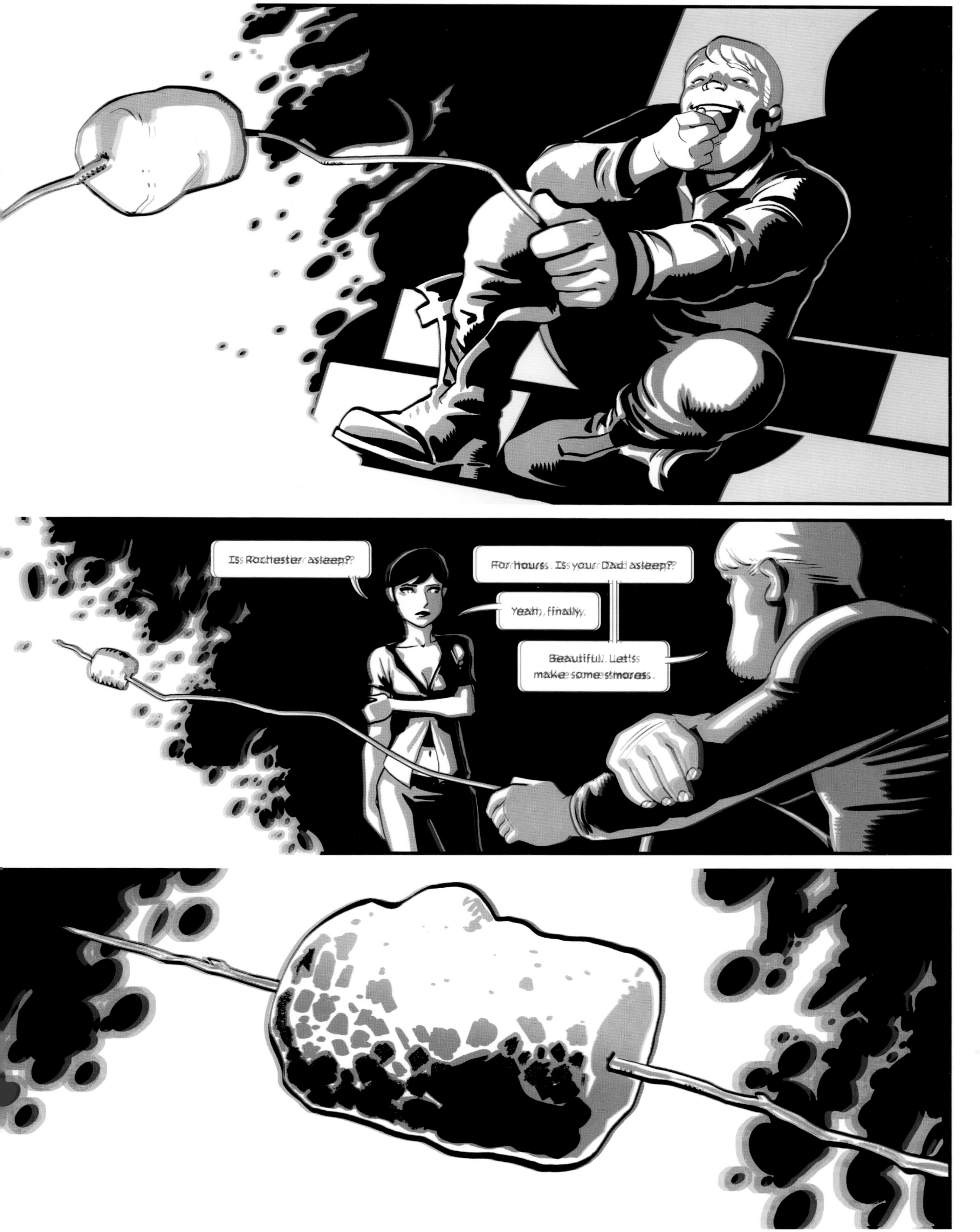
Is Rochester asleep?
For hours. Is your Dad asleep?
Yeah, finally.
Beautiful. Let's make some s'mores.

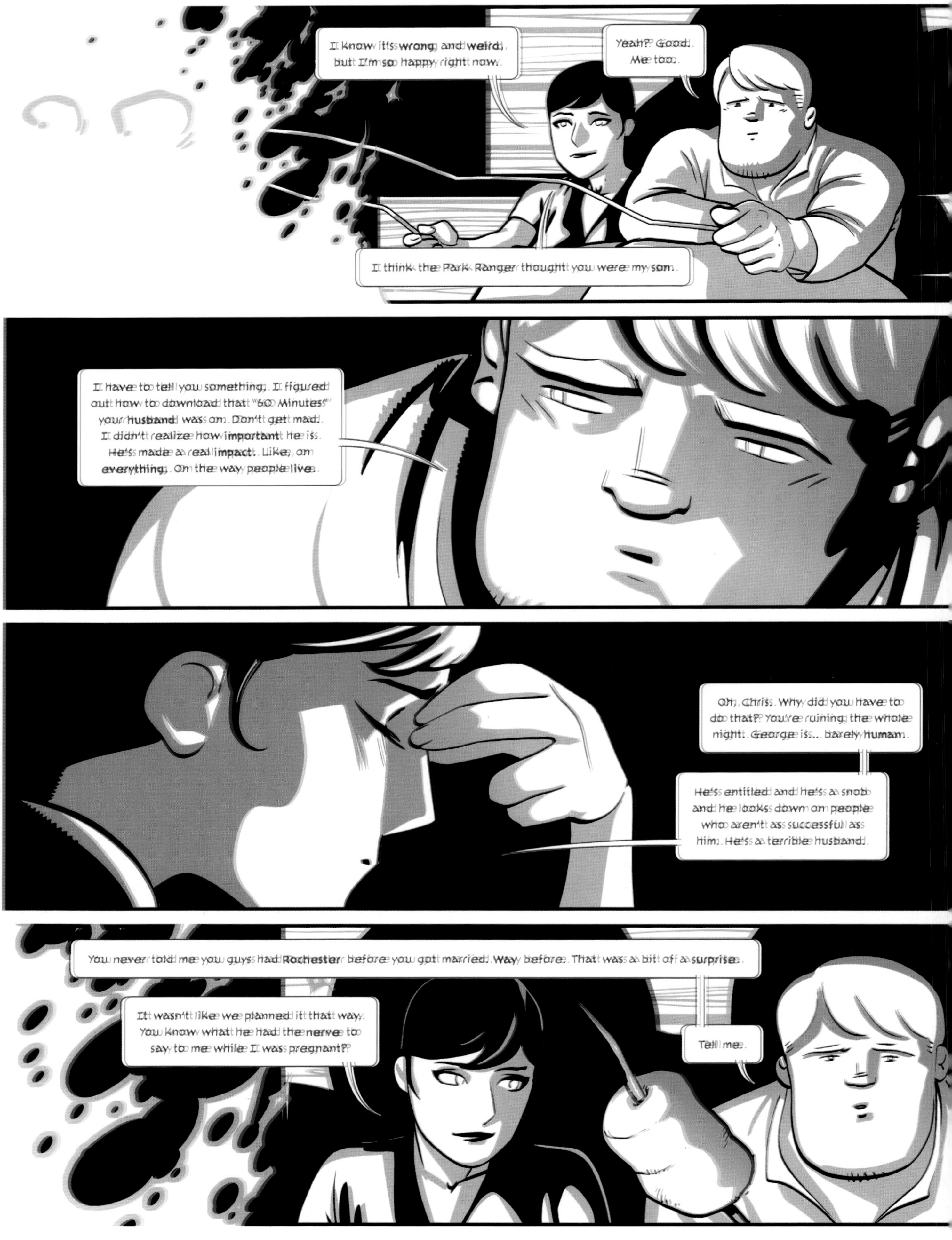

I know it's wrong and weird, but I'm so happy right now.
Yeah? Good. Me too.
I think the Park Ranger thought you were my son.
I have to tell you something. I figured out how to download that "60 Minutes" your husband was on. Don't get mad. I didn't realize how important he is. He's made a real impact. Like, on everything. On the way people live.
Oh, Chris. Why did you have to do that? You're ruining the whole night. George is... barely human.
He's entitled and he's a snob and he looks down on people who aren't as successful as him. He's a terrible husband.
You never told me you guys had Rochester before you got married. Way before. That was a bit of a surprise.
It wasn't like we planned it that way. You know what he had the nerve to say to me while I was pregnant?
Tell me.

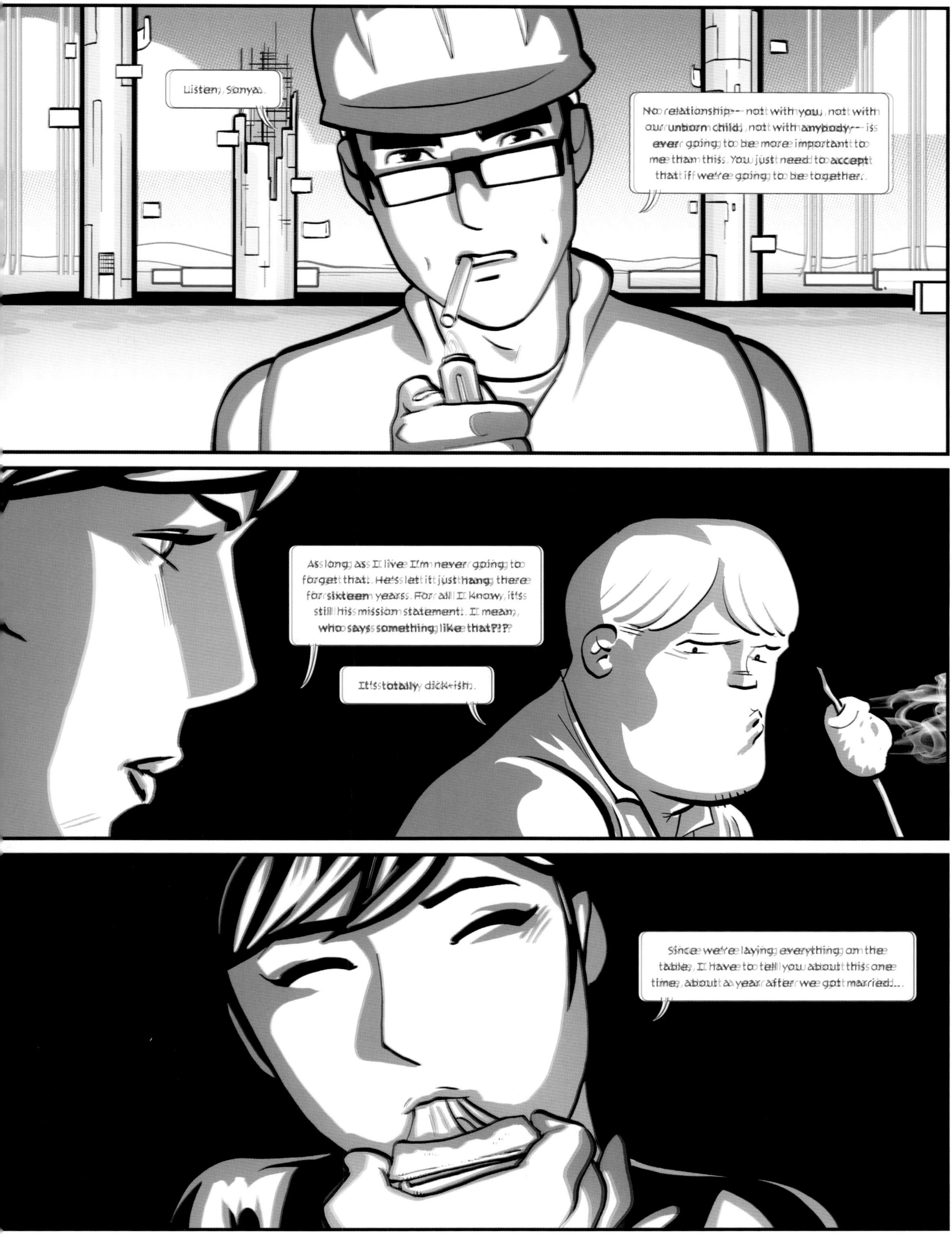
Listen, Sonya.
No relationship-- not with you, not with our unborn child, not with anybody-- is ever going to be more important to me than this. You just need to accept that if we're going to be together.
As long as I live I'm never going to forget that. He's let it just hang there for sixteen years. For all I know, it's still his mission statement. I mean, who says something like that?!?
It's totally dick-ish.
Since we're laying everything on the table, I have to tell you about this one time, about a year after we got married...

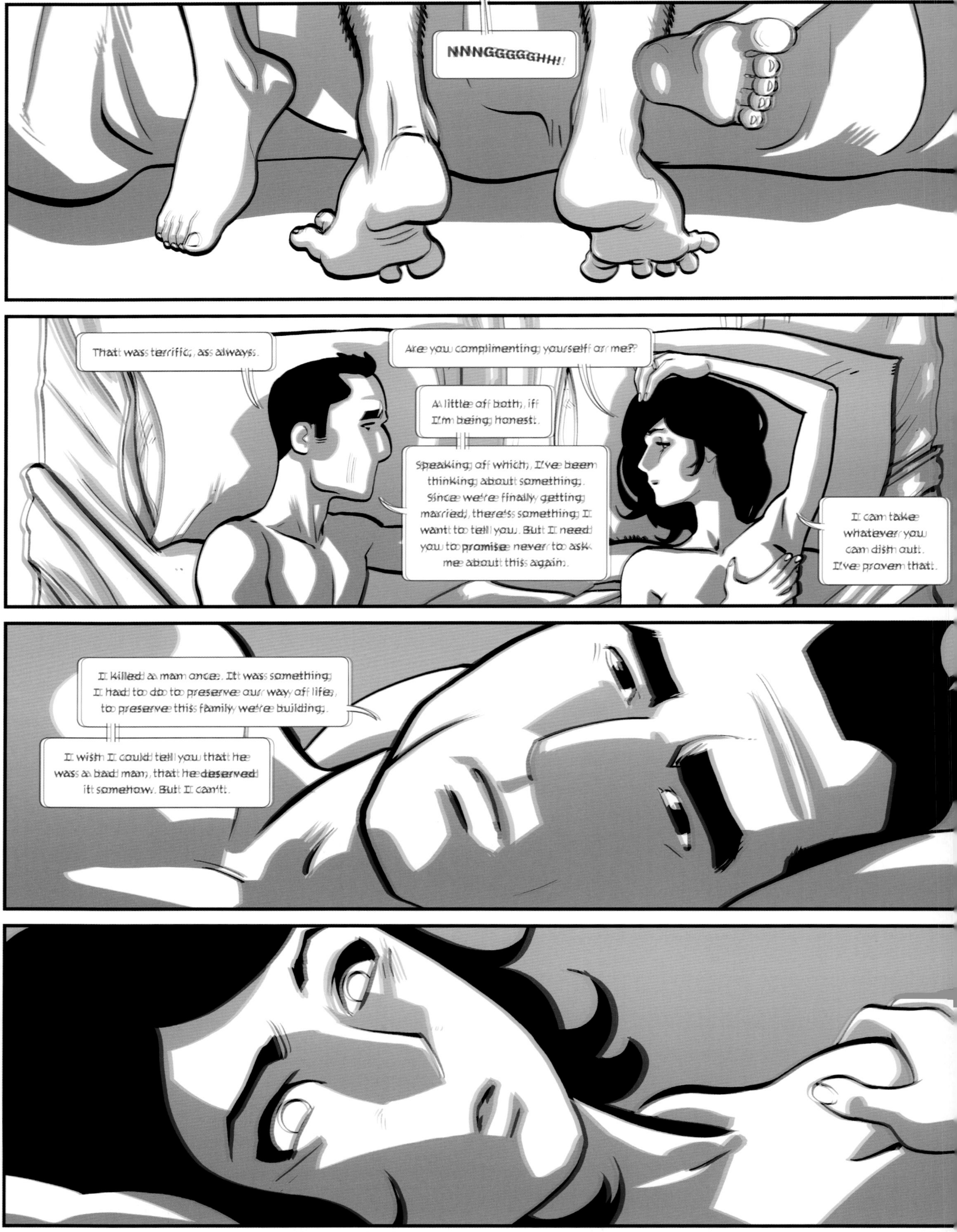
NNNGGGGGHH!!
That was terrific, as always.
Are you complimenting yourself or me?
A little of both, if I'm being honest.
Speaking of which, I've been thinking about something. Since we're finally getting married, there's something I want to tell you. But I need you to promise never to ask me about this again.
I can take whatever you can dish out. I've proven that.
I killed a man once. It was something I had to do to preserve our way of life, to preserve this family we're building.
I wish I could tell you that he was a bad man, that he deserved it somehow. But I can't.

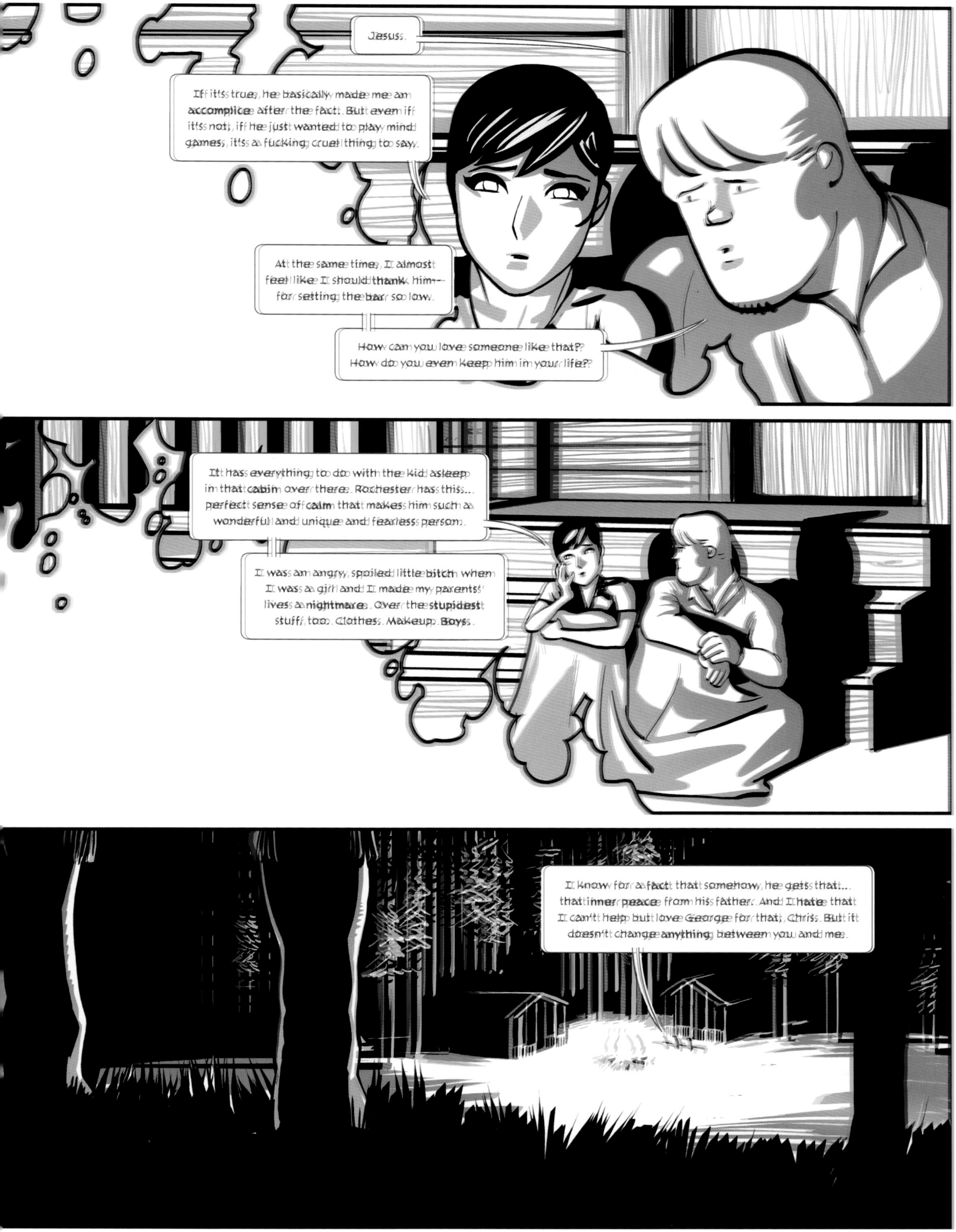
Jesus.
If it's true, he basically made me an accomplice after the fact. But even if it's not, if he just wanted to play mind games, it's a fucking cruel thing to say.
At the same time, I almost feel like I should thank him-- for setting the bar so low.
How can you love someone like that? How do you even keep him in your life?
It has everything to do with the kid asleep in that cabin over there. Rochester has this... perfect sense of calm that makes him such a wonderful and unique and fearless person.
I was an angry, spoiled little bitch when I was a girl and I made my parents' lives a nightmare. Over the stupidest stuff, too. Clothes. Makeup. Boys.
I know for a fact that somehow, he gets that... that inner peace from his father. And I hate that I can't help but love George for that, Chris. But it doesn't change anything between you and me.

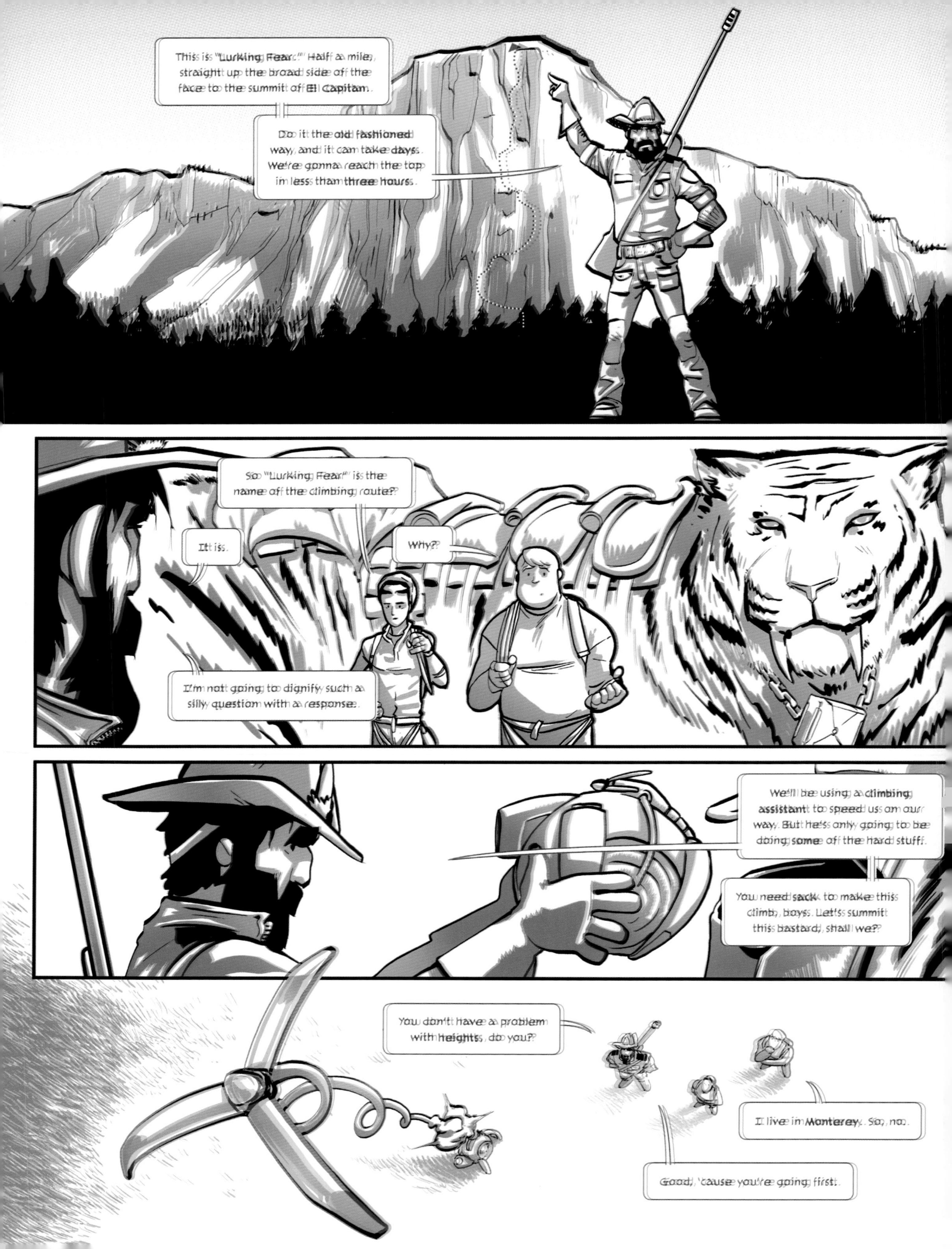
This is "Lurking Fear." Half a mile, straight up the broad side of the face to the summit of El Capitan.
Do it the old fashioned way, and it can take days. We're gonna reach the top in less than three hours.
So "Lurking Fear" is the name of the climbing route?
It is.
Why?
I'm not going to dignify such a silly question with a response.
We'll be using a climbing assistant to speed us on our way. But he's only going to be doing some of the hard stuff.
You need sack to make this climb, boys. Let's summit this bastard, shall we?
You don't have a problem with heights, do you?
I live in Monterey. So, no.
Good, 'cause you're going first.

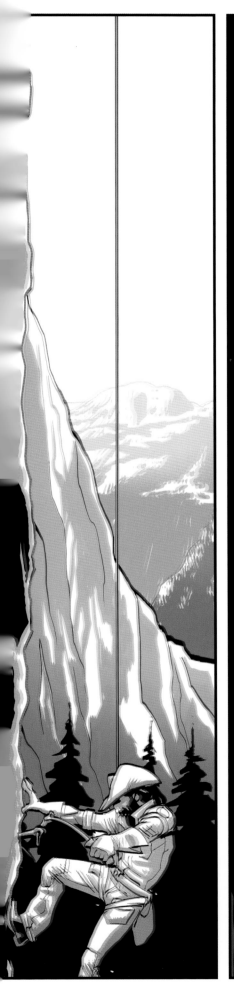

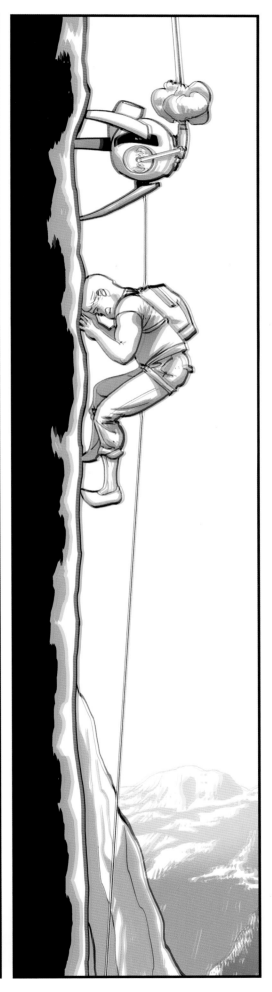

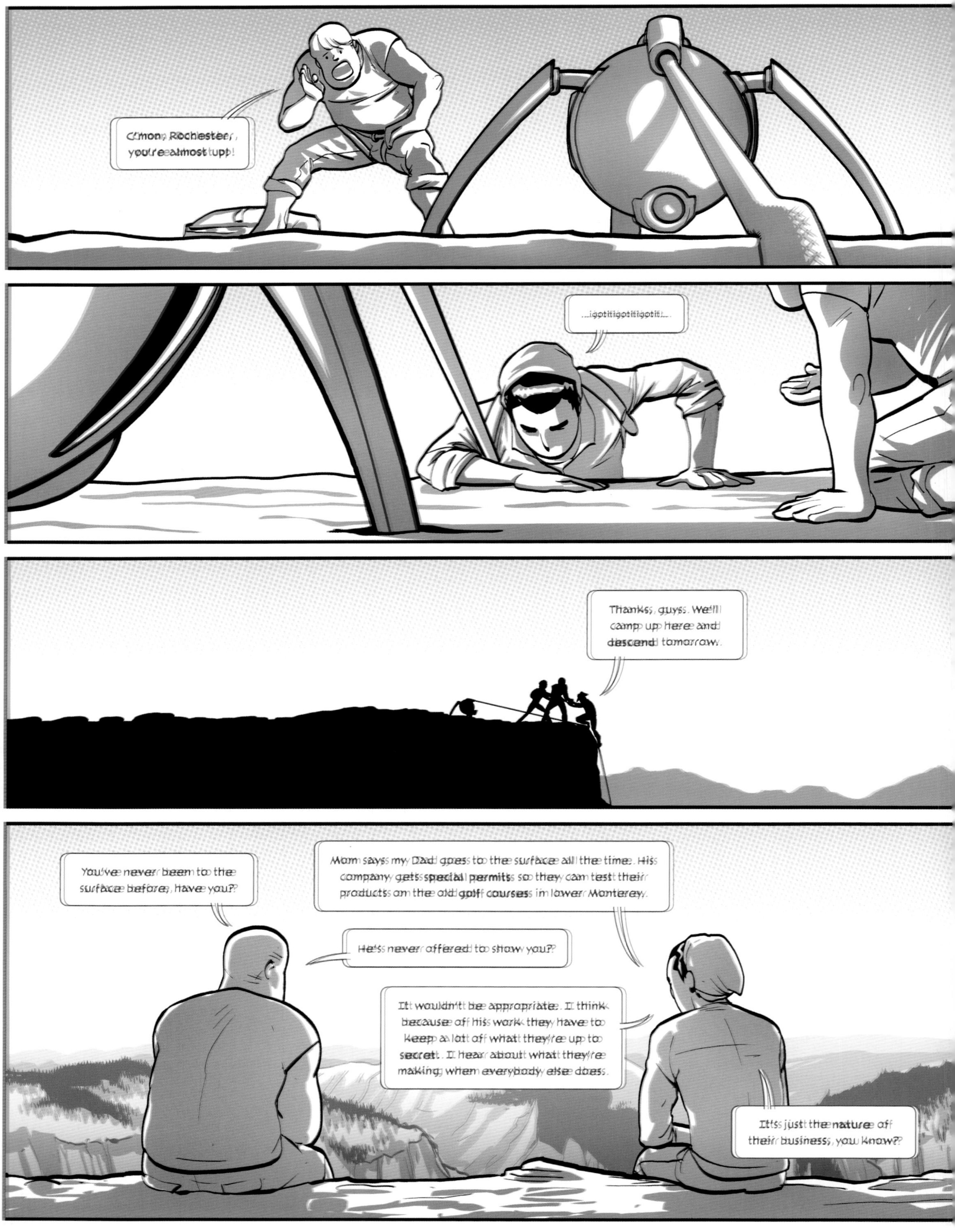
C'mon, Rochester, you're almost up!
...igotitigotitigotit...
Thanks, guys. We'll camp up here and descend tomorrow.
You've never been to the surface before, have you?
Mom says my Dad goes to the surface all the time. His company gets special permits so they can test their products on the old golf courses in lower Monterey.
He's never offered to show you?
It wouldn't be appropriate. I think because of his work they have to keep a lot of what they're up to secret. I hear about what they're making when everybody else does.
It's just the nature of their business, you know?

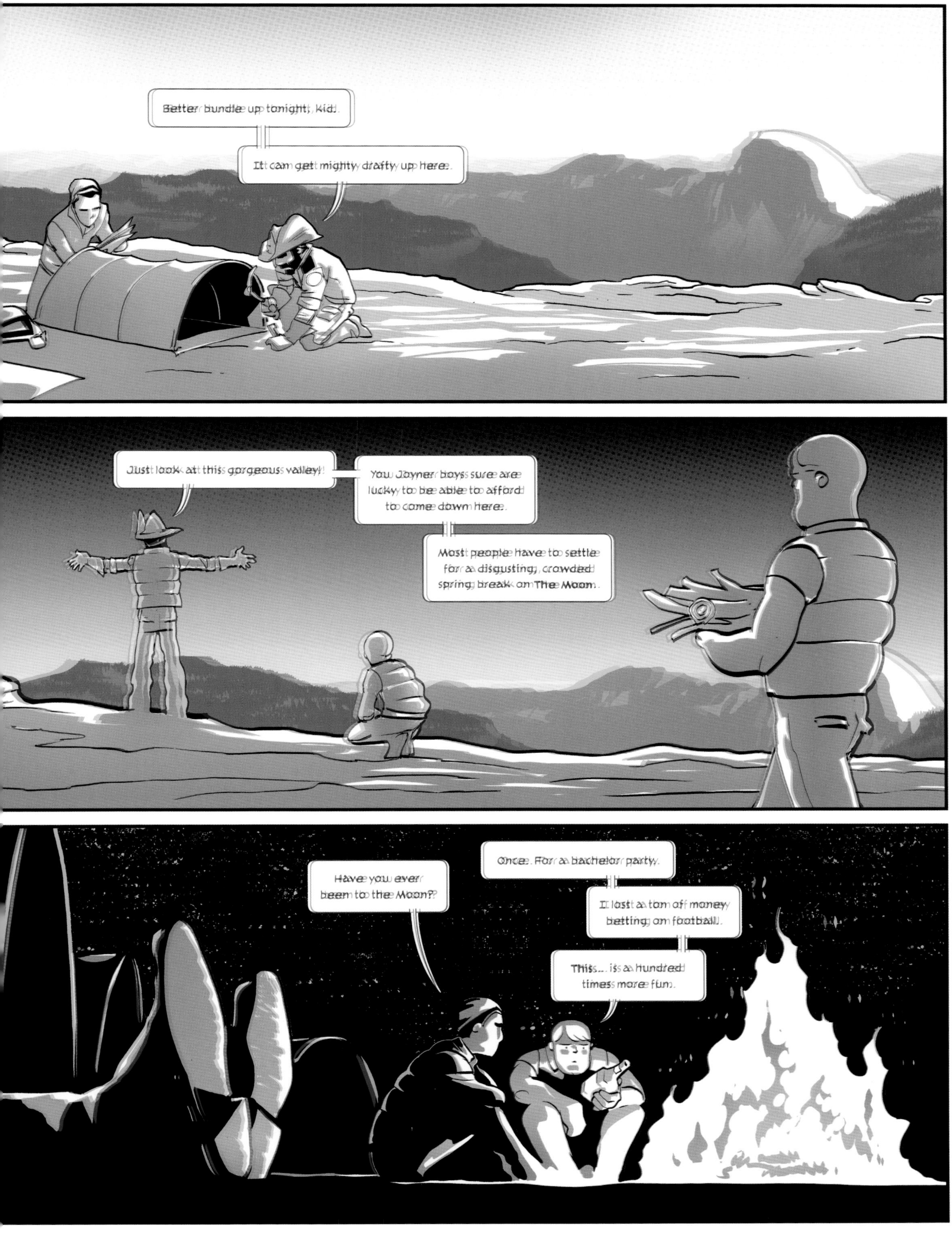

Better bundle up tonight, kid.
It can get mighty drafty up here.
Just look at this gorgeous valley!
You Joyner boys sure are lucky to be able to afford to come down here.
Most people have to settle for a disgusting, crowded spring break on The Moon.
Have you ever been to the Moon?
Once. For a bachelor party.
I lost a ton of money betting on football.
This... is a hundred times more fun.

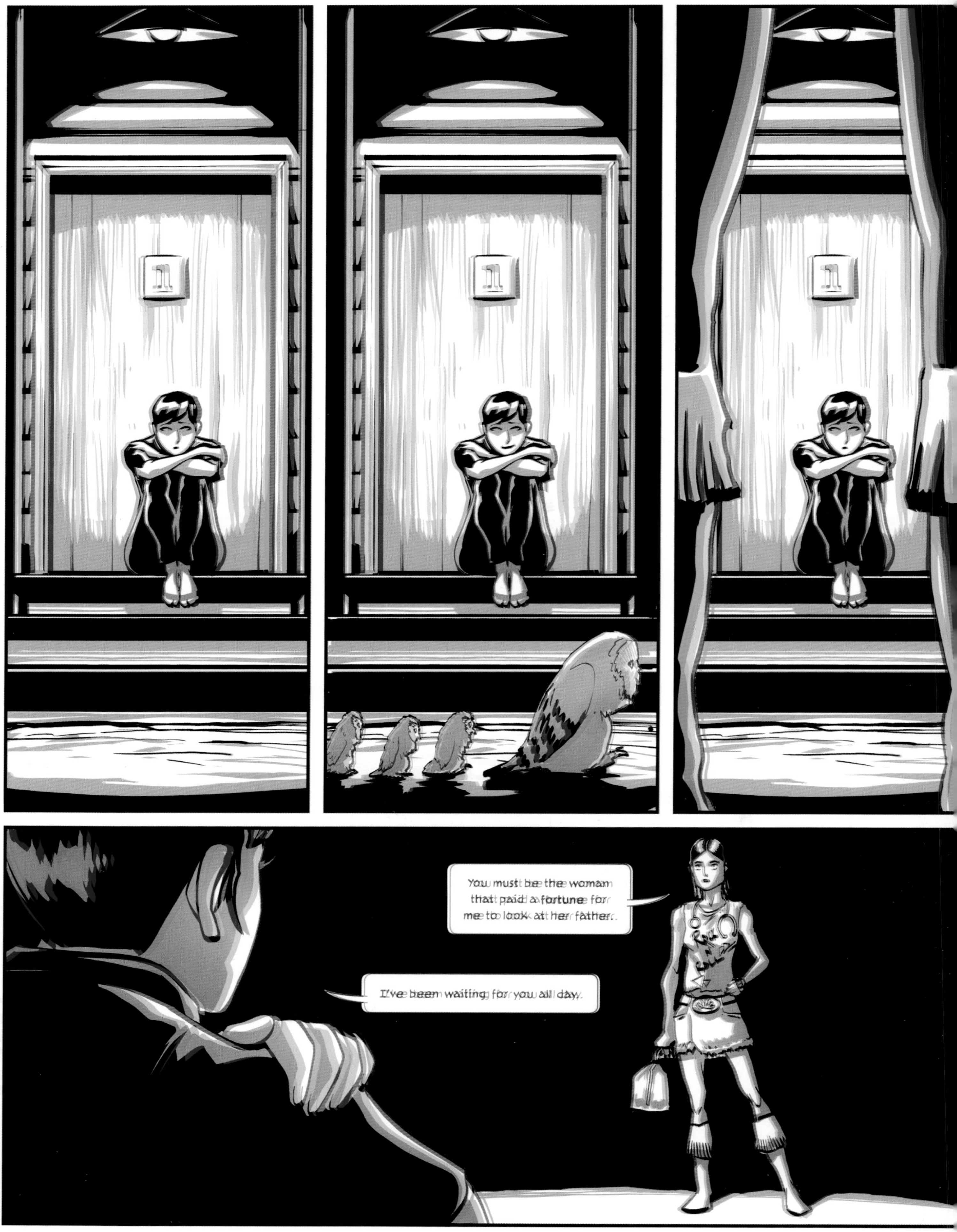
You must be the woman that paid a fortune for me to look at her father.
I've been waiting for you all day.

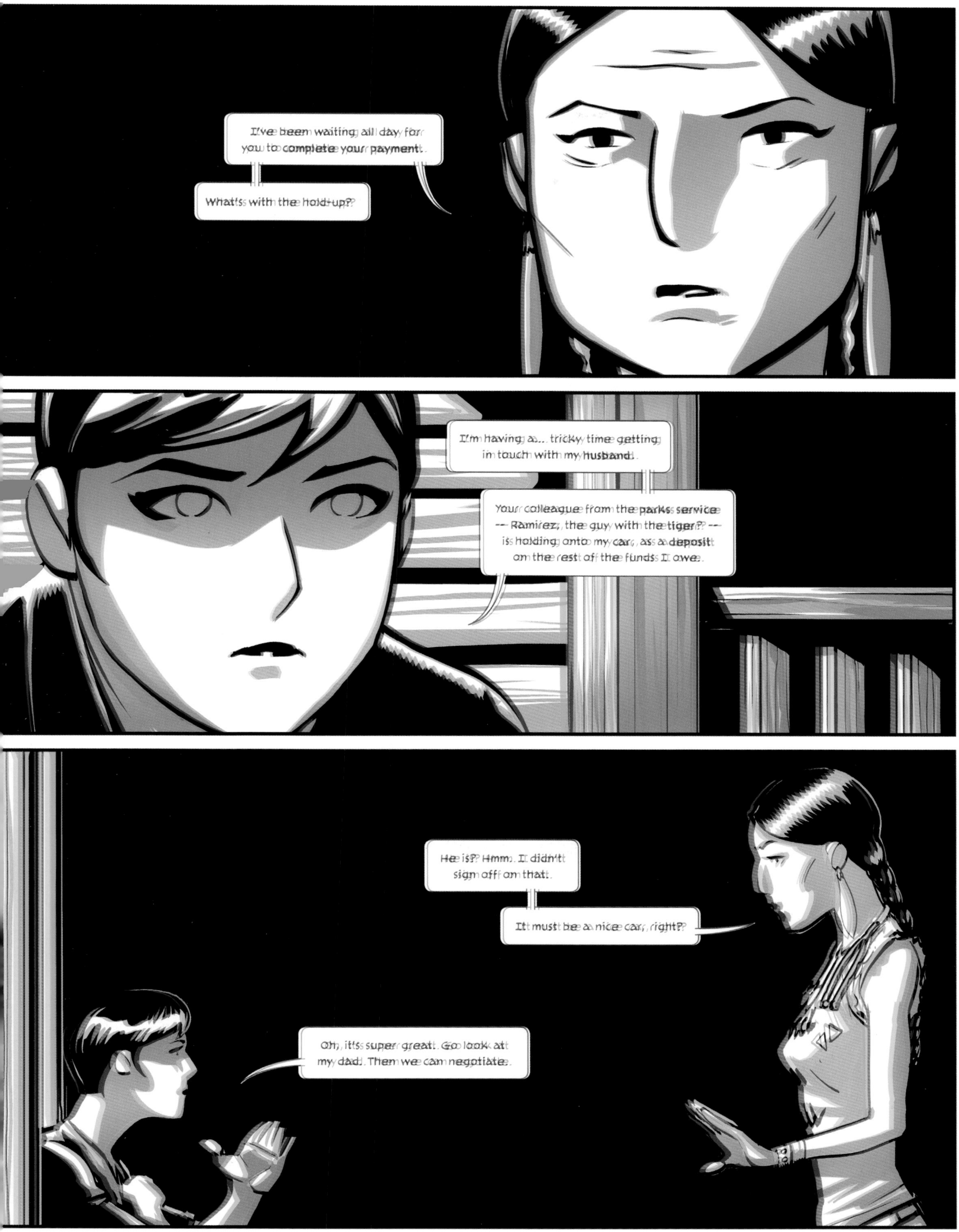
I've been waiting all day for you to complete your payment.
What's with the hold-up?
I'm having a... tricky time getting in touch with my husband.
Your colleague from the parks service -- Ramirez, the guy with the tiger? -- is holding onto my car, as a deposit on the rest of the funds I owe.
He is? Hmm. I didn't sign off on that.
It must be a nice car, right?
Oh, it's super great. Go look at my dad. Then we can negotiate.

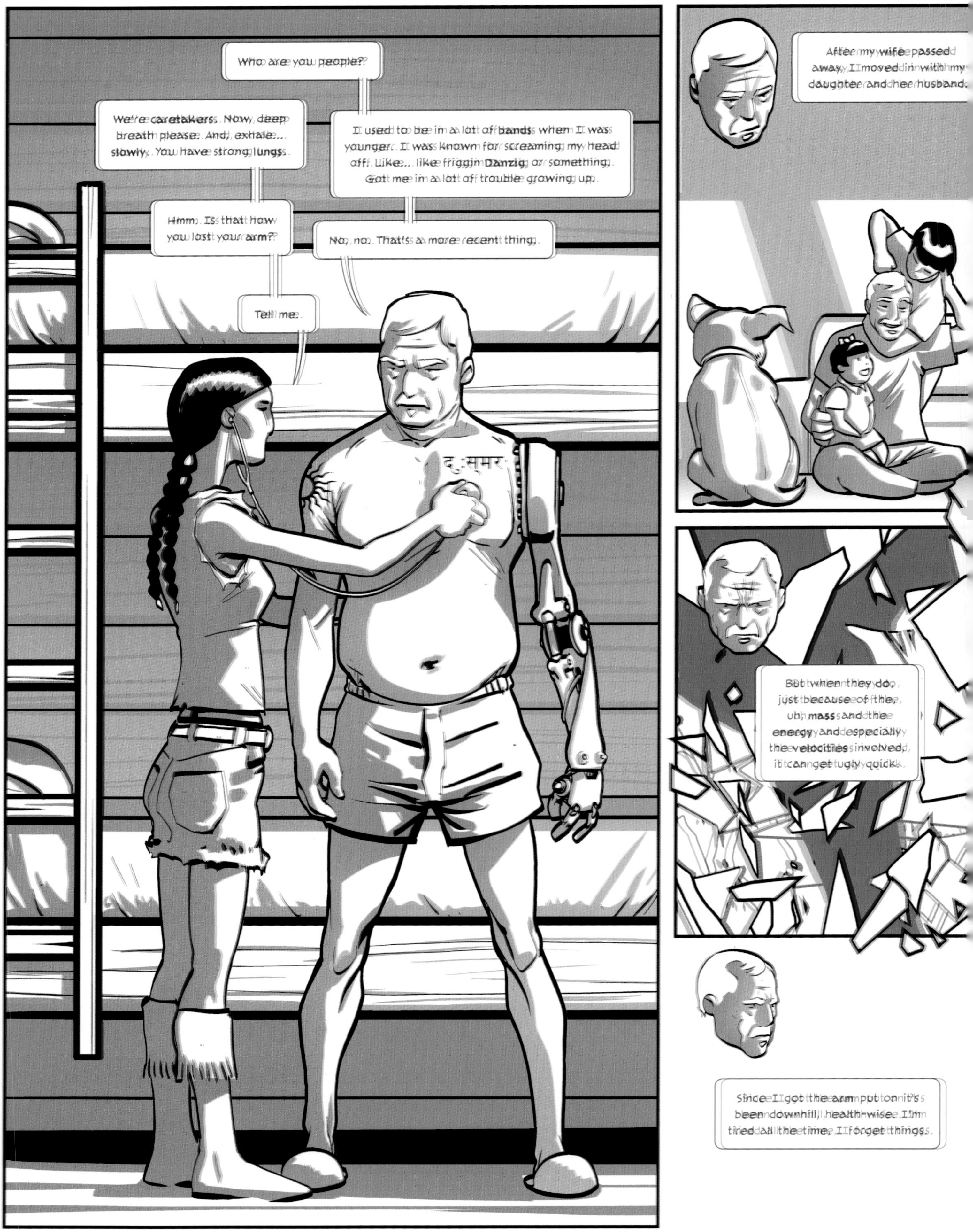
Who are you people?
We're caretakers. Now, deep breath please. And, exhale... slowly. You have strong lungs.
I used to be in a lot of bands when I was younger. I was known for screaming my head off. Like... like friggin Danzig or something. Got me in a lot of trouble growing up.
Hmm. Is that how you lost your arm?
No, no. That's a more recent thing.
Tell me.
After my wife passed away, I moved in with my daughter and her husband.
But when they do, just because of the, uh, mass and the energy and especially the velocities involved, it can get ugly quick.
Since I got the arm put on it's been downhill, health-wise. I'm tired all the time, I forget things.

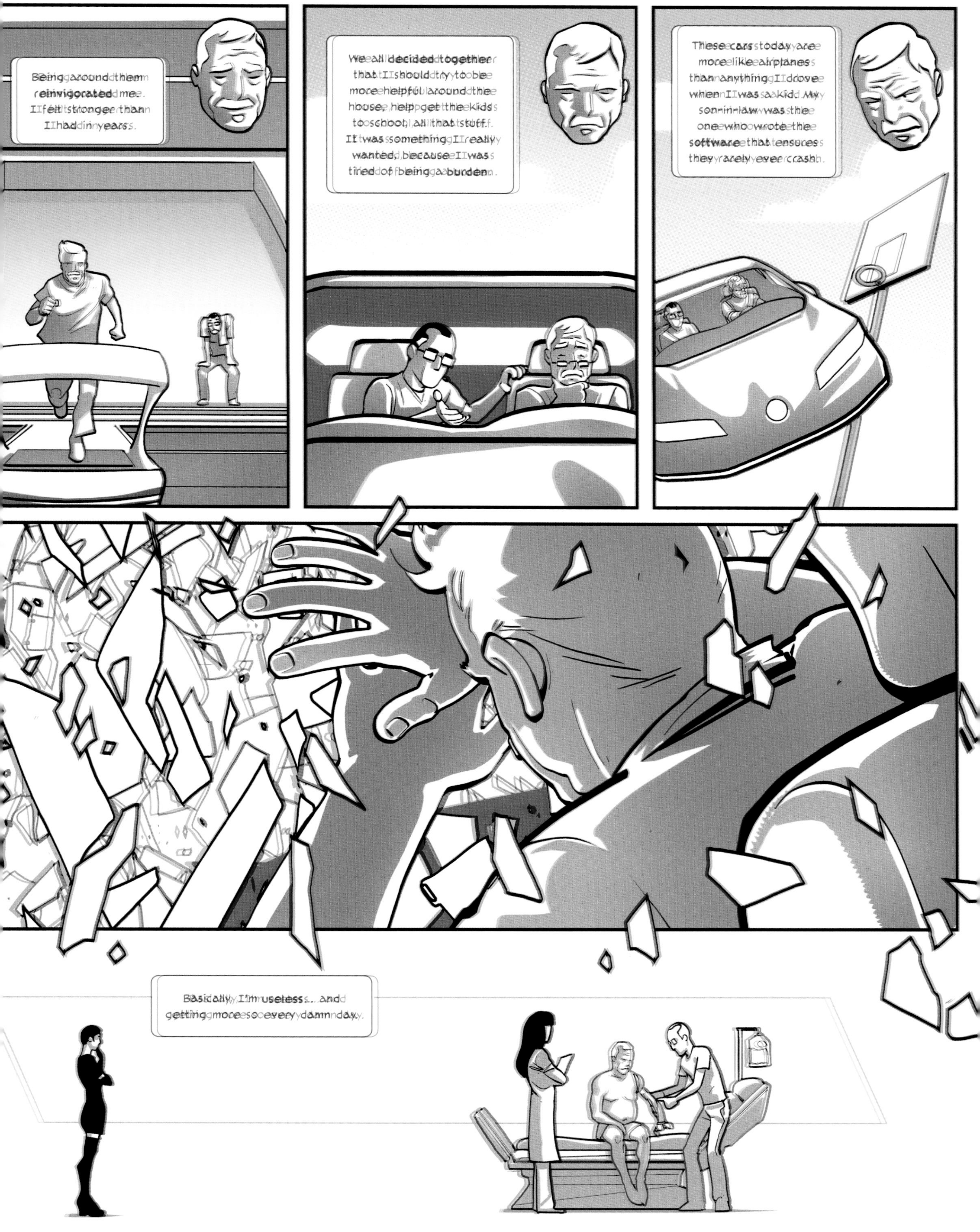
Being around them reinvigorated me. I felt stronger than I had in years.
We all decided together that I should try to be more helpful around the house, help get the kids to school, all that stuff. It was something I really wanted, because I was tired of being a burden.
These cars today are more like airplanes than anything I drove when I was a kid. My son-in-law was the one who wrote the software that ensures they rarely ever crash.
Basically, I'm useless... and getting more so every damn day.

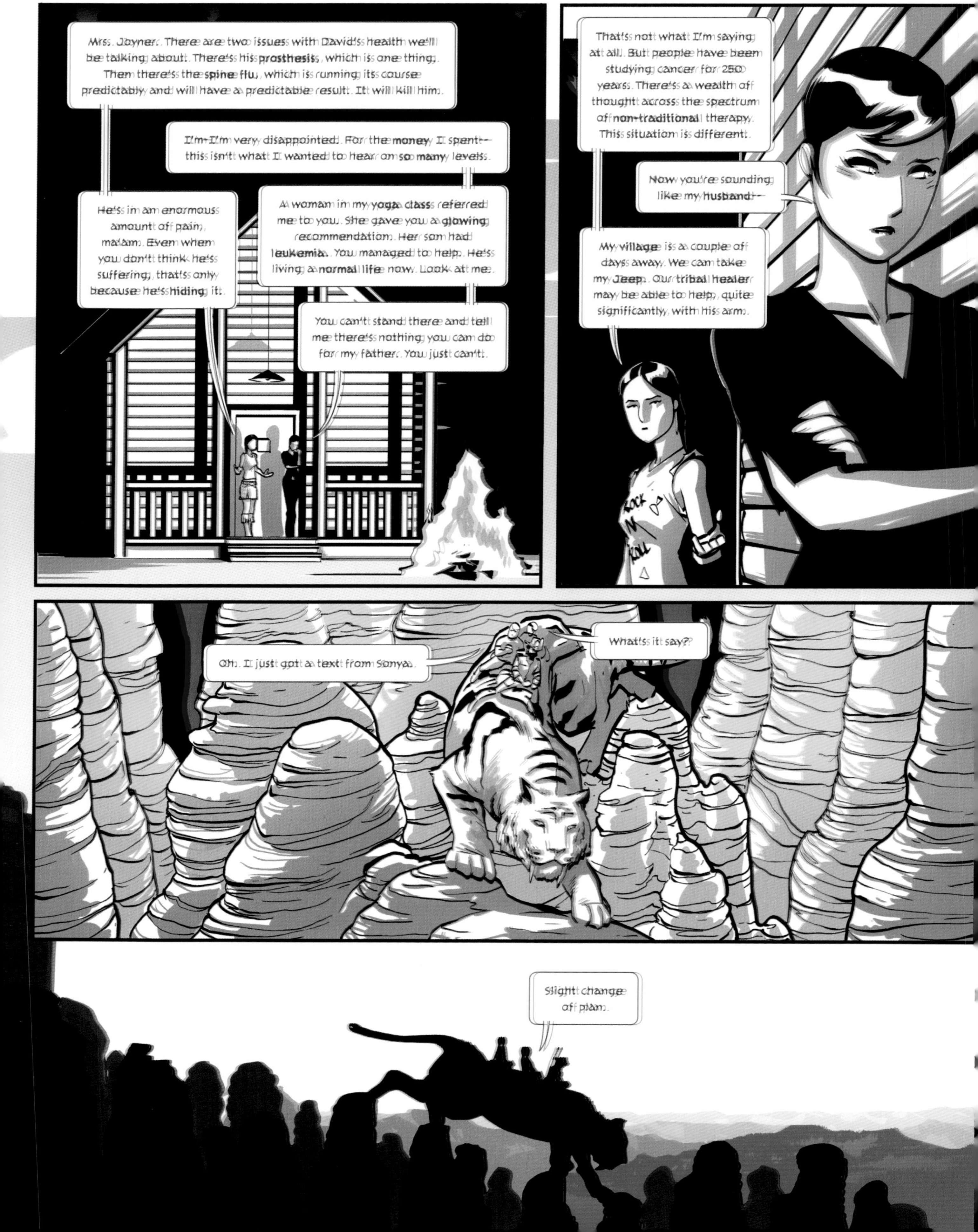
Mrs. Joyner. There are two issues with David's health we'll be talking about. There's his **prosthesis**, which is one thing. Then there's the **spine flu**, which is running its course predictably and will have a predictable result. It will kill him.
I'm--I'm very disappointed. For the **money** I spent--this isn't what I wanted to hear on **so many** levels.
He's in an enormous amount of pain, ma'am. Even when you don't think he's suffering, that's only because he's **hiding** it.
A woman in my **yoga class** referred me to you. She gave you a **glowing** recommendation. Her son had **leukemia**. You managed to help. He's living a **normal life** now. Look at me.
You can't stand there and tell me there's nothing you can do for my father. You just can't.
That's not what I'm saying at all. But people have been studying cancer for 250 years. There's a wealth of thought across the spectrum of **non-traditional** therapy. This situation is different.
Now you're sounding like my **husband**--
My **village** is a couple of days away. We can take my **Jeep**. Our **tribal healer** may be able to help, quite significantly, with his arm.
Oh. I just got a text from Sonya.
What's it say?
Slight change of plan.

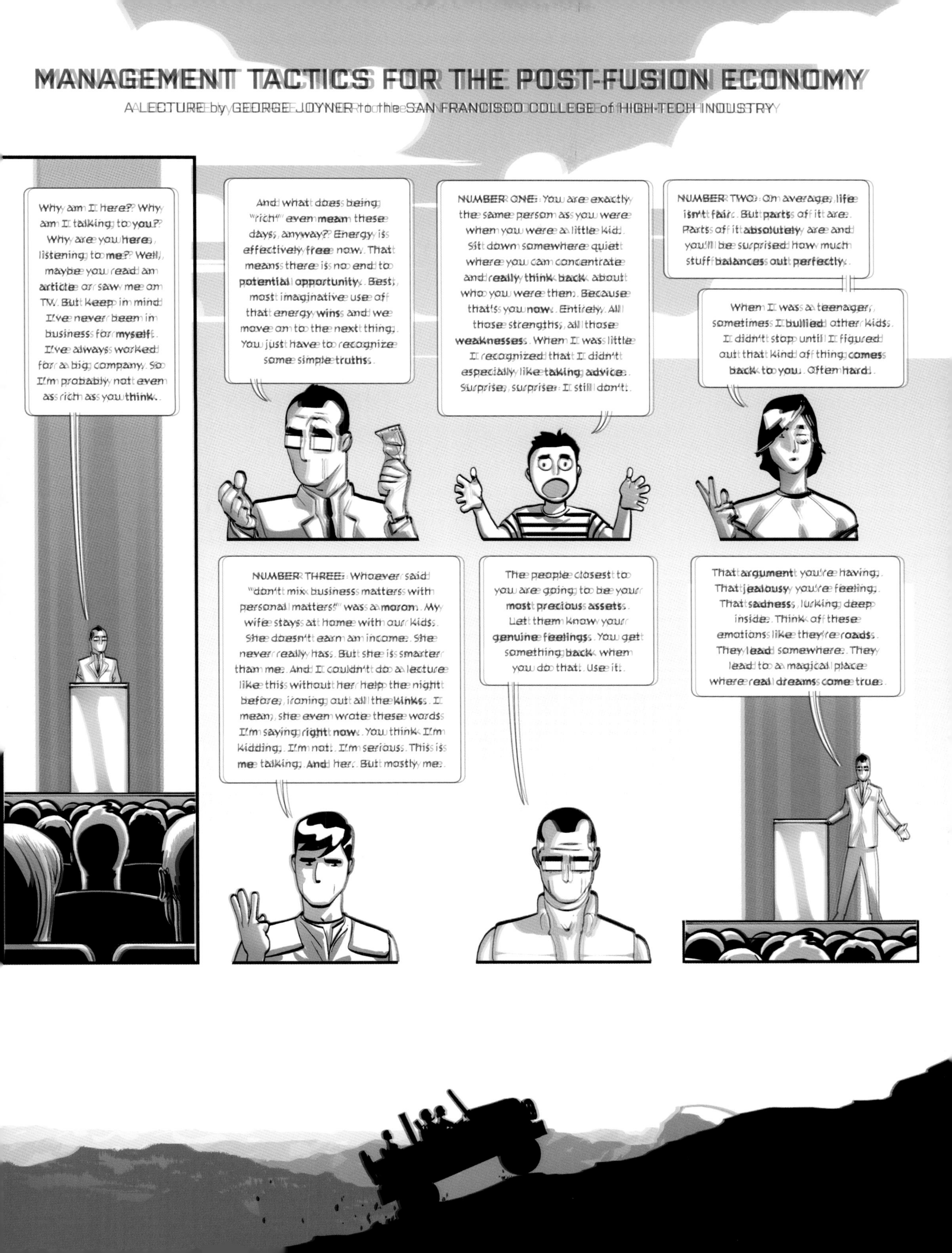
MANAGEMENT TACTICS FOR THE POST-FUSION ECONOMY
A LECTURE by GEORGE JOYNER to the SAN FRANCISCO COLLEGE of HIGH-TECH INDUSTRY
Why am I here? Why am I talking to you? Why are you here, listening to me? Well, maybe you read an article or saw me on TV. But keep in mind I've never been in business for myself. I've always worked for a big company. So I'm probably not even as rich as you think.
And what does being "rich" even mean these days, anyway? Energy is effectively free now. That means there is no end to potential opportunity. Best, most imaginative use of that energy wins and we move on to the next thing. You just have to recognize some simple truths.
NUMBER ONE: You are exactly the same person as you were when you were a little kid. Sit down somewhere quiet where you can concentrate and really think back about who you were then. Because that's you now. Entirely. All those strengths, all those weaknesses. When I was little I recognized that I didn't especially like taking advice. Surprise, surprise: I still don't.
NUMBER TWO: On average, life isn't fair. But parts of it are. Parts of it absolutely are and you'll be surprised how much stuff balances out perfectly.
When I was a teenager, sometimes I bullied other kids. I didn't stop until I figured out that kind of thing comes back to you. Often hard.
NUMBER THREE: Whoever said "don't mix business matters with personal matters" was a moron. My wife stays at home with our kids. She doesn't earn an income. She never really has. But she is smarter than me. And I couldn't do a lecture like this without her help the night before, ironing out all the kinks. I mean, she even wrote these words I'm saying right now. You think I'm kidding. I'm not. I'm serious. This is me talking. And her. But mostly me.
The people closest to you are going to be your most precious assets. Let them know your genuine feelings. You get something back when you do that. Use it.
That argument you're having. That jealousy you're feeling. That sadness, lurking deep inside. Think of these emotions like they're roads. They lead somewhere. They lead to a magical place where real dreams come true.

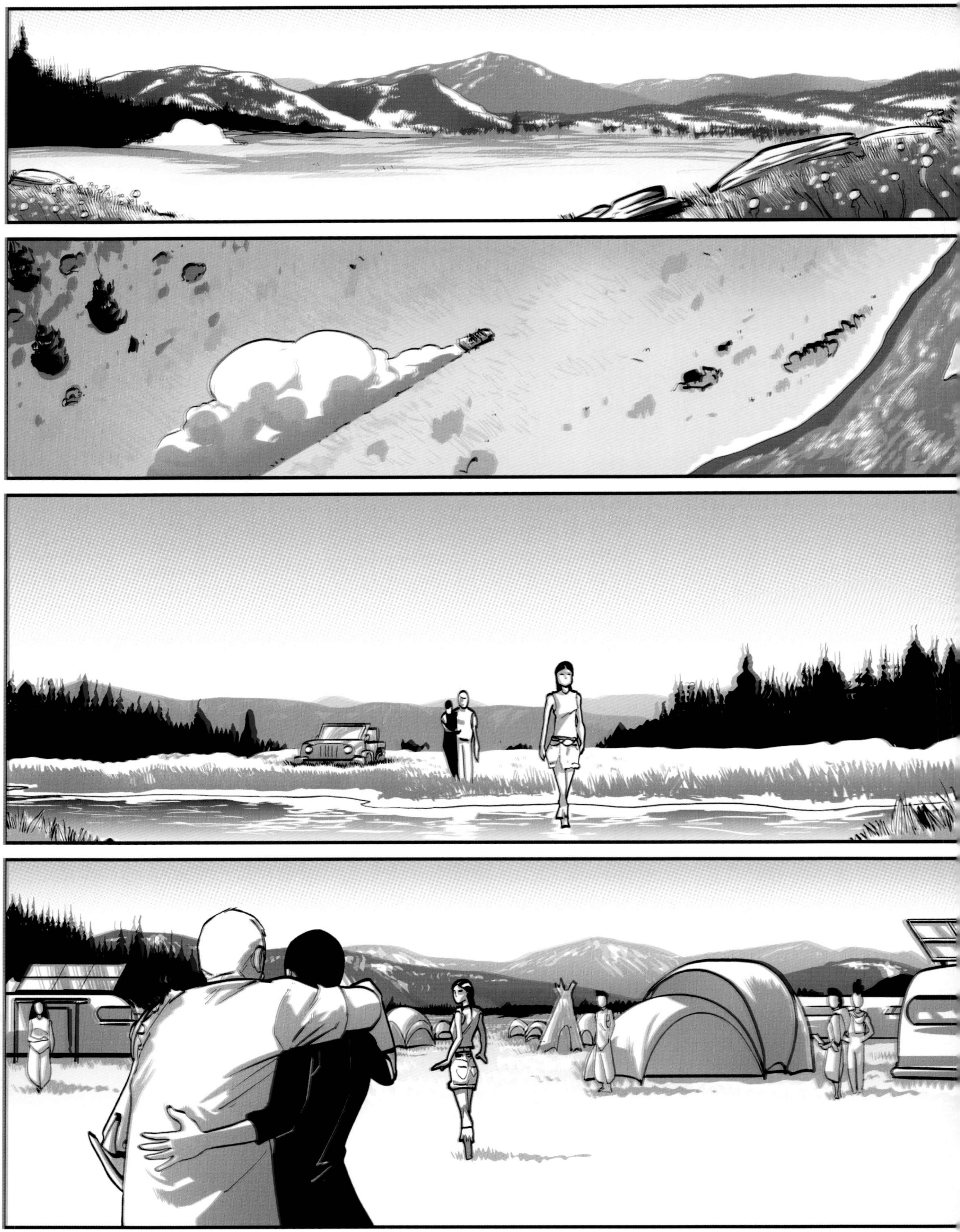

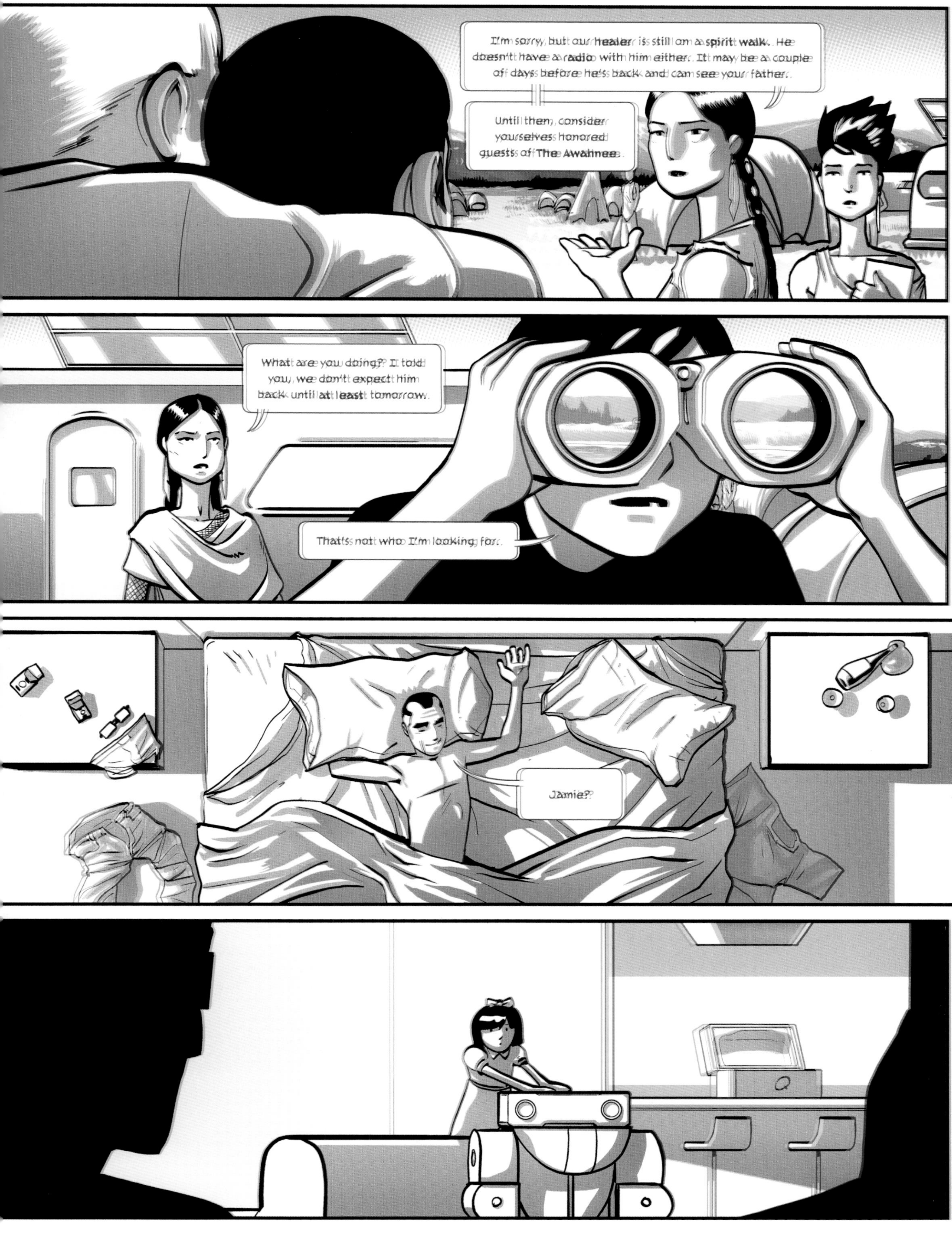
I'm sorry, but our healer is still on a spirit walk. He doesn't have a radio with him either. It may be a couple of days before he's back and can see your father.
Until then, consider yourselves honored guests of The Awahnee.
What are you doing? I told you, we don't expect him back until at least tomorrow.
That's not who I'm looking for.
Jamie?

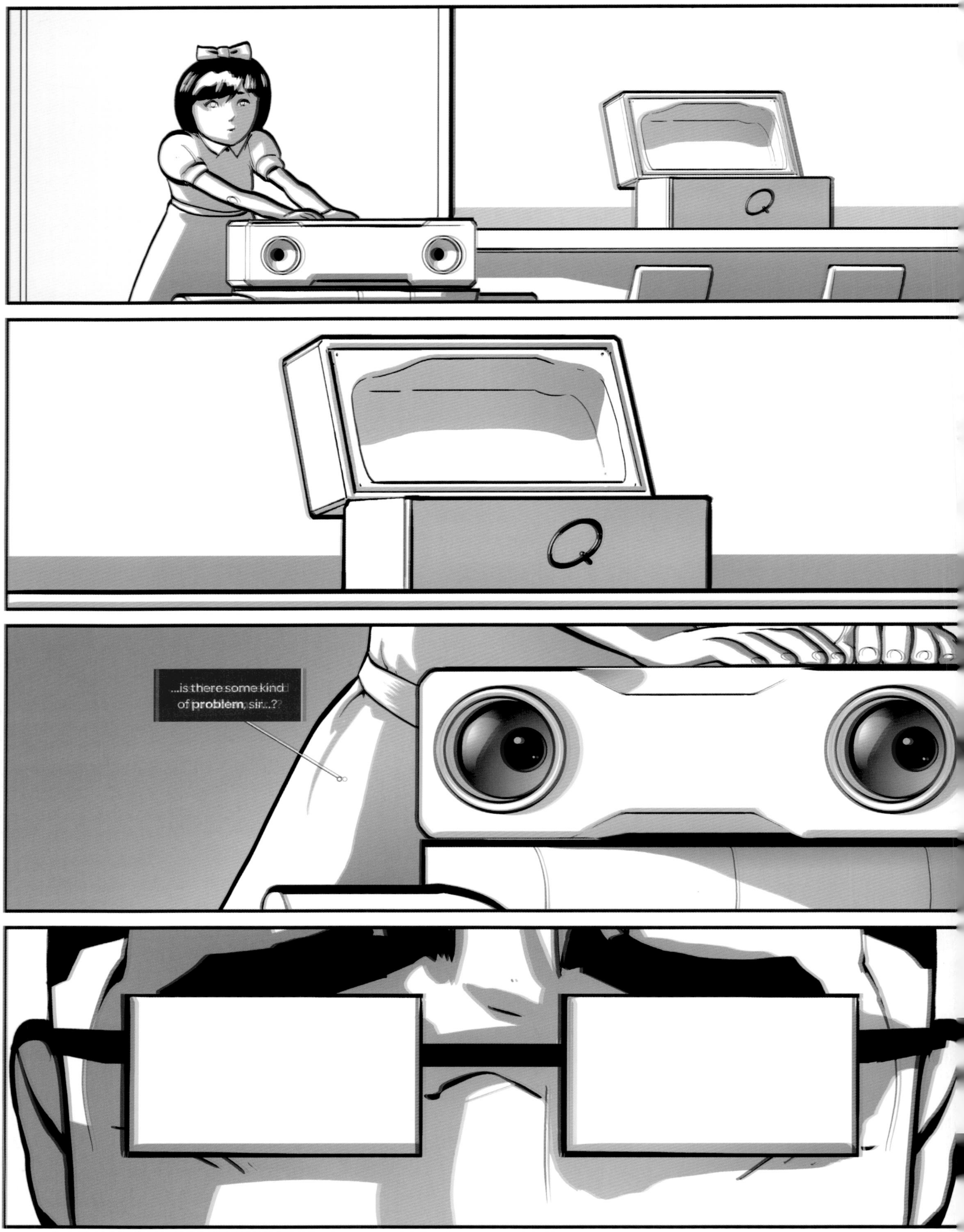
...is there some kind of problem, sir...?

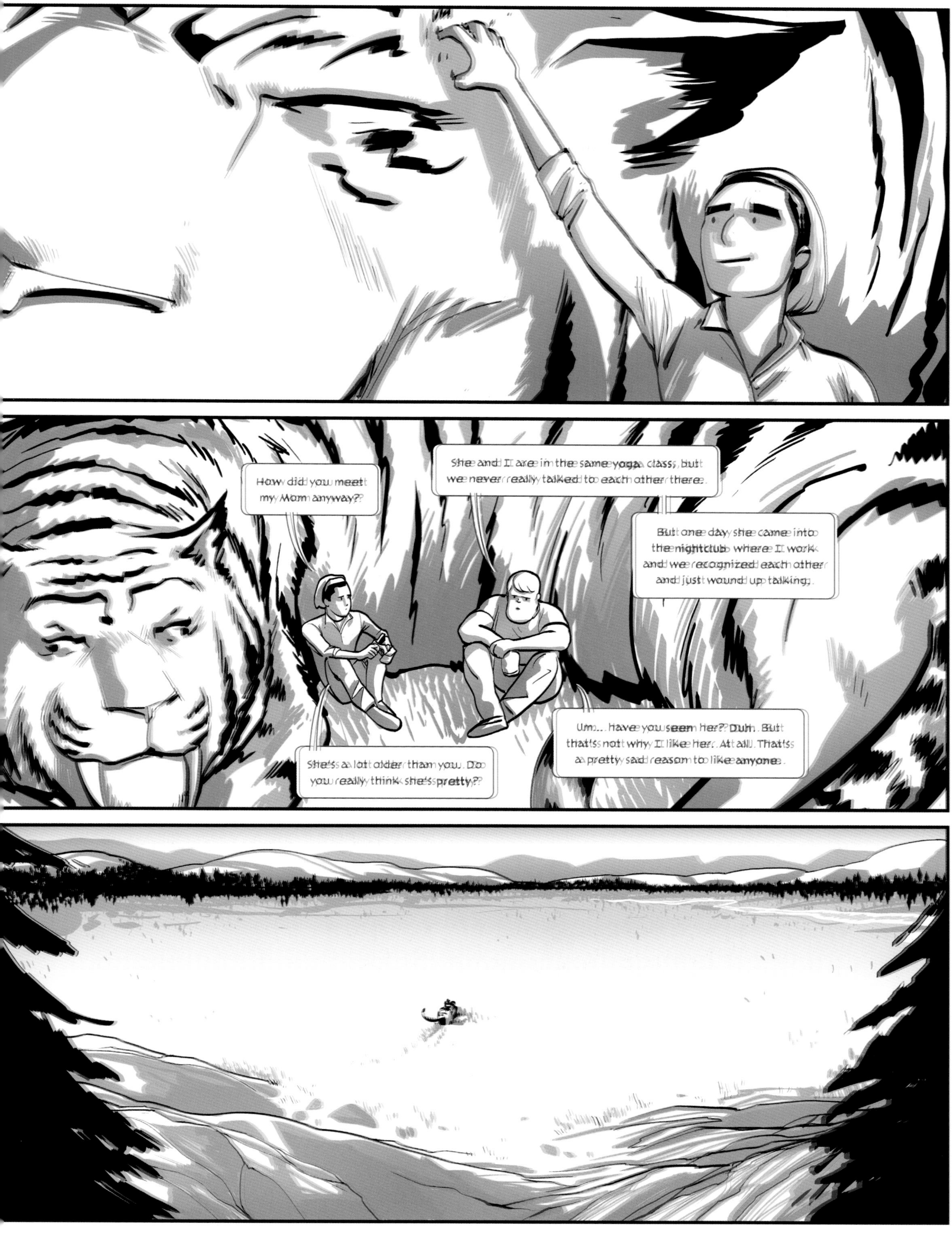
How did you meet my Mom anyway?
She and I are in the same yoga class, but we never really talked to each other there.
But one day she came into the nightclub where I work and we recognized each other and just wound up talking.
She's a lot older than you. Do you really think she's pretty?
Um... have you seen her? Duh. But that's not why I like her. At all. That's a pretty sad reason to like anyone.

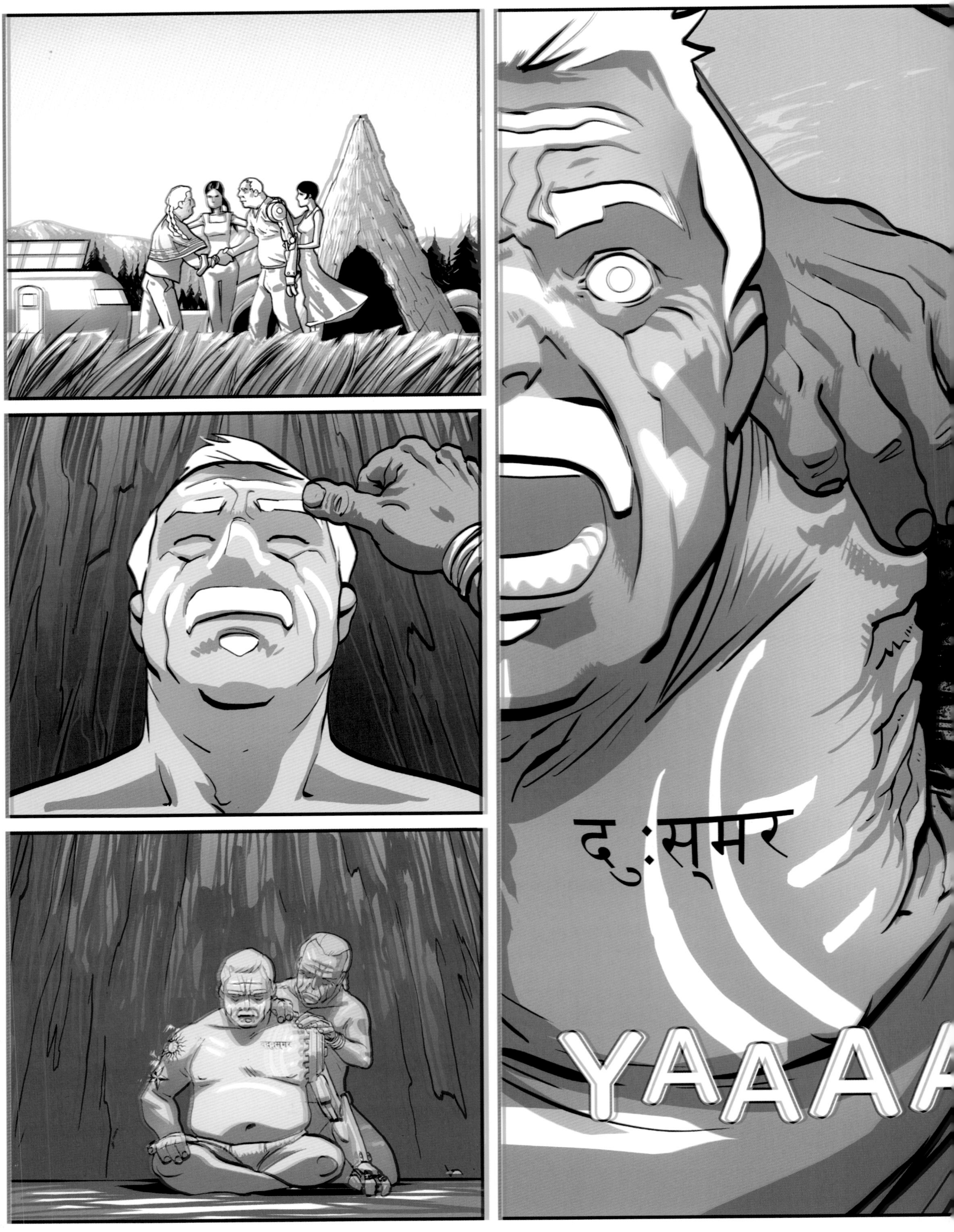

दुःस्मर
YAAAA

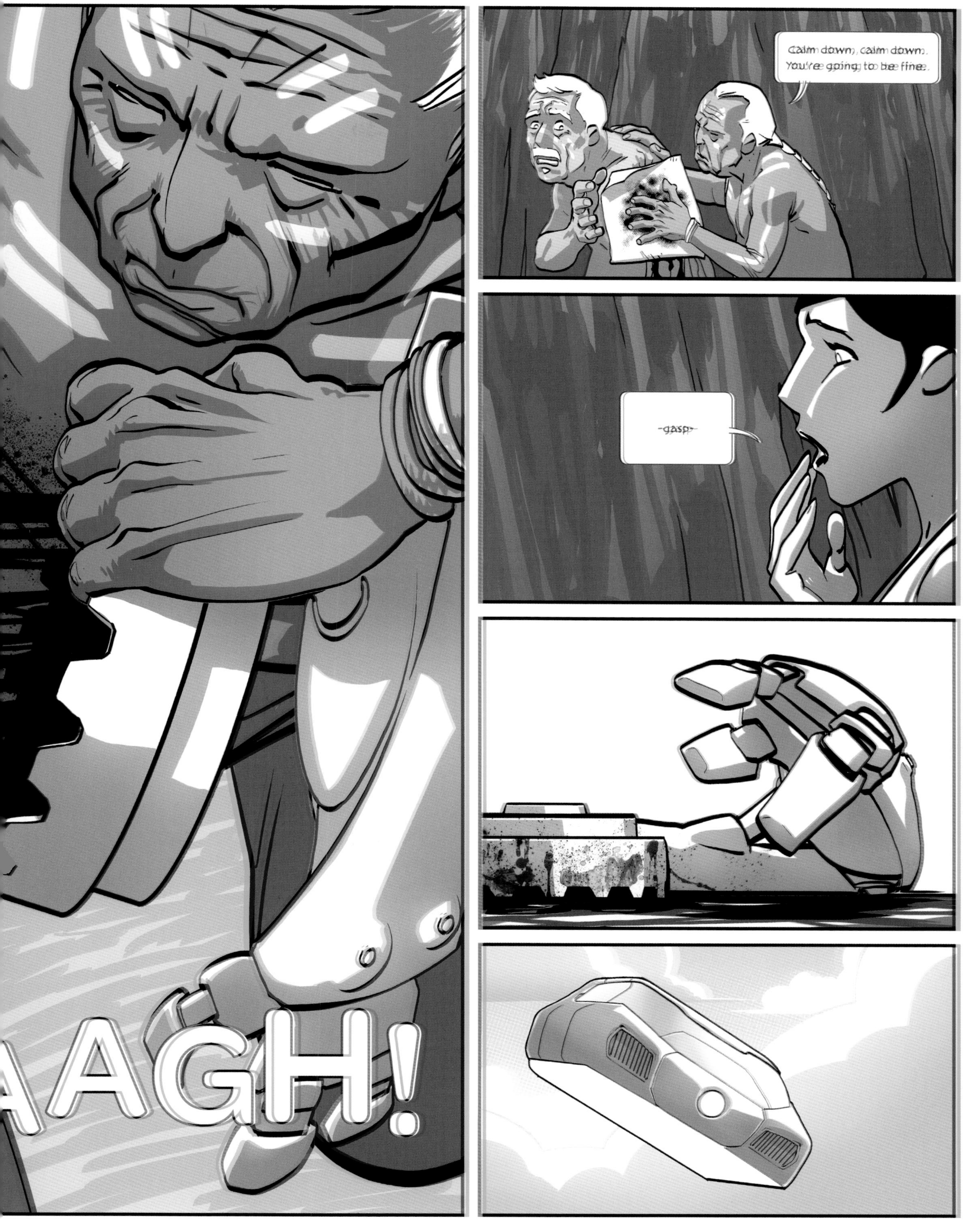
AAGH!
Calm down, calm down.
You're going to be fine.
gasp

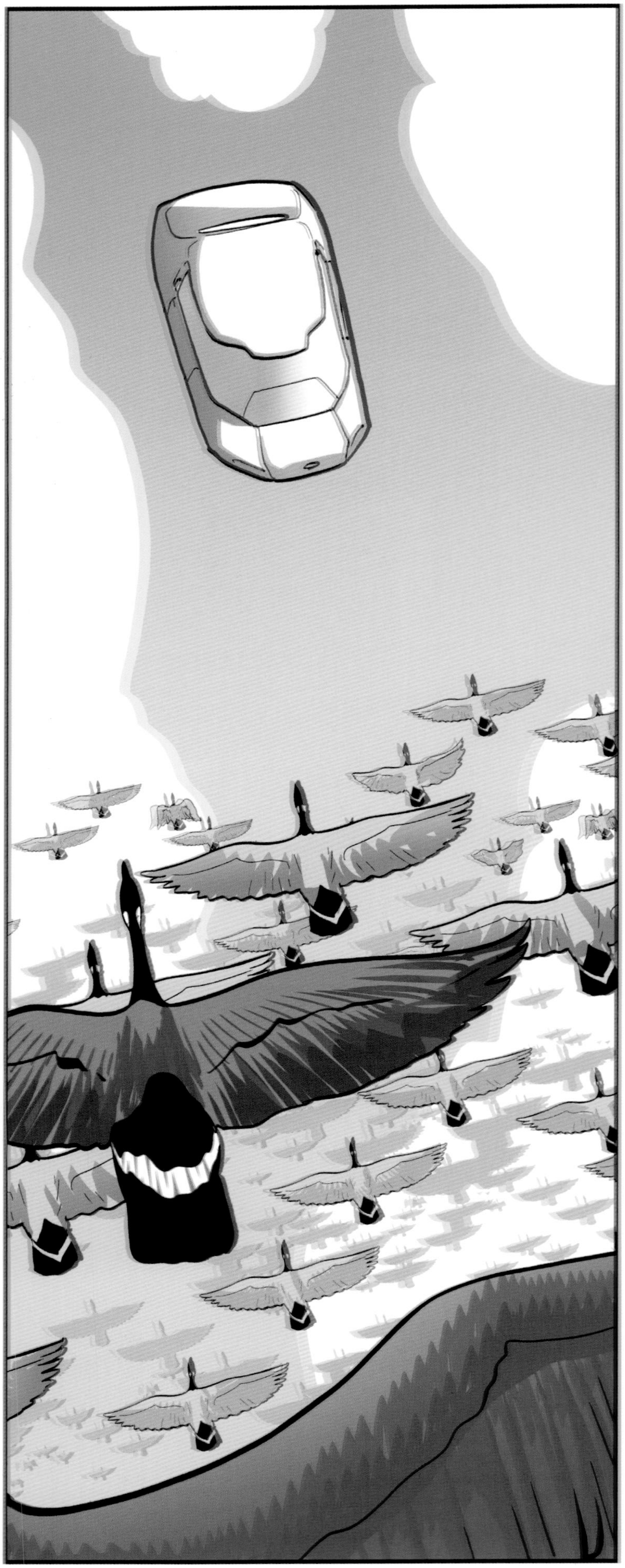

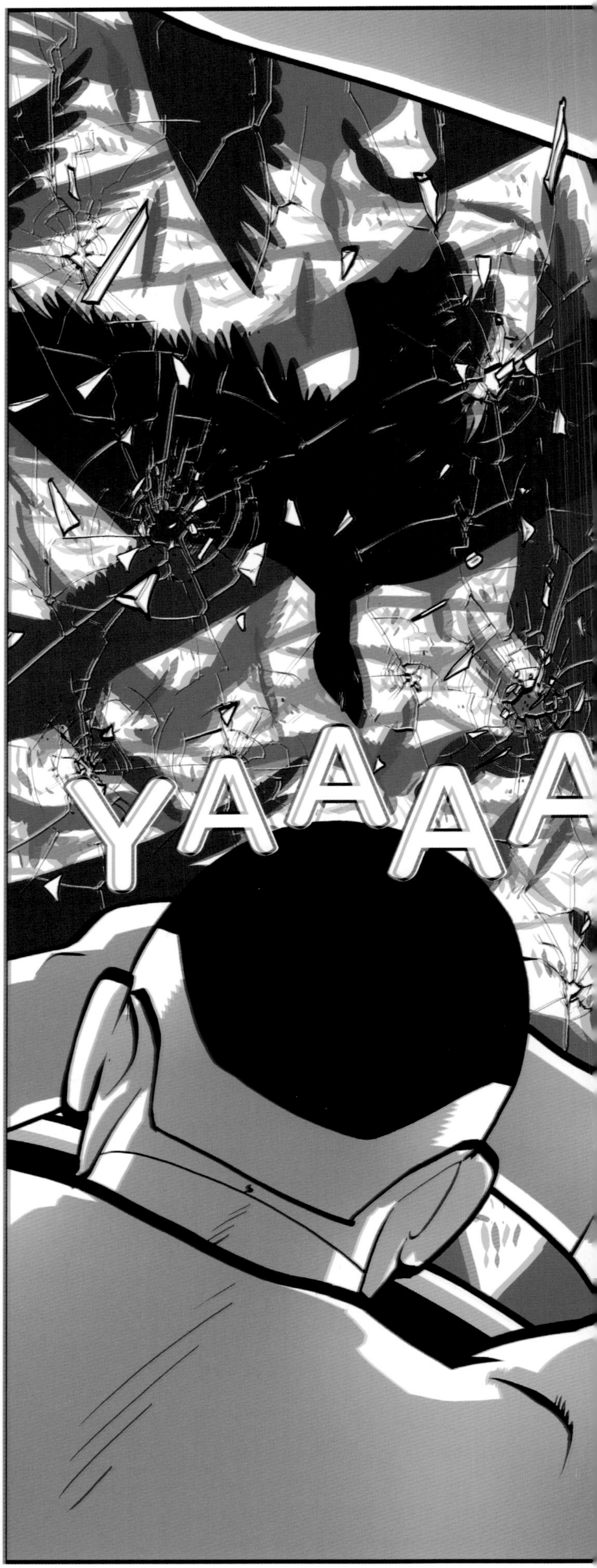
YAAAA

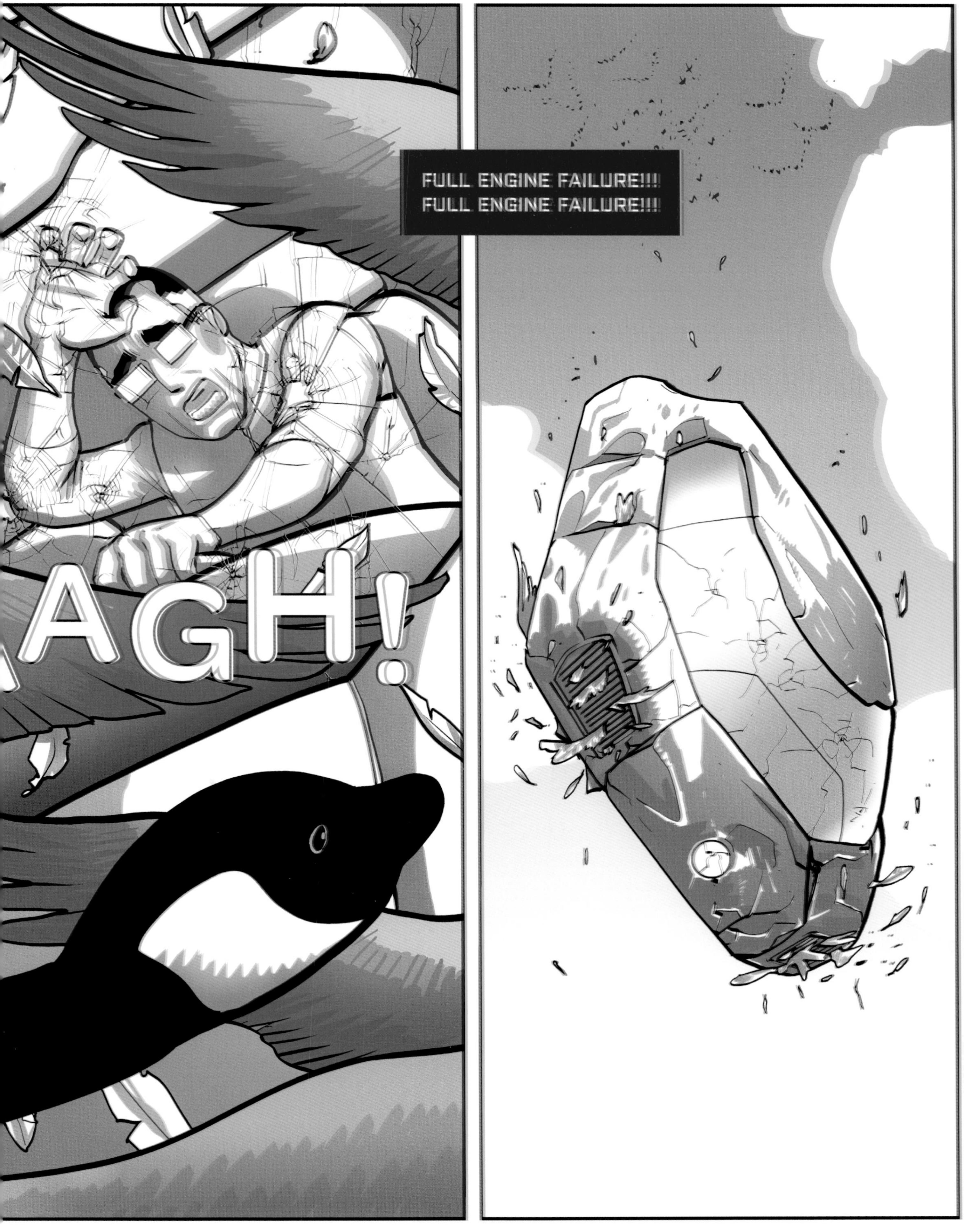
FULL ENGINE FAILURE!!!
FULL ENGINE FAILURE!!!
AGH!

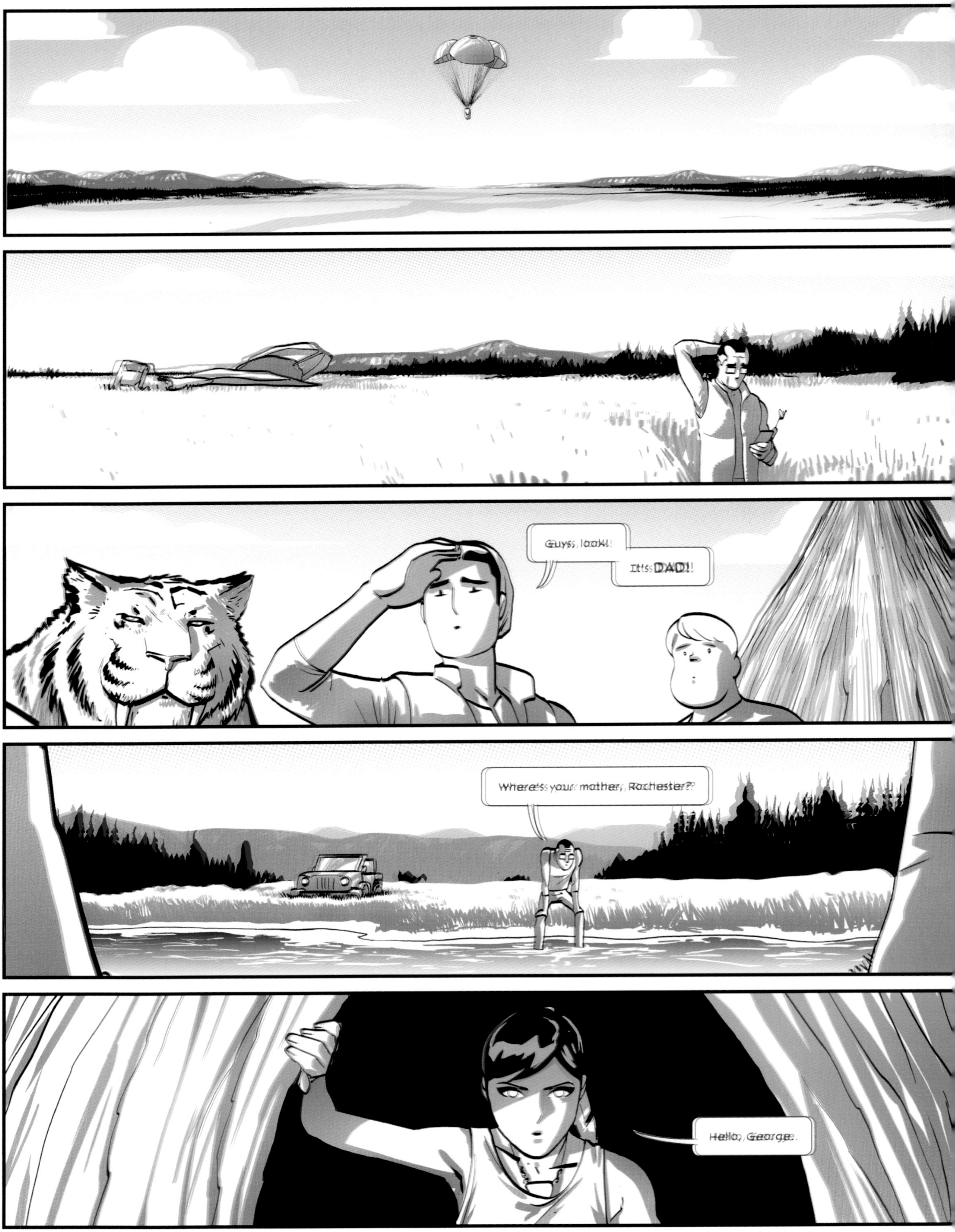
Guys, look!
It's DAD!
Where's your mother, Rochester?
Hello, George.

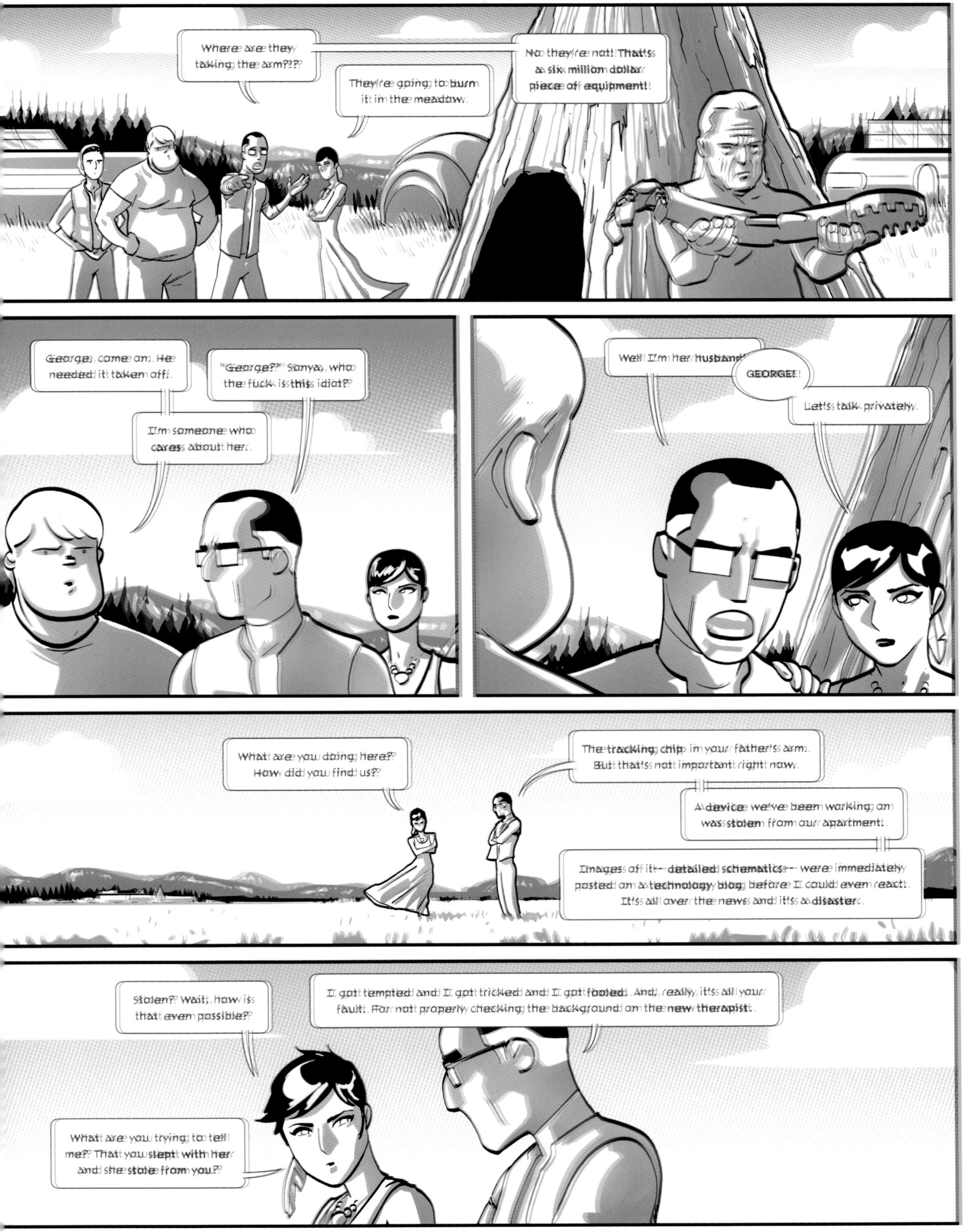
Where are they taking the arm?!?
They're going to burn it in the meadow.
No they're not! That's a six million dollar piece of equipment!
George, come on. He needed it taken off.
"George?" Sonya, who the fuck is this idiot?
I'm someone who cares about her.
Well I'm her husband!
GEORGE!
Let's talk privately.
What are you doing here? How did you find us?
The tracking chip in your father's arm. But that's not important right now.
A device we've been working on was stolen from our apartment.
Images of it—detailed schematics—were immediately posted on a technology blog before I could even react. It's all over the news and it's a disaster.
Stolen? Wait, how is that even possible?
I got tempted and I got tricked and I got fooled. And, really, it's all your fault. For not properly checking the background on the new therapist.
What are you trying to tell me? That you slept with her and she stole from you?

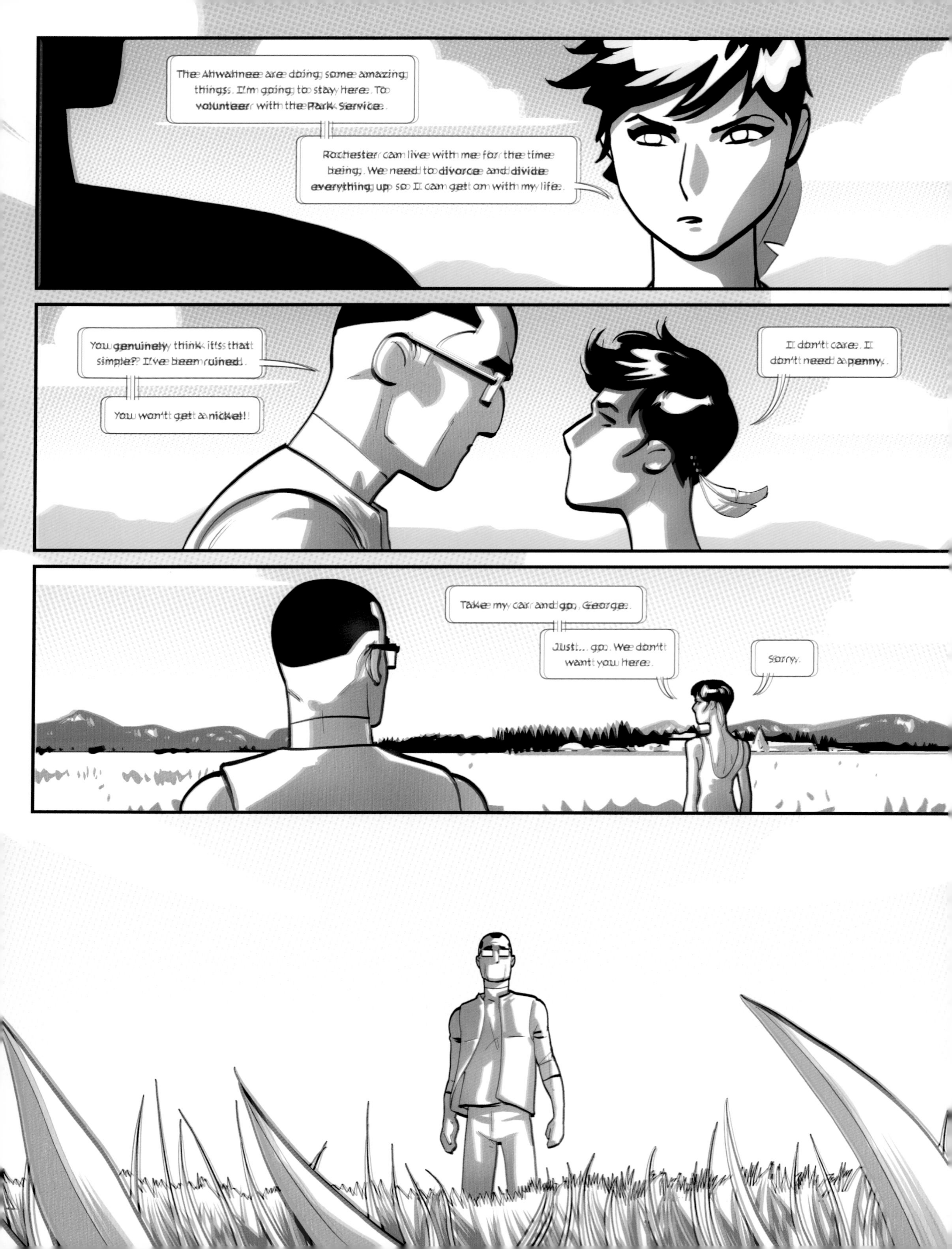
The Ahwahnee are doing some amazing things. I'm going to stay here. To volunteer with the Park Service.
Rochester can live with me for the time being. We need to divorce and divide everything up so I can get on with my life.
You genuinely think it's that simple? I've been ruined.
You won't get a nickel!
I don't care. I don't need a penny.
Take my car and go, George.
Just... go. We don't want you here.
Sorry.

CHAPTER FOUR

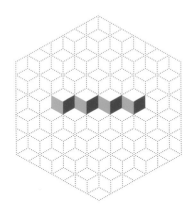

LE VOYAGE DANS LA LUNE

CHAPTER FOUR
LE VOYAGE DANS LA LUNE

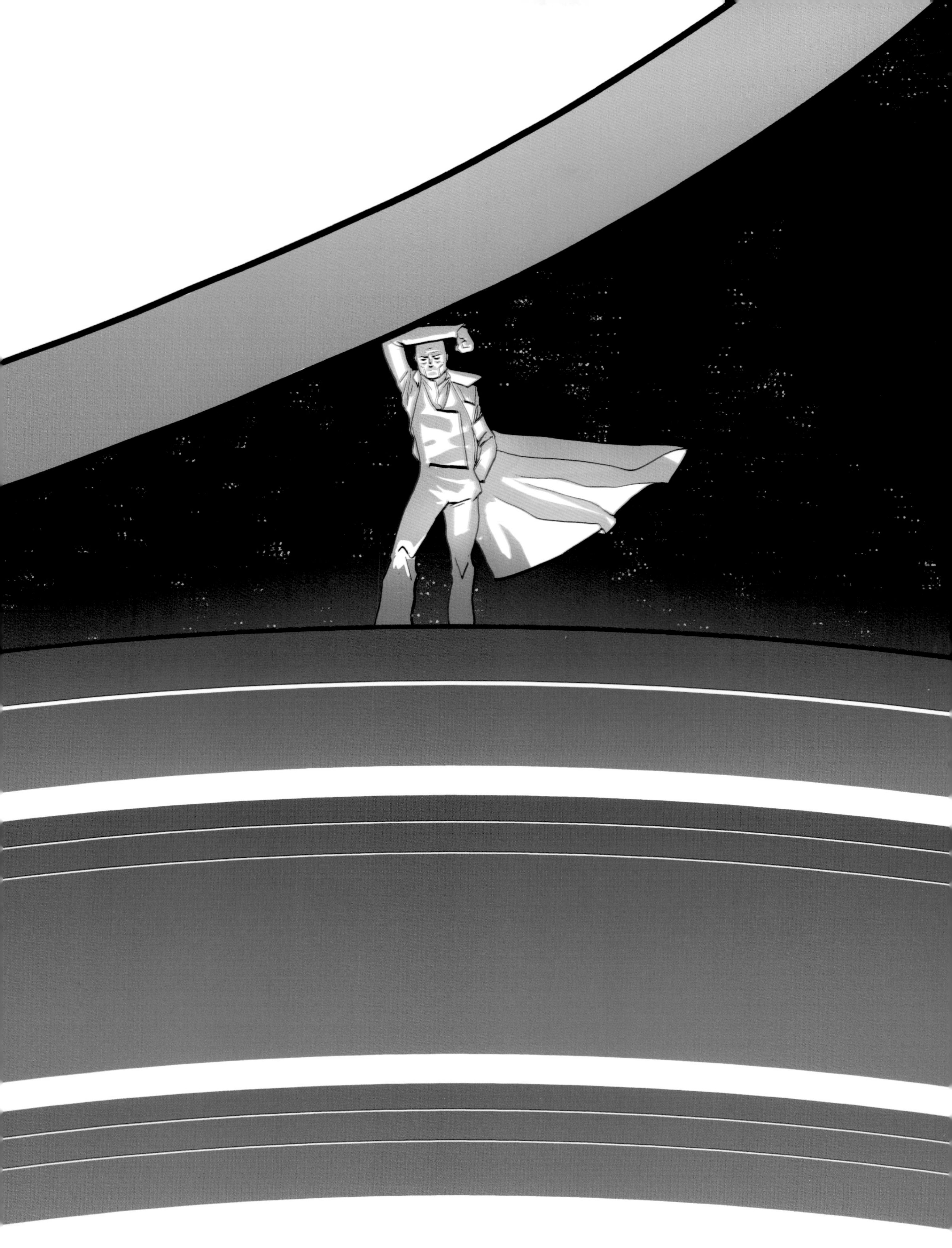

You asked to see me, sir?

Tomorrow at 5 a.m. Pacific, 8 a.m. Eastern, a press release goes out announcing that George Joyner has resigned his post as Chief Products Officer and has vacated his seat on the Board of Directors.

You will be named as his successor.

He didn't want to go. He begged to stay. But his contract had a morals clause and we're supposed to be a family company.

Jeremy Quattrone.

Erica Baxter.

It's exhilarating to finally put a face to the name.

Likewise. And for the record, I accept.

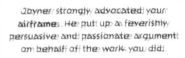

Joyner strongly advocated your airframe. He put up a feverishly persuasive and passionate argument on behalf of the work you did.

I need to know if that argument was strictly merit-based. You're single, correct? Tell me right now if you are-slash-were sleeping with him. Ever.

Did someone say that to you?

Beginning tonight, I --- have resolved to change my entire management style.

I want to get my hands dirty. Get down there in the bullpen with the product engineers. Like how I did it when I started out.

No, never. Not if my life depended on it.

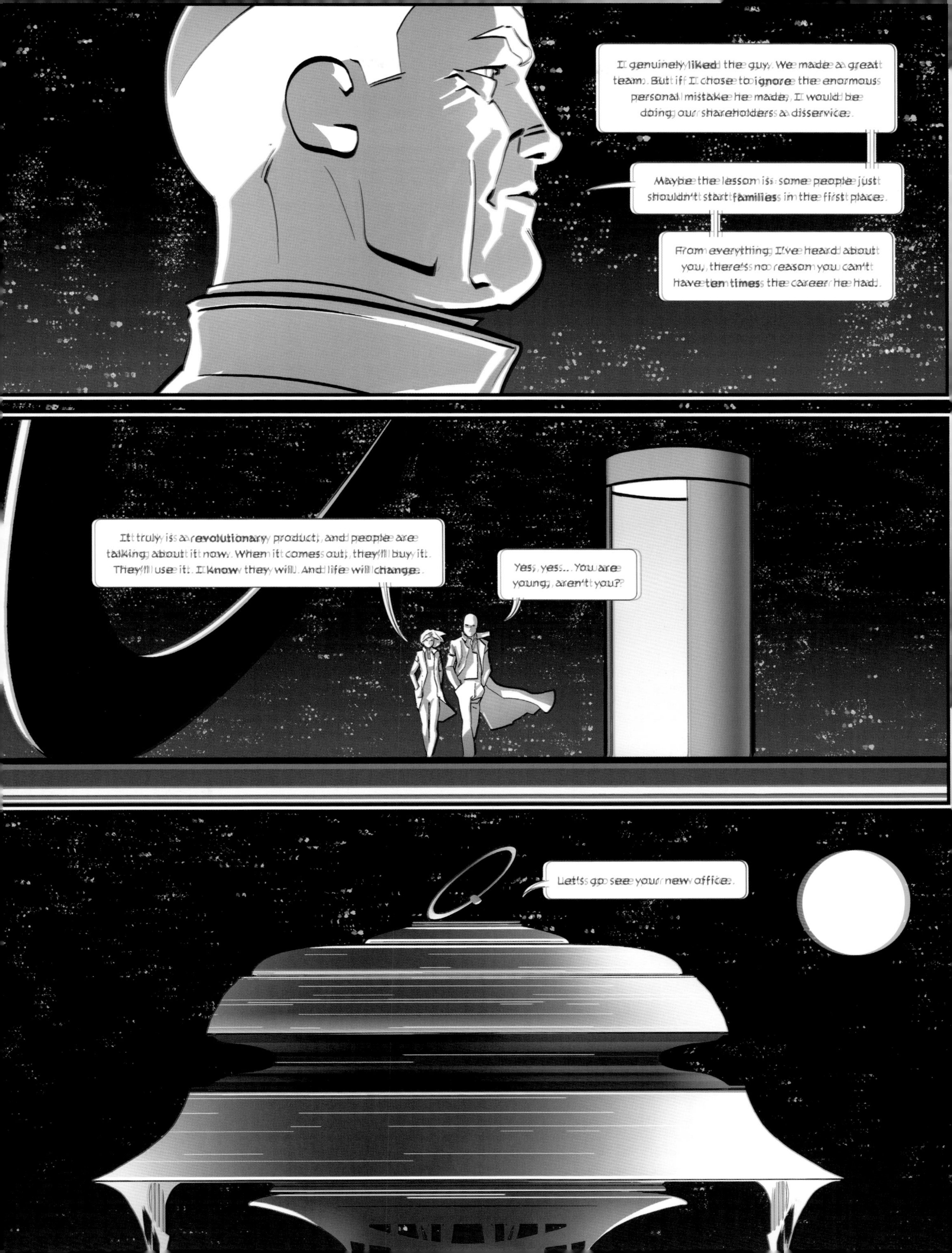
I genuinely liked the guy. We made a great team. But if I chose to ignore the enormous personal mistake he made, I would be doing our shareholders a disservice.
Maybe the lesson is some people just shouldn't start families in the first place.
From everything I've heard about you, there's no reason you can't have ten times the career he had.
It truly is a revolutionary product, and people are talking about it now. When it comes out, they'll buy it. They'll use it. I know they will. And life will change.
Yes, yes... You are young, aren't you?
Let's go see your new office.

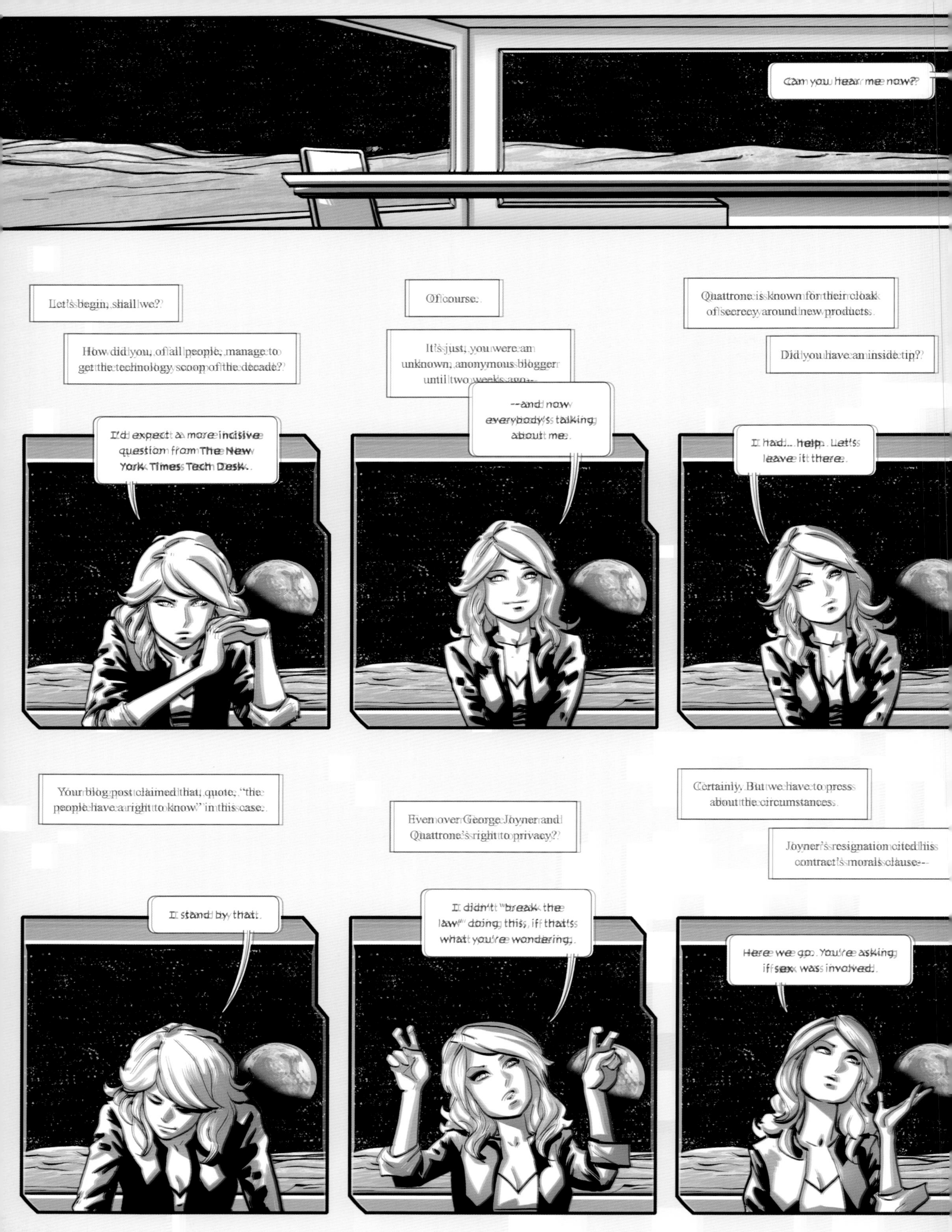

Can you hear me now?
Let's begin, shall we?
How did you, of all people, manage to get the technology scoop of the decade?
I'd expect a more incisive question from The New York Times Tech Desk.
Of course.
It's just, you were an unknown, anonymous blogger until two weeks ago--
--and now everybody's talking about me.
Quattrone is known for their cloak of secrecy around new products.
Did you have an inside tip?
I had... help. Let's leave it there.
Your blog post claimed that, quote, "the people have a right to know" in this case.
I stand by that.
Even over George Joyner and Quattrone's right to privacy?
I didn't "break the law" doing this, if that's what you're wondering.
Certainly. But we have to press about the circumstances.
Joyner's resignation cited his contract's morals clause--
Here we go. You're asking if sex was involved.

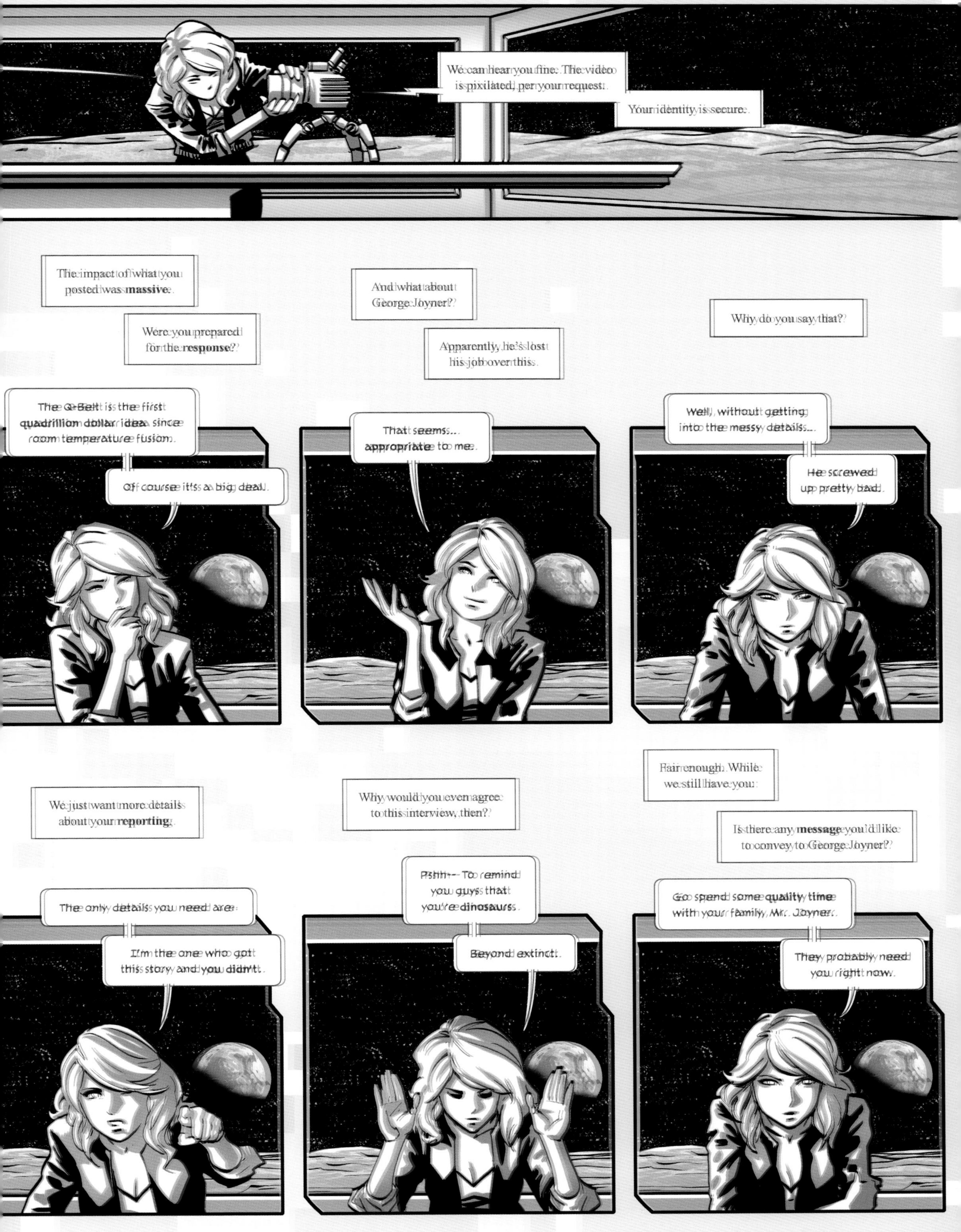
We can hear you fine. The video is pixilated, per your request.
Your identity is secure.
The impact of what you posted was **massive**.
Were you prepared for the **response**?
The Q-Belt is the first quadrillion dollar idea since room temperature fusion.
Of course it's a big deal.
And what about George Joyner?
Apparently, he's lost his job over this.
That seems... **appropriate** to me.
Why do you say that?
Well, without getting into the messy details...
He screwed up pretty bad.
We just want more details about your **reporting**.
The only details you need are:
I'm the one who got this story and **you didn't**.
Why would you even agree to this interview, then?
Pshh--- To remind you guys that you're **dinosaurs**.
Beyond extinct.
Fair enough. While we still have you:
Is there any **message** you'd like to convey to George Joyner?
Go spend some **quality time** with your family, Mr. Joyner.
They probably need you right now.

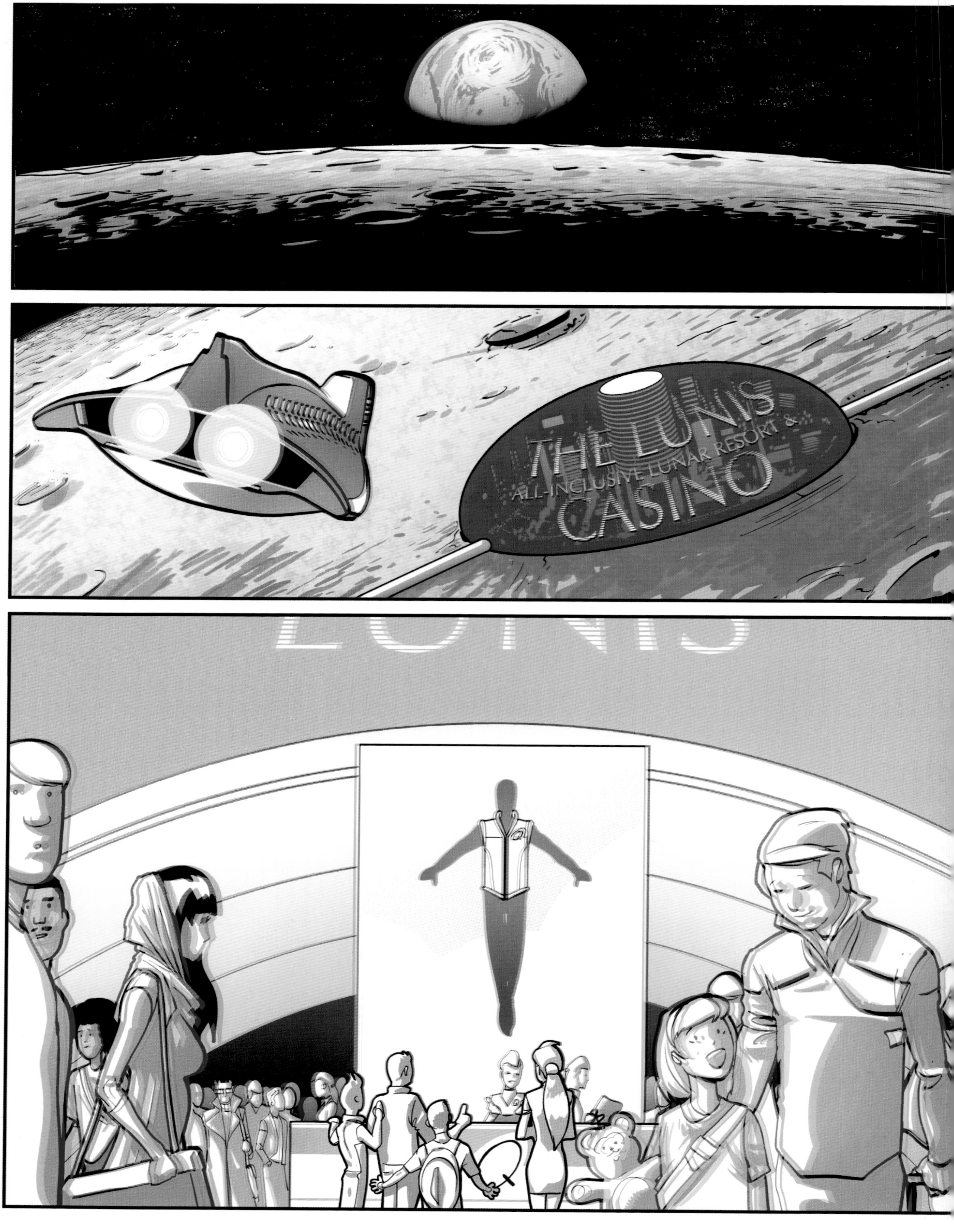
THE LUNIS
ALL-INCLUSIVE LUNAR RESORT &
CASINO

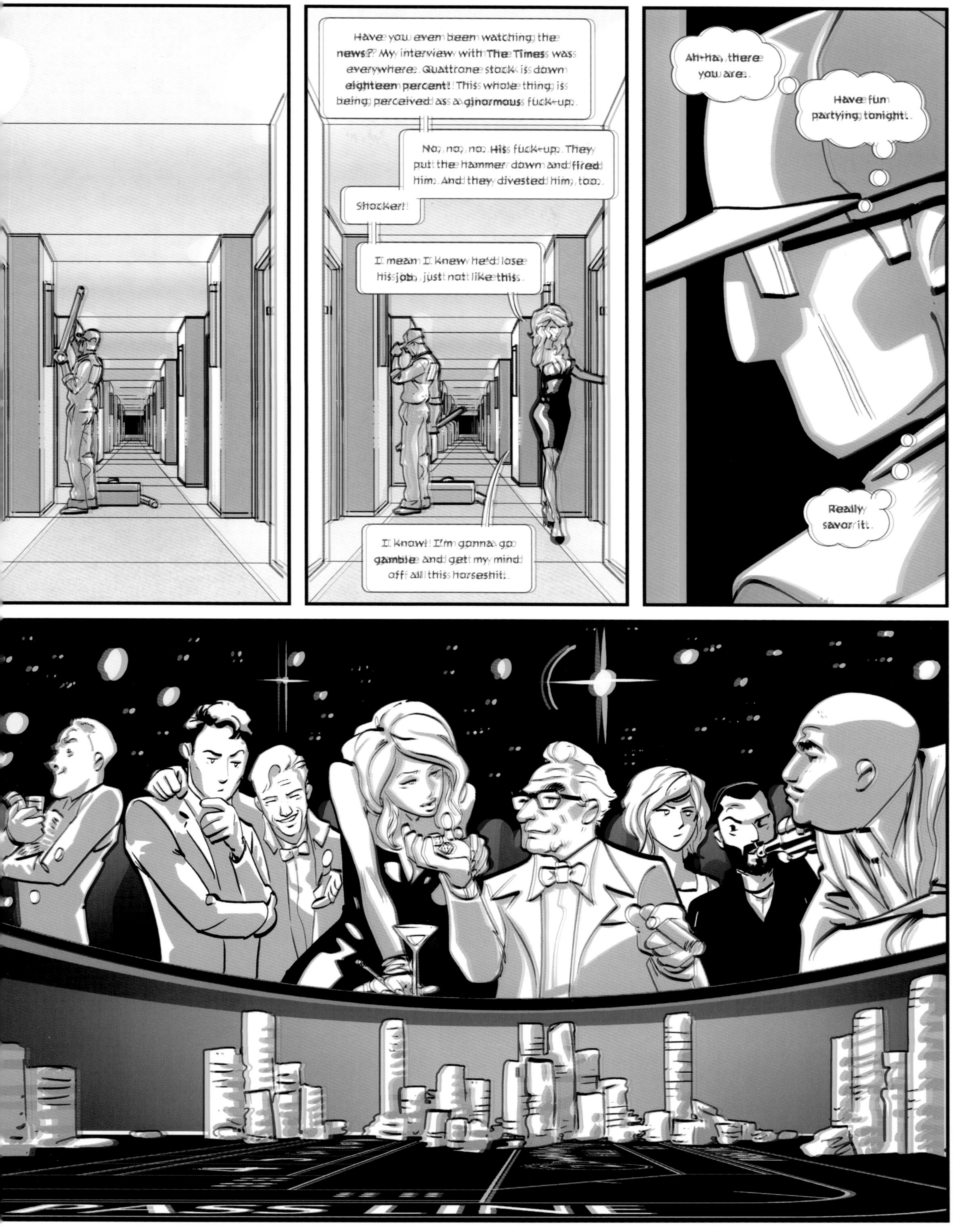
Have you even been watching the news? My interview with The Times was everywhere. Quattrone stock is down eighteen percent! This whole thing is being perceived as a ginormous fuck-up.
No, no, no. His fuck-up. They put the hammer down and fired him. And they divested him, too.
Shocker!
I mean I knew he'd lose his job, just not like this.
I know! I'm gonna go gamble and get my mind off all this horseshit.
Ah-ha, there you are.
Have fun partying tonight.
Really savor it.
PASS LINE

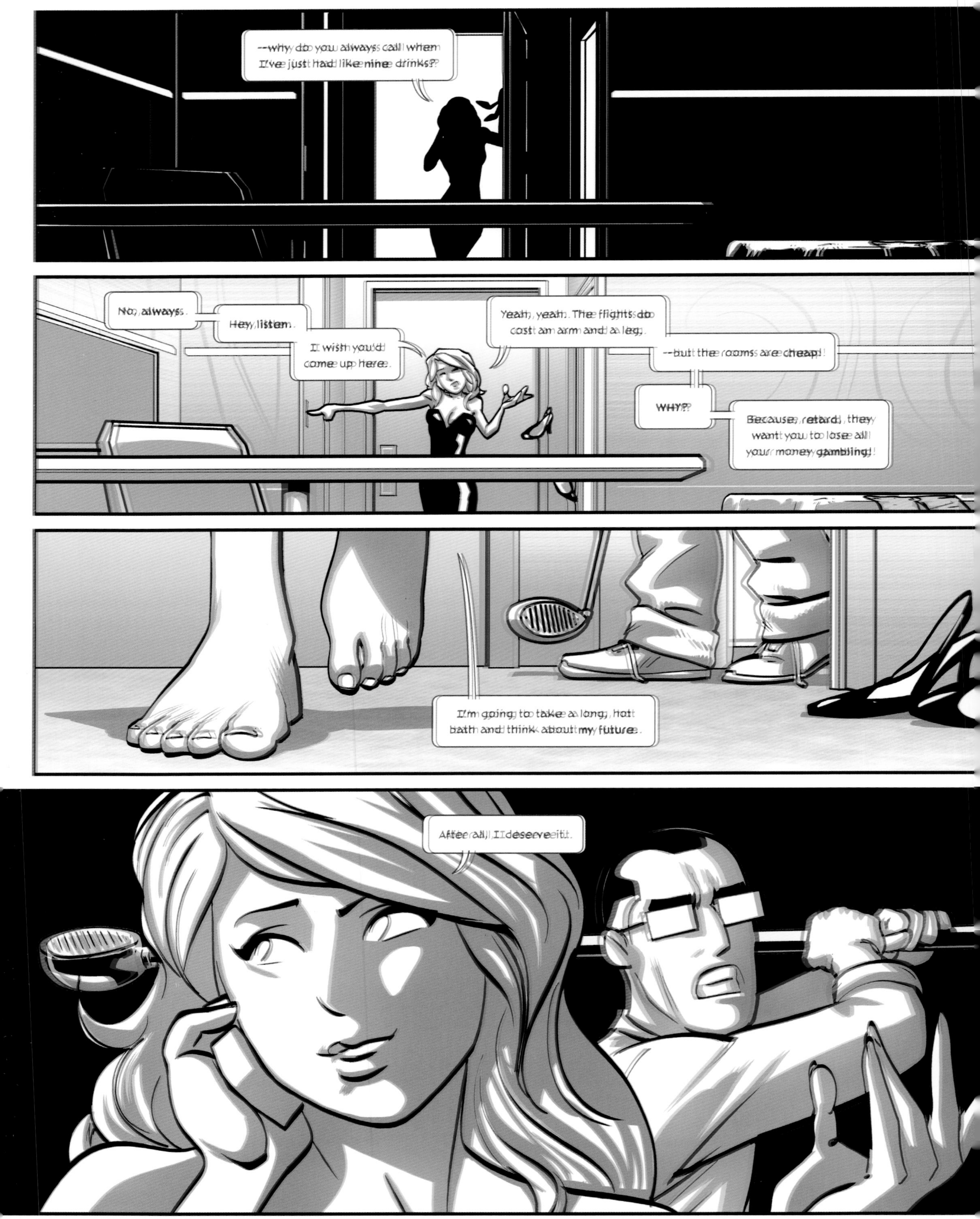
--why do you always call when I've just had like nine drinks?
No, always.
Hey, listen.
I wish you'd come up here.
Yeah, yeah. The flights do cost an arm and a leg.
--but the rooms are cheap!
WHY?
Because, retard, they want you to lose all your money gambling!
I'm going to take a long, hot bath and think about my future.
After all, I deserve it.

THE MAKERS OF THIS BOOK

R.J. RYAN is best known for his and David Marquez's debut graphic novel, 2010's acclaimed psychological thriller *Syndrome*. He lives and works in Los Angeles, CA.

DAVID MARQUEZ is the *New York Times* bestselling artist of *Ultimate Comics Spider-Man*, *All-New X-Men*, and *Fantastic Four: Season One*, and made his comics debut with R.J. Ryan in 2010 with the graphic novel *Syndrome*. David is based in Portland, OR.

TARA RHYMES earned her BFA at the University of Texas at Austin with a focus in Studio Art and Transmedia. *The Joyners in 3D* marks her comics debut. She lives and works in Portland, OR.

JON ADAMS is the writer and artist of the Eisner-nominated *Truth Serum*. He's currently writing, drawing, and designing a children's book for McSweeney's, tentatively titled, *Demon Flesh Cannibals*. hisportfolio.com.

THE AUTHORS WOULD LIKE TO THANK

All of our families and our friends near and far who helped make this project possible. This book would not exist without the careful, patient eye of our longtime editor, Stephen Christy. Nobody is better at putting together beautiful comics. Stephen's assistant Cameron Chittock provided a critical jolt of energy to THE JOYNERS IN 3D during the most labor-intensive leg of the production process. Our brilliant designer Jon Adams has amazed us for years with his own comics work, making it an honor and an true education to collaborate with the man on this book. A massive and heartfelt thanks to Tara Rhymes for supporting us throughout the process with her invaluable insight and feedback, and for stepping up to the plate when it became clear the 3D art was too much for one person to handle. Thanks to friend-of-JI3D Dimitry Elyashkevich for generous, countless insights and inspiration from the world of stereography, and much gratitude to writers Daniel Quantz, Jon Dorsey and Pete Szilagyi for lending their time and considerable vision to our production and post-production in Los Angeles. Thank you to Jonathan Koa for life-modeling during pre-production. At Archaia, thanks to Mel Caylo, keeper of the flame during a long, complicated process. At BOOM! Studios, thank you to Ross Richie for the support of the book when he bought Archaia right before we went to the printer. Thanks to famous creators over the years who have been generous with their time, insights and encouragement: David Eick, Michael Crichton, Matthew Weiner.

RJR & DM

Published
by Archaia
A Division of BOOM! Studios
5670 Wilshire Blvd. Ste. 450
Los Angeles, California,
90036
ARCHAIA.COM

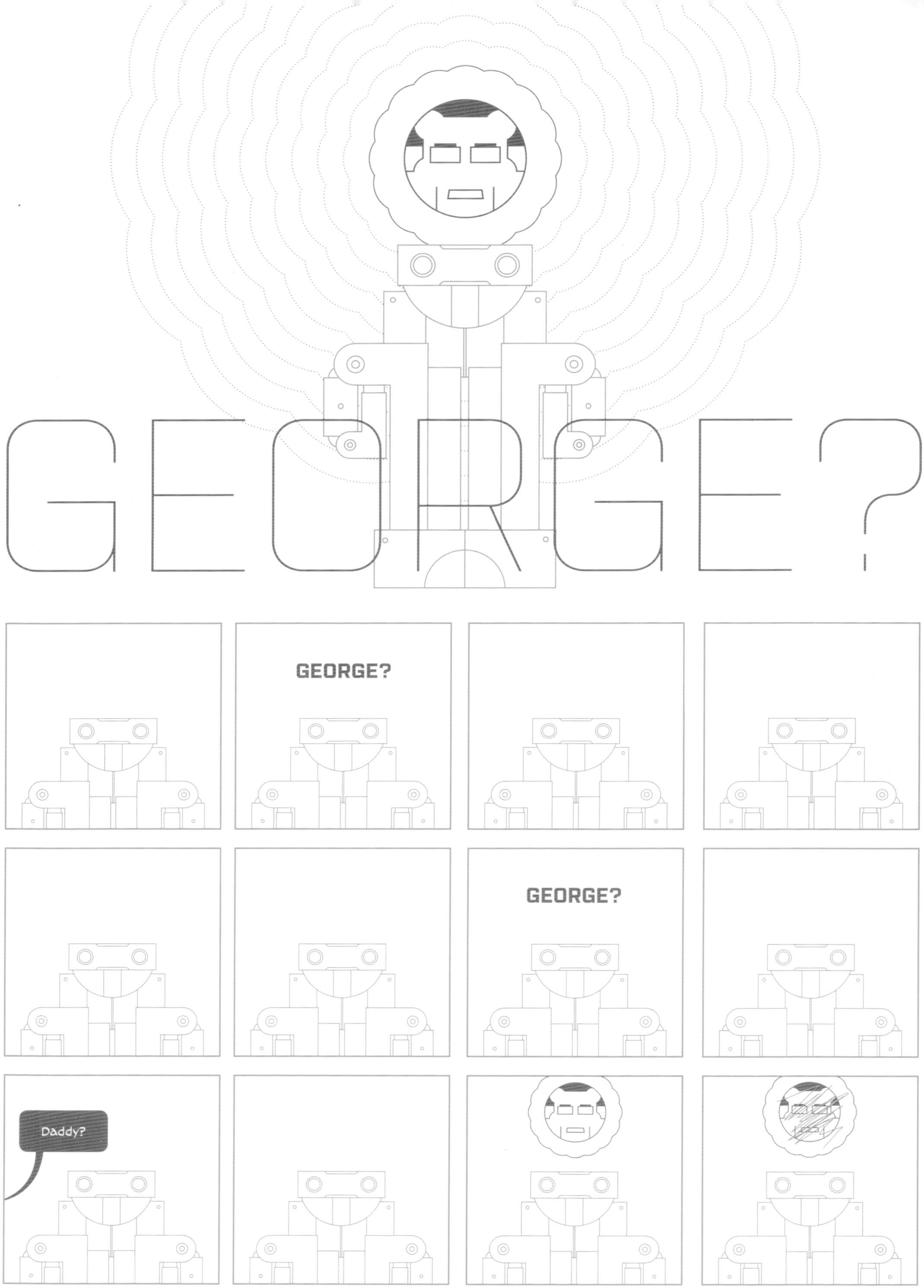
GEORGE?
GEORGE?
GEORGE?
Daddy?